Making Antique Furniture

MAKING
ANTIQUE
FURNITURE

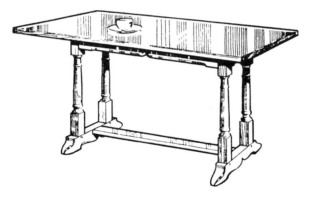

TAB BOOKS

BLUE RIDGE SUMMIT, PA. 17214

FIRST EDITION
FIRST PRINTING

Copyright © 1988 in North America by TAB BOOKS Inc.
Printed and bound in Great Britain

Library of Congress Cataloging in Publication Data
1. Furniture making.

2. Furniture – Reproduction.

1. Woodworker Magazine
TT194.M347 1988
749′.1′0287–dc19   87–33581
                         CIP

ISBN 0-8306-0356-5: $25.95
ISBN 0-8306-9356-4 (pbk):$15.95

TAB BOOKS Inc. offers software for
sale. For information and a catalog,
please contact TAB Software
Department, Blue Ridge Summit,
PA 17294-0850.

Phototypesetting by En to En, Tunbridge Wells
Printed and bound by Richard Clay Ltd, Chichester, Sussex

Contents

Introduction

Since it first appeared over eighty years ago, *Woodworker* magazine has published an enormous number of furniture designs. The range is vast and extends from antique designs of the 17th, 18th, and 19th centuries to the most modern contemporary furniture. It also includes furniture of all types for all parts of the home.

Obviously, such a mass of information is an invaluable asset, and our problem was to find the best way to present it in book form so that it would be at once coherent, stimulating, and informative.

One aspect of the problem solved itself. Designs which were modern in the 1920's, say, are now well on their way to becoming antiques in their own right, just as today's *avant-garde* examples will be antiques in sixty years' time. The choice, therefore, was narrowed down to reproductions of antique pieces which are, to all intents and purposes, timeless.

Another obstacle we had to surmount was the difference in styles of drawings and text which is bound to occur in any selection of articles spread over a long period of time. To achieve a degree of conformity all designs now have cutting lists in a standard format; both imperial and metric equivalent dimensions are given; annotations and captions on drawings have been standardized; and the layouts have been altered to conform to a general editorial theme.

As far as possible we have tried to accommodate all levels of craftsmanship from the enthusiastic beginner to the professional, and to include exercises in skill from simple basic designs such as a gate-leg table to a complicated and elegant Carlton House table. Those who prefer country-style furniture, such as Windsor and ladder-back chairs, will also find much to inspire them.

This then, is a book containing thirty-six designs of reproduction antique furniture which will surely appeal to those who cherish a sense of heritage and who believe that the craftmanship built up over the centuries should not be allowed to wither and die.

OAK COFFEE TABLES

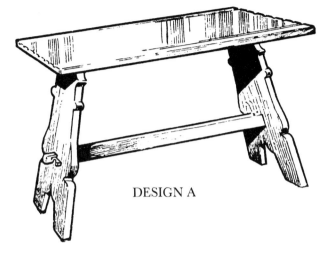

DESIGN A

Choose which design suits you best – it's a matter of taste, equipment, and the timber you can find. Design (A) can be made entirely in flat timber, $\frac{1}{2}$ to $\frac{7}{8}$in thick. For design (B) $1\frac{1}{2}$in squares are needed, and a lathe is essential – or the legs will have to be specially made up. In both cases the sizes could be varied a little.

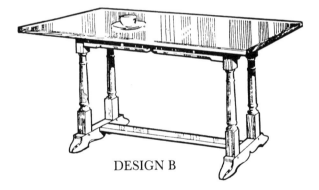

DESIGN B

Fig. 1.1.

DESIGN A

It's advisable to set out one half of the elevation in full size, working to the sizes in Fig. 1.3. This will enable you to get exact shoulder lengths, and will give you the angle required for them and for the slots and mortises in the sloping ends. No attempt is made to cut the shaping at an angle; it is cut through square.

ENDS

Owing to their shape these should be cut out to finish 20 in long. This allows for the slight reduction in height due to the angle at which they lean, and for bevelling top and bottom edges. Mark the notches to receive the top rails and the through mortises for the stretcher rail. Both of these are at an angle, for which you should set an adjustable bevel. Square the marks across the face and use the bevel to mark the edges, so giving the line for the inner face.

Saw down the sides of the notches and cut away the waste short of the line with a coping saw used at an angle. Finally pare with a chisel up to the line. Much of the mortise waste can be bored away and the remainder partly chopped and partly pared. Remember the angle of top and bottom edges.

The shaped edges can be plotted out map fashion from the 1 in squares shown in Fig. 1.2. Owing to the angularity the length will not align exactly, but the difference is small and is easily allowed for. A good plan is to mark one side on a piece of card, cut it out, and use it as a template, working to a centre line.

Use a band saw, jig saw, bow saw or coping saw for the shape, and clean up with rasp and file followed by the scraper and glass-paper. The latter should be used with suitably shaped rubbers so that the corners are not dubbed over. Do not leave the edges dead sharp, but run the glasspaper over them. There are two reasons for this. A sharp edge is easily damaged, and it is almost impossible to polish a really sharp corner.

RAILS

Take the lengths from the full size drawing, and mark the shoulders with the adjustable bevel at the same angle as for the ends. The width of the bridle joints should be taken from the wood of the ends themselves. They should be a nice hand tight fit because no glue is used when assembling. Cut the wedge holes in the stretchers so that the wedges bear against the ends and so pull the shoulders tightly home.

TOP

Cut the top to size and work the quarter round hollows along near the edges. A router, a small plane or a scratch stock can be used. They could also be omitted – they are entirely decorative. The notching at the ends can be done with a small gouge. Fix the top with screws driven upwards through the rails.

DESIGN B

The ends are framed up first, as shown in Fig. 1.5. Tenon the top rail into the legs, and mortise the foot

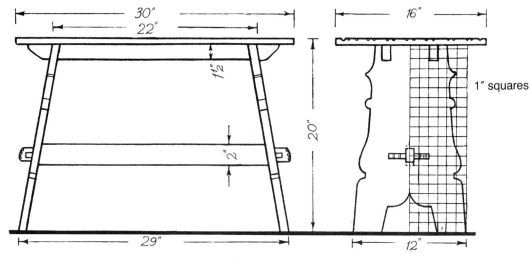

1″ squares

Fig. 1.2.

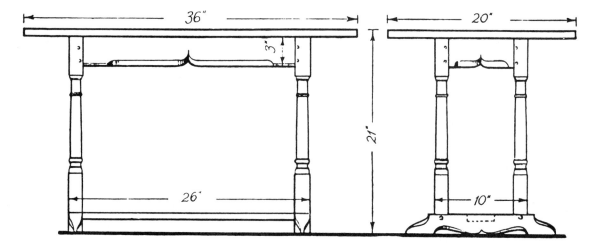

Fig. 1.3.

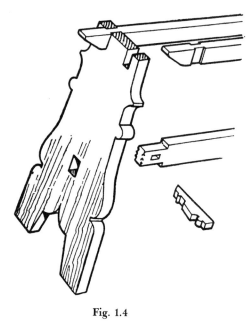

Fig. 1.4

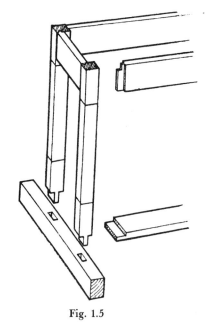

Fig. 1.5

pieces to receive tenons at the bottom ends of the legs. The mortises at the top meet in the thickness of the wood. Do not work the shaping or chamfers until after the joints have been cut and fitted.

FEET

The shaping can be with a bandsaw, coping saw, jig saw or bow saw, or, if preferred, the wasting-away method. Many prefer this when wood is thick; a series of saw cuts is made across the grain, and the waste chopped out with chisel and gouge. Use rasp and file to bring down to the line, and finish with scraper and glasspaper.

All the joints are pegged, and it saves the use of

cramps if they are draw-bored. Fit all the joints independently, try the whole job together, and test for squareness and freedom from winding. Bore the holes through the pieces with the mortises, push the joints tightly home, and mark the tenons by inserting the bit in the holes. Bore the holes through the tenons slightly nearer the shoulders.

All parts are now cleaned up finally and the whole job assembled. If the ends of the pegs are slightly tapered they will enter the staggered holes easily and pull the joints tightly home. Those who prefer can leave the pegs projecting slightly, in which case they are neatly rounded over. Alternatively they can be planed flush. In any case the ends are put together independently, and the side rails and stretchers added after the glue has set.

The top is fixed with pocket screws driven through the rails, the holes generously sized to allow for possible movement.

FINISH

The tables can be finished in various ways. Those who prefer natural wood can give a few coats of white or transparent french polish and finish with wax. The french polish builds up a preliminary shine and helps to keep out dirt. For a dark finish use one of the proprietary stains, or one made from Vandyke crystals dissolved in warm water with a little ammonia added immediately before use. French polish is essential when wax polish is used after an oil stain, as otherwise the wax polish may lift the stain unevenly in patches. Yet another plan is to fume the table. The advantages are a fine colour and entire freedom from any rising of the grain such as that often caused by water stain.

If an antique effect is desired add some lamp black powder to the wax polish whilst it is molten. This leaves a dark deposit in the grain and in the corners and so on. Modern plastic lacquers would be ideal for these tables, being heat- and water-proof and abrasion resistant. Apply the lacquer in strict accordance with the manufacturer's instructions. A satin-like finish can be achieved by allowing the last coat to set really hard and then rubbing it lightly with finest grade wire wool dipped in a good furniture wax.

CUTTING LIST

	INCHES			MM		
	L	W	T	L	W	T
DESIGN A						
1 Top	30½	16¼	½ or ⅝	775	413	12 or 16
2 Ends	20½	12¼	¾ or ⅞	521	311	19 or 22
2 Rails	27½	1¾	⅞	699	45	22
1 Stretcher	30	2¼	⅞	762	58	22
DESIGN B						
1 Top	36½	20¼	¾ or ⅞	927	514	19 or 22
4 Legs (square finished)	20	—	1⅜ or 1½	508	—	35 or 38
2 Rails	25	3¼	⅞	635	83	22
2 Rails	9	3¼	⅞	229	83	22
2 Feet	16½	2¼	1½	419	58	38
1 Stretcher	25	3¼	⅝ or ¾	635	83	16 or 19

Working allowances have been made to lengths and widths; thicknesses are net.

REGENCY-STYLE DRESSING TABLE

Fig. 2.1

Furniture of the Regency period is always sought after. Fig. 2.1 shows a sofa-table design adapted for use as a dressing table, while Fig. 2.5 is a similar design but fitted with end leaves supported by brackets. The triple mirror in Fig. 2.1 would look particularly glamorous in gilt compo; an alternative shield-shape toilet mirror is illustrated in Fig. 2.2.

Fig. 2.2 gives alternative elevations and plans for the two types of table and, to assist in setting-out, enlarged details of top and legs are given in Figs. 2.3, 2.4 and 2.6. At the outset it should be realised that much of the work is very fine and calls for properly prepared working detail. Although the tables vary in size, most of the construction is common to both. We are taking the table with flaps for specification, therefore, and only a few points vary with the other.

PILASTERS

A joint calling for fine work is that between the pilasters (B) and end rails (F) of the table frame. From Fig. 2.4 it will be observed that the pilaster is half-lapped with the end rail right up through on the inside, finishing flush. You may prefer to make a better joint of this by cutting it as a dovetail, but half-lapping can be made perfectly secure later on by screwing through from the inside, as indicated in Fig. 2.4. Externally, the small half of the fork stops under the supporting swing bracket which carries the flap.

In the case of the table without flaps the pilasters are flush with the outside of the rails. No fork pieces are

required, but the pilasters continue up to the top at the inside in the halving cut in the rails.

FRAMEWORK

Cut these joints before squaring up the end rails for tonguing them to the uprights (E), which finish $1\frac{5}{8}$ in in thickness to allow the $\frac{7}{8}$ in rails and $\frac{3}{4}$ in brackets ultimately to finish flush with them. Knock the joints apart and leave them dry until later.

Note from Fig. 2.4 that in the table with fixed top, uprights (E) are flush at the outside with rails (F). At the back no uprights are needed. Instead the back rail (G) can be dovetailed into the end rails — or better still be mitre-dovetailed.

Cut $\frac{1}{2}$ in tongues on the back rail to enter the uprights and work rebates $\frac{1}{2}$ in deep on the lower edges of the end and back rails right through to receive the bottom frame. In the flapless table the bottom frame is thicker to allow for the rim moulding. Trench the back rail $\frac{1}{8}$ in deep across grain to receive the centre division (Fig. 2.3). Two top rails (H) are dovetailed down to the table frame and run right through from end to end. The front one is wide enough to allow a good hold into the uprights, with a secondary dovetail into the end rails. The centre one should be chopped into the top edges of the half-lapped pilasters.

BOTTOM FRAME

This consists of stiles and rails (I and J, Figs. 2.3) mortised and tenoned together. Allow the centre rail some-

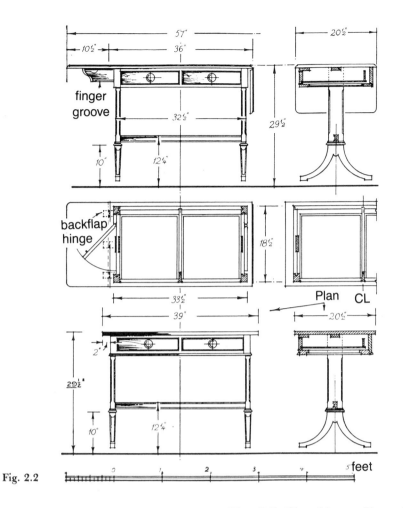

finger groove

backflap hinge

51"
10½"
36"
32½"
29½"
10"
12¼"

20½"

backflap hinge

18½"

33½"
Plan CL
39"
20½"

2"
29½"
10"
12¼"

Fig. 2.2

0 1 2 3 4 5 feet

what wider and notice that panels (K) are rebated in from the underside – they can thus be screwed up finally after the top has been secured and the drawers fitted. Front and back rails are longer than the main frame dimensions to allow for dovetailing into the uprights. The centre division clamp (L) might be tenoned through the top and bottom rails, and the division (M) housed in $\frac{1}{8}$ in deep into the centre rail and tongued $\frac{3}{8}$ in into the clamp. It should be notched away to allow the centre top rail to run through. Fit the end rails of the bottom frame accurately around the pilasters and do not cut away anything of the latter at this point.

LEGS
Plot the shape of one of the legs (A) from the grid in

Fig. 2.7. Use thin card or plywood and make a template for cutting. Notice that joints occur centrally under the pilasters, and timber should be left on in the form of squares (Fig. 2.4) so the trued faces of the legs can be pulled up tightly with cramps later. The half-round shapes between the legs can also be fretted away with the squares later. Scheme the grain of the timber to fall along the line of the shape. Fret-cut the legs, and glue and cramp them together to form shaped pairs. When dry remove surplus wood left on and clean up. Complete the half round shaping falling across the joint. The taper from $1\frac{5}{8}$ in to $1\frac{1}{8}$ in on front elevation can be worked with the plane. Recesses, a bare $\frac{1}{8}$ in deep, might be worked next, these being finished with a sharp gouge cut at the top to half-circular pattern. As an alternative fine reeds might be worked.

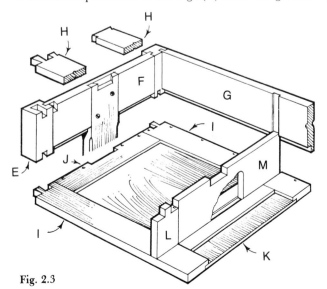

Fig. 2.3

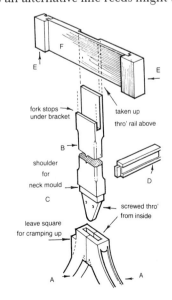

Fig. 2.4

5

Fig. 2.5

PILASTER-LEG JOINTS

The pilasters (B) are shouldered to receive the necking mould (C), the latter being finely worked to detail in Fig. 2.4 and mitred around (leave dry until ultimate assembly). Further shoulders on the pilasters immediately below those just mentioned provide the bevelled tenons that enter mortises in the paired legs (see Figs.

2.4 and 2.7). Careful work is necessary at this stage. The thickness of the tenons should be one-third that of the top of the legs. When satisfied with the joints, remove the pilasters for further work. Notice that, ultimately and to give additional strength, fine brass screws can be driven through the inside faces of the legs to lock the tenons, the screwheads sunk $\frac{1}{8}$ in below the surface and the holes filled with mahogany pellets flushed off.

The corners of the pilasters might be provided with a chamfered edge or ovolo as indicated in Fig. 2.6, but stop either about $\frac{3}{4}$ in below the table frame and lineable with the stretcher (D). Alternative sections for the face edge of this item are given in Fig. 2.6. Either will look fine. Stub-tenons $\frac{1}{2}$ in in length should ultimately be cut on the ends to enter the pilasters.

ASSEMBLING

Gluing and cramping should be carried out in the following order: (a) end rails to uprights, (b) pilasters to paired shaped legs and table frame rails. This will give complete end units. When dry proceed to (c); pull up the back rail and stretcher to end units, (d) insert bottom frame from the underside and screw end and back rails to table frame rails, (e) erect division and clamp, and (f) glue and pin the top rails down. Test for squareness and standing before the glue chills after completing (c) and (d).

DRAWER CONSTRUCTION

Fine cocked beads, $\frac{1}{8}$ in in thickness at the most, surround the fronts. Those at the top edges run right over, whilst others are stepped back to the line of the dovetailed sides only. Cut neat mitres and glue on after all

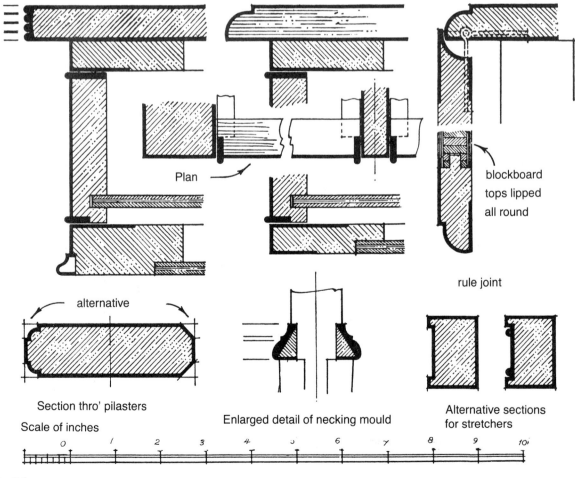

Plan

blockboard
tops lipped
all round

rule joint

alternative

Section thro' pilasters

Scale of inches

Enlarged detail of necking mould

Alternative sections
for stretchers

| 0 | 1 | 2 | 3 | 4 | 5 | 6 | 7 | 8 | 9 | 10 |

Fig. 2.6

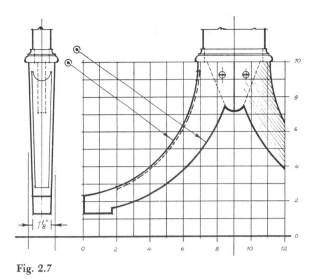

Fig. 2.7

the other work in regard to construction and running has been completed. Make allowance for the top bead when setting-out the lap-dovetailing of sides to fronts and continue with the through-dovetailing of backs and sides.

Drawer bottoms of $\frac{1}{4}$ in plywood may be grooved into the fronts and sides and run out under the backs to which they are screwed. To conform to customary practice, solid bottoms of mahogany, grooved into the fronts and taken into slips glued and pinned to the sides, would be the alternative. After the drawers have run in, glue and pin kickers between the top rails, gluing to end rails and division.

TOP AND FLAP CONSTRUCTION

The grain of these items, if allowed in the solid, should run from front to back to facilitate the working of the rule joints and so conform to traditional practice. Prime seasoned mahogany is, therefore, essential. One should look out for any old stock which might have seen previous service over the years and whose standing qualities are in no doubt. With new stock it is advisable to purchase as early as possible, match and joint the boards to obtain the necessary width, and leave to stand, suitably battened, whilst other work on the table is in progress. Fig. 2.8 gives the overall sizes required for tops, either in the solid or blockboard. It also shows the mitred lippings of solid timber required when blockboard is used.

Enlarged sections are given in Fig. 2.6. Using solid timber, the first task is to square the top and flaps, but do not trim finally until after the rule joints have been worked. Notice particularly the centres of the rule-joint hinges, of which three per flap will be required. These should be bought early and worked to for thicknesses, etc., and positioned 2 in in from the front and back edges, the others in the centre.

Develop a full-size section of the joint on paper and

watch the all-important centre of the hinge from which is struck the hollow and thumb sections that have to work smoothly in together. The square to the hollow of the flaps should have a good overlap on the thumb mould of the top to ensure an easy start to the upward movement and also to cover the cutting away of the top for the recessing of the hinges.

Some people arrange that the square of the thumb moulding falls $\frac{3}{16}$ in at least behind the centre of the hinge when viewed vertically. Always arrange a trial run with some odd bits of softwood before moulding the selected boards. When these joints have been moulded and hinged to run well, square the completed top of three boards, shoot the edges true and mould the same thumb section all round.

BLOCKBOARD

The same procedure is adopted for tops made up in blockboard and lipped with solid mahogany — a section appears in Fig. 2.6, showing tongues worked on the lippings to enter grooves in the blockboard. The joints at the ends should be mitred. Make a note that the joint of the lippings and blockboard should fall centrally under any inlaid banding that may be introduced.

BRACKETS

Before mounting the top and flaps it is necessary to provide the swing brackets (N) details of which appear in Fig. 2.9. Again, for this type of table, nothing but the knuckle joint satisfies if we are to adhere to traditional methods. Short pieces are glued and screwed to the end frame rails as in Figs. 2.2 and 2.9, with hinged longer ones swinging out to support the flaps. Dowel stops are fitted, projecting about $\frac{1}{4}$ in. The scribing and cutting of the knuckle joints calls for fine cutting and workmanship. A $\frac{1}{8}$ in steel pin passes down through the centre, and upon the latter depends the tightness or sloppiness of the joint. In the finished width of $3\frac{1}{4}$ in to the bracket, five knuckles are suggested, but this could be increased to seven if desired. Fret cut the ends of the swinging brackets to a nice shape and work stopped finger groves inside. Mount the finished members to the table frame and try for

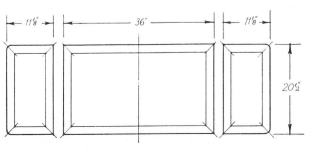

Fig. 2.8

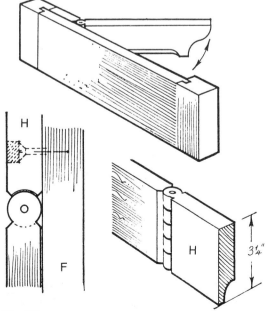

Fig. 2.9

level in the open position with a straight-edge across carcase and brackets.

Secure the top (and associated flaps) to the table frame by passing screws up through the top front rail, and pocket screws through the end and back rails. For a blockboard top the screwing can be firm and tight, but clearance is desirable for a solid top that might move a little.

VENEERING

The use of blockboard for the tops obviously calls for the use of veneers, and a fiddleback pattern is recommended, with the grain running from back to front. Fig. 2.5 shows a crossband edge to the outsides and the joint could be broken with the introduction of a fine black inlaid line, say $\frac{3}{32}$ in wide. Alternatively, any period banding not more than $\frac{1}{4}$ in wide – say in satinwood, or tulipwood, with fine black lines to the outside – might be introduced. Veneering would be undertaken before the rule-joint and other edges are moulded, and calls for toothing and sizing.

The appearance of the drawer fronts will be considerably enhanced if selected small knife-cut curls are introduced and would well repay the additional time and labour involved.

FITTINGS

Brass ring handles with supporting back plates of period pattern and not more than 2 in diameter should be chosen. Locks are not essential and might, indeed, call for rearrangement of handles according to depth to centre of lock pin. Brass plate castors are required and any slight deviation from the height allowed will be immaterial as the table height at $29\frac{1}{2}$ in allows for such adjustment.

TABLE WITH FIXED TOP

As mentioned earlier the making-up of this table is practically the same as the other. To recapitulate the exceptions: (a) increased length of top to 39 in and a reeded edge all round – overhang 2 in at ends and 1 in back and front; (b) the pilasters finish level with the outside faces of the uprights in elevation; (c) the bottom frame is stouter in thickness to allow for a rim moulding housed in $\frac{1}{8}$ in front, ends, and back and neatly mitred at the corners; and (d) no uprights are needed at the back for the table frame.

FINISH (BOTH TABLES)

It should be borne in mind that a sofa table had occasional use as a centre table, and so the workmanship was the same all round. For that reason we have suggested moulded tops on all sides. The joints of table frames should be clean, thus facilitating the work of staining and french polishing.

CUTTING LIST

Part			INCHES			MM		
			L	W	T	L	W	T
Table with flaps								
A	2	pieces for 4 legs (or schemed in any other way to enable shapes to be plotted)						
	4	Legs	14	7	$1\frac{5}{8}$	356	178	42
B	2	Pilasters	$22\frac{1}{2}$	4	$1\frac{1}{8}$	572	102	29
C	1	Piece for neck moulding	36	1	$\frac{9}{16}$	915	25	14
D	1	Stretcher	$32\frac{1}{2}$	$1\frac{3}{4}$	$1\frac{1}{8}$	825	45	29

CUTTING LIST (continued)

Part			INCHES			MM		
			L	W	T	L	W	T
E	4	Uprights	5	$2\frac{1}{4}$	$1\frac{5}{8}$	127	58	42
F	2	End rails	17	5	$\frac{7}{8}$	432	127	22
G	1	Back rail	$32\frac{1}{2}$	5	$\frac{7}{8}$	825	127	22
H	2	Top rails	$33\frac{1}{2}$	3	$\frac{5}{8}$	851	76	16
I	2	Bottom frame rails	$33\frac{1}{2}$	3	$\frac{5}{8}$	851	76	16
J	3	Bottom frame rails	18	3	$\frac{5}{8}$	457	76	16
K	2	Panels	15	15	$\frac{1}{4}$	381	381	6
L	1	Division clamp	5	3	$\frac{5}{8}$	127	76	16
M	1	Division	17	5	$\frac{5}{8}$	432	127	16
N	2	Pieces for brackets	16	4	$\frac{3}{4}$	407	102	19
O	1	Top	21	$36\frac{1}{2}$	$\frac{5}{8}$	533	927	16
P	2	Flaps	21	12	$\frac{5}{8}$	533	305	16
Q	2	Drawer fronts	$15\frac{1}{2}$	$3\frac{1}{2}$	$\frac{13}{16}$	394	89	21
R	4	Drawer sides	17	$3\frac{1}{2}$	$\frac{3}{8}$	432	89	10
S	2	Drawer backs	$15\frac{1}{2}$	3	$\frac{3}{8}$	394	76	10
T	2	Drawer bottoms	15	17	$\frac{1}{4}$	381	432	6
U	1	Piece for cocked beads	17	6	$\frac{1}{8}$	432	153	3
V	4	Kickers	8	$1\frac{1}{2}$	$\frac{5}{8}$	203	38	16

For blockboard top and flat construction omit parts (O) and (P) and substitute the following:

			INCHES			MM		
1	Top		$33\frac{1}{2}$	18	$\frac{3}{4}$	851	457	19
2	Flaps		$8\frac{1}{2}$	18	$\frac{3}{4}$	216	457	19
2	Lippings		38	$2\frac{1}{2}$	$\frac{3}{4}$	965	64	19
4	Lippings		$13\frac{1}{8}$	$2\frac{1}{2}$	$\frac{3}{4}$	333	64	19
6	Lippings		$22\frac{1}{2}$	$2\frac{1}{2}$	$\frac{3}{4}$	572	64	19

Fixed top table

			INCHES			MM		
2	Pieces for legs		14	7	$1\frac{5}{8}$	356	178	42
2	Pilasters		$22\frac{1}{2}$	4	$1\frac{1}{8}$	572	102	29
1	Piece for neck moulding		36	1	$\frac{9}{16}$	915	25	14
1	Stretcher		35	$1\frac{3}{4}$	$1\frac{1}{8}$	889	45	29
4	Uprights		6	2	$1\frac{5}{8}$	153	51	42
2	End rails		18	6	$\frac{7}{8}$	457	153	22
1	Back rail		36	6	$\frac{7}{8}$	915	153	22
2	Top Rails		35	3	$\frac{5}{8}$	889	76	16
2	Bottom frame rails		35	3	$1\frac{1}{16}$	889	76	27
3	Bottom frame rails		18	4	$1\frac{1}{16}$	457	102	27
2	Panels		15	15	$\frac{1}{4}$	381	381	6
1	Piece for moulding		39	4	$\frac{7}{16}$	990	102	11
1	Division clamp		6	3	$\frac{5}{8}$	153	76	16
1	Division		17	5	$\frac{5}{8}$	432	127	16
4	Kickers		8	$1\frac{1}{2}$	$\frac{5}{8}$	203	38	16
1	Top		40	$21\frac{1}{2}$	$\frac{3}{4}$	1016	546	19
2	Drawer fronts		$16\frac{1}{2}$	$3\frac{1}{2}$	$\frac{13}{16}$	419	89	21

Sides, backs, and bottoms, similar to those of the other table will also be required.

As a guide to timber, choose prime straight-grained Honduras mahogany for parts (A) to (G) inclusive; one part of (H), (I), (L), (N), (O), (P), (Q), (R), (S), and (U). Birch plywood (6 mm thickness) could be suitably stained and used for parts (K) and (T), and deal for the remainder.
Working allowances have been made to lengths and widths; thicknesses are net.

SHIELD MIRROR

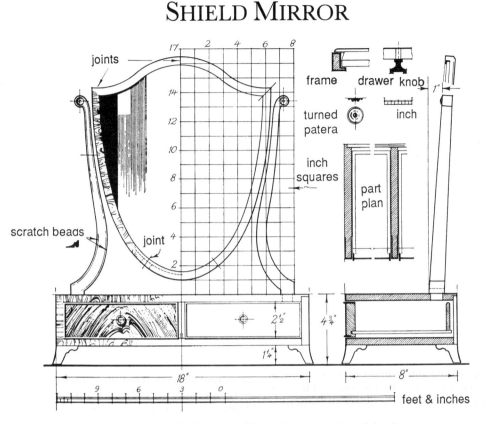

Fig. 3.1. Front elevation, side section, and enlarged detail.

The reproduction mirror on the Regency-style dressing table, design No 2, Fig. 2.5, although small, calls for a high standard of workmanship. Elevations and construction are shown in Figs. 3.1, 3.2 and 3.3. Make a full-sized drawing of at least the mirror frame and standards from the inch-square detail given in Fig. 3.1, preferably on plywood (the ultimate mirror back could be used for this purpose if allowed somewhat larger than in the cutting list, and suitably pinned down to keep it flat).

Whilst making the drawing, also prepare a full-sized card template of the mirror and give it to the glass manufacturer for a quotation. The edge can be left square but if a bevel is preferred it is advisable not to exceed a width of ⅝ in in order to keep the result fine after insertion in the frame. It may well be that the overall mirror frame size of 15½ × 12¾ in is considered to be too small, in which case proportional enlargement can be made regarding the inch squares as 1⅛ in or 1¼ in as desired. This will call for an increase in the length of the base portion, but the depth can be kept the same.

SHIELD FRAME
The method of making up a shield-shaped frame and the best places for joints has always formed the subject of discussion between experienced makers. The method shown in Fig. 3.3 is orthodox, but the centre joint at the top of the shield could be dispensed with in favour of one piece from end to end if desired.

The guiding principle is to arrange as much long grain in the individual members as possible, otherwise there is the risk of casting and brittleness. The same thing applies to the standards. Normally one would arrange to cut one from the other to save timber, but some may prefer to make a centre joint with the grain as a broad V-shape from top to bottom.

Reverting to the frame, two methods of making up are possible: (a) to roughly shape the individual members to the required lines and accurately cut each joint on top of the working template before inserting cross-tongues or keys of mahogany veneer or (b) to make up a complete jointed frame, cross-tongued and glued as in Fig 3.3 and cut to shape afterwards. This method is recommended for the less experienced, in that it provides a complete unit to handle from the start. Keep the cross-tongues or keys as fine as possible, using veneer about ³⁄₃₂ in thick, or thin hard mahogany. Make one accurate cut with the tenon saw about ½ in deep and in line each side of the joint for each key, and glue well in when bringing the parts together.

Check the actual outline of the mirror with the working template of the frame to ensure accuracy, and fretsaw the inside line of the frame, leaving about ¹⁄₁₆ in on for final cleaning up with the spokeshave. From this finished edge accurately gauge the rebate for the glass and work this next. From the same inside edge, again gauge the outside line of the frame, leaving a little on for cleaning up.

STANDARDS
When shaping the standards, leave rough squares at

9

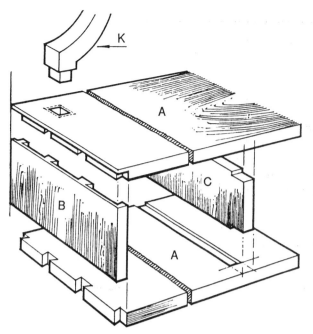

Fig. 3.2. Drawer carcase construction.

the tops until after the turned paterae have been applied, then fret them to follow the line. The timber for the paterae, incidentally, should be hard to ensure fine outlines of the section when turning. They are applied straight from the lathe without additional cleaning up. An alternative is to use ivory left natural colour. Taper the standards from $1\frac{1}{8}$ in at the bottom to $\frac{3}{4}$ in at the top. Notice the ultimate rake of 1 in out of the vertical when viewed from the ends. This will involve the accurate cutting of shoulders and tenons to enter the top of the jewel box carcase.

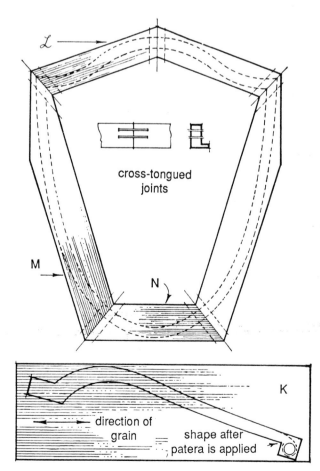

cross-tongued joints

Fig. 3.3. How frame is made, with detail of standard.

direction of grain

shape after patera is applied

Beads, if worked on the faces of the standards, should commence just above the squares at the bottom and run out just below the turned paterae at the top.

DRAWER CARCASE

The jewel drawer carcase consists of a top, ends, bottom, division, and back. The latter is rebated into back edges of the top and ends, these members being secret lap-dovetailed together as indicated in Fig. 3.2. Alternatively, fine mitre-dovetailed joints could be effected. The bottom is lap-dovetailed up to the ends. The housings required across top and bottom for the division are worked to a depth of $\frac{1}{8}$ in and stopped approximately $\frac{3}{4}$ in from the front. Before assembling the carcase cut the mortises required in the top for tenons of the standards, taking particular care to correctly establish their position. In effect, it means a check of the working position of the mirror frame between the standards, correctly sighting the latter both from front and ends, and a dead-tight fit of the tenons into their mortises. Leave the latter dry until the carcase has been completely finished.

Glue and cramp the carcase together and screw the back temporarily in position, and decide the amount of veneering. The mirror frame face, for example, could have a cross-banded pattern in fiddleback mahogany, and the edges overlaid lengthwise with the same veneer to hide the keyed joints. The standards, if cut in firm, figured mahogany should need no further embellishment. The top and ends of the jewel box carcase might be veneered after assembling, or alternatively, the ends only if secret lap-dovetailing has been employed. Certainly the drawer fronts should have fine curls, after which they can be trimmed up and prepared for fine cocked beads — the drawer construction is identical to that of the sofa tables, but is, of course, on a reduced scale. Knobs, again of hard mahogany or ivory, should be turned complete with pins.

The feet can be fret cut and mitred together. If the carcase is bow-shaped remember to make the front ones at an angle to suit the curve.

FITTING

Finally, erect the standards and glue well into position. The glass mirror should be mounted in its frame with softwood wedge-shaped blocks glued in, and the plywood back secured with fine brass screws. The fixing of the glass centres, which might be selected from a reproduction pattern, is an accurate job and should only be undertaken when the balance of the completed mirror frame has been established. Take a position for the centre of the glass centres just above the balancing joint.

An added refinement to the design as a whole would, of course, be the introduction of a bowed front to the jewel drawer carcase, say about 1 in at most.

CUTTING LIST

				INCHES			MM		
Part				L	W	T	L	W	T
A	2	Top and bottom pieces		$18\frac{1}{2}$	$8\frac{1}{4}$	$\frac{1}{2}$	470	210	12
B	2	Ends		4	$8\frac{1}{4}$	$\frac{1}{2}$	102	210	12
C	1	Division		$3\frac{1}{4}$	$8\frac{1}{4}$	$\frac{1}{2}$	83	210	12
D	1	Piece for feet		18	$1\frac{3}{8}$	$\frac{1}{2}$	457	35	12

CUTTING LIST (continued)

Part			INCHES			MM		
			L	W	T	L	W	T
E	2	Drawer fronts	8¾	2¾	¾	223	70	19
F	4	Drawer sides	7½	2¾	¼	191	70	6
G	2	Drawer backs	8¾	2	¼	223	51	6
H	2	Drawer bottoms	8¾	7½	⅛	223	191	3
I	1	Piece for cocked beads	18	6	⅛	457	153	3
J	1	Piece for two knobs	6	⅝	⅝	153	16	16
K	2	Standards	16	5	1⅛	406	127	29
L	2	Pieces for mirror frame	8	1½	⅝	203	38	16
M	2	Pieces for mirror frame	15½	2½	⅝	394	64	16

CUTTING LIST (continued)

Part			INCHES			MM		
			L	W	T	L	W	T
N	1	Piece for mirror frame	9	2½	⅝	229	64	16
O	1	Mirror back	16	13	3/16	406	330	5
P	1	Piece for two paterae	6	⅝	⅝	153	16	16

Working allowances have been made to lengths and widths; thicknesses are net. With the exception of the mirror back, carcase back, and drawer bottoms (all of which are birch plywood suitably stained), select sound, well-figured and close-grained mahogany.

SHERATON-STYLE SIDEBOARD WITH SERPENTINE FRONT

This sideboard is made in the same manner as an original Sheraton in construction, with the exception that the timber used in certain parts is mahogany ply rather than mahogany veneered pine or solid mahogany; for example the ends of the sideboard in the original would have been made of veneered pine, and the back of the sideboard just solid pine.

The reason for the use of ply is that it reduces the risk of shrinkage, such as might occur in a house with central heating. The doors in this particular sideboard are made in the original way but here again an alternative method of ply doors, using a jig to shape them is also described. The inlay used is a boxwood white line.

Four small trays fit into the left-hand side of the sideboard, the other side being left so that larger articles can be stored. The large centre drawer can be lined with baize when finished and the small trays could also be treated in the same way if desired.

Begin work on the sideboard by first setting out half the serpentine shape shown in Fig. 4.1 on to a thin piece of ply or stout card; when satisfied that you have obtained the right shape transfer it on to the top rail (already cut and planed to size). Reverse the pattern over at the centre line and mark the other half, to obtain an even and equal shape. Another rail is temporarily panel-pinned to the underneath of the top rail and both are cut together and finished off with a spokeshave. The second rail will become the three bottom rails, but by cutting together you will have exactly the same shape of rail for top and bottom.

Now mark out all shoulder sizes, including tenon and dovetail lengths, on to these two rails, marking the top rail first and squaring off to the bottom rail to maintain accuracy. The two rails can then be separated and the marking-out completed.

Now cut the bottom rail to make up the three bottom rails. Using a mortise gauge and gauging from the back edges, gauge mortises for the bridle joints and stub tenons. Also the dovetails can be marked on to the top rail: Fig. 4.2 shows all joints used on these rails.

Next, the ply ends of the sideboard are cut to size and veneered with a good quality mahogany veneer so that the grain runs from the front leg to the back leg. It is left to you to decide how to veneer these; either by hand using Scotch glue, or by cramping the two ends under some stout waste ply using a resin or PVA glue.

The back is cut next, using the top front rail to transfer shoulder sizes on to the back. The housing joints are now cut $\frac{3}{16}$ in into the back, and also the semi-circular shape is cut between these two joints. Fig. 4.1 (plan) shows this shape. Drill four $\frac{3}{16}$ in holes equally spaced through each housing joint and countersink from the back. These will be used to screw the divisions in place later.

After this operation is complete, work can be carried out on the six legs. Four are made in the same manner but the two centre legs are shaped to follow the front rails. This alters the shape of the toe: Fig. 4.3 shows details of how the toes are set out and also three different methods of making the toes.

The best of these is the leg and toe made from one piece of timber, as in an original Sheraton. The least difficult to make is the toe by itself which is then dowelled on to the leg after the latter has been tapered. If this method is accurately carried out no joint will be seen and the finished result should be quite acceptable.

The inlay of white line can be cut into the four front legs at this stage: Fig. 4.4 shows the method used, a scratch gauge and chisel scribed around a jig made specially for the purpose. This is held against one side of the leg and can also be reversed to the other side so that a complete shape can be cut into each leg. Care must be taken to make the scratch gauge just the right

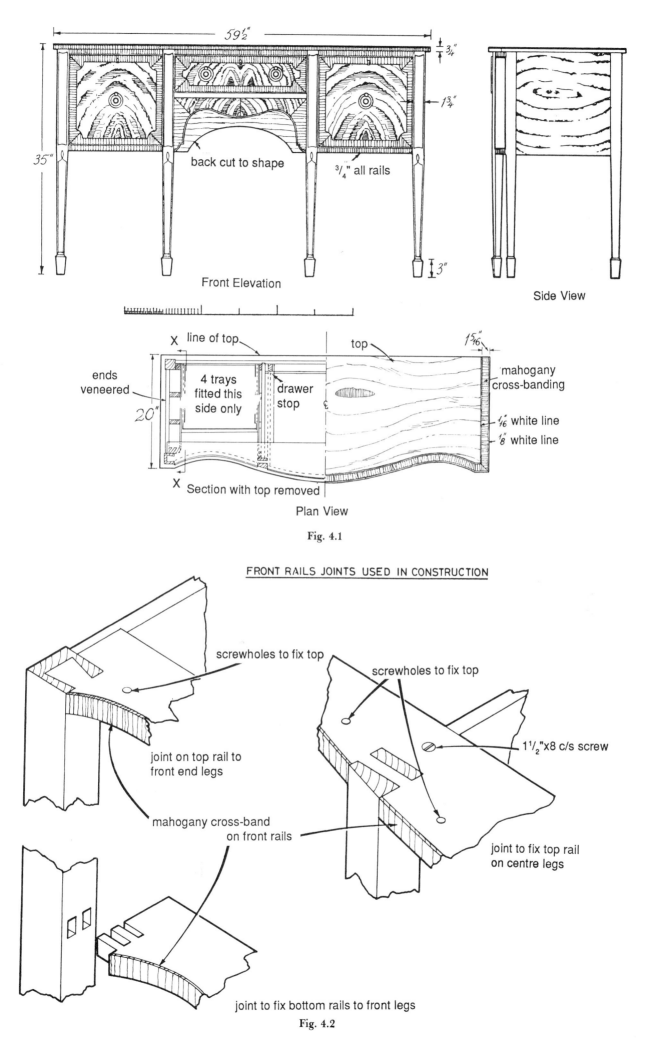

59½"

¾"

1¾"

35"

back cut to shape

¾" all rails

3"

Front Elevation

Side View

X line of top

top

15/16"

ends veneered

4 trays fitted this side only

drawer stop

mahogany cross-banding

20"

1/16" white line

1/8" white line

X Section with top removed

Plan View

Fig. 4.1

FRONT RAILS JOINTS USED IN CONSTRUCTION

screwholes to fix top

screwholes to fix top

1½"x8 c/s screw

joint on top rail to front end legs

mahogany cross-band on front rails

joint to fix top rail on centre legs

joint to fix bottom rails to front legs

Fig. 4.2

13

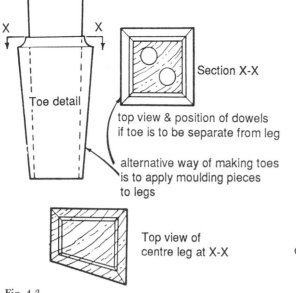

Toe detail

X   X

Section X-X

top view & position of dowels
if toe is to be separate from leg

alternative way of making toes
is to apply moulding pieces
to legs

Top view of
centre leg at X-X

Fig. 4.3

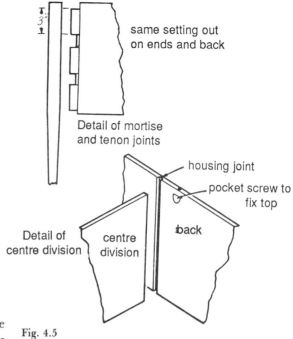

$\frac{3}{1}$"

same setting out
on ends and back

Detail of mortise
and tenon joints

housing joint

pocket screw to
fix top

Detail of
centre division

centre
division

back

Fig. 4.5

size and also to use the right size of chisel. Test these first on an odd piece of wood before work is commenced on the legs themselves.

Glue the line in with Scotch glue so that any imperfection filled by the glue will take polish when finished. If a PVA or resin glue is used the probability is that it will show badly in the grain when polished. Use a hammer head to push the line into the slots and keep the head hot by dipping it into boiling water. This will help to keep the glue workable. After allowing the legs to dry for 24 hours, clean them up to a good finish.

Now all the mortise and tenon joints are marked and cut, making sure that they are a good fit; Fig. 4.5 shows the setting out of these joints. At the same time the stub tenon and mortise joints can also be cut.

Note that all the front rails are set back $\frac{1}{8}$in from the front legs to allow for the mahogany crossbanding later in construction. Both the ends and the two centre divisions can then be glued up and allowed to dry. Note the two centre divisions are cut longer than required and can be trimmed to the exact length later.

When these have set, fit the back into the two ends. This will now stand on its own and allow you to mark the dovetails on to the ends from the top rail. You can also mark and cut the bridle joints to take the centre divisions. By temporarily fitting the top rail into the dovetails at the two ends you will now be able to measure the correct length of the centre divisions and these can be cut to length.

This completes the whole carcase which can then be fitted together dry, and checked for squareness. When you're quite satisfied, the carcase can be taken apart and glued and cramped together. This is then left to dry and afterwards the surplus glue is cleaned off and the whole carcase glass-papered up.

Fit the runners, kickers, and drawer guides to take the centre drawer. These are glued and screwed in place, apart from the guides which are just glued and pinned into position. Screw in place the support pieces for the ply cupboard bottoms shown in Fig. 4.6.

Now the front rails are crossbanded and this will bring the front rails flush with the front legs. After the crossbanding has been cleaned off, fit the ply bottoms into each side of the sideboard. Note that these are set back about 1 in from the front rail and should act as stops for the doors. The bottoms are not glued but pinned in position with panel pins.

Four small trays are fitted into the left-hand cupboard after first fitting the interior with packing pieces to each side. Fig. 4.8 shows in detail how this is achieved. This will ensure that the trays will clear the door. When this side has been fitted out, the small trays can be made and fitted; Fig. 4.6 shows the details of this and no more explanation should be necessary.

Doors, drawer front, and spandrel are next to be made, starting with the doors. There are two methods of making these. The first is the same way in which the original would have been made – solid wood (in this case obeche), shaped and built up in brick fashion as in Fig. 4.10. Cleats are loose-tongued on to each side of the doors only.

The other method is to make up jigs to form 4 mm ply into door, drawer and spandrel shapes; Fig. 4.9 shows the jig for making the doors. This is made from blockboard glued and screwed together with rubber

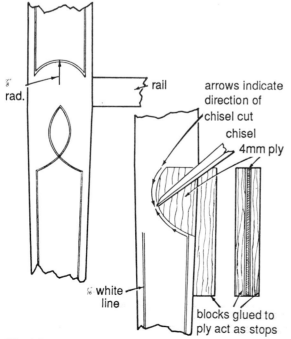

$\frac{1}{8}$"
rad.

rail

arrows indicate
direction of
chisel cut

chisel

4mm ply

$\frac{1}{16}$" white
line

blocks glued to
ply act as stops

Fig. 4.4

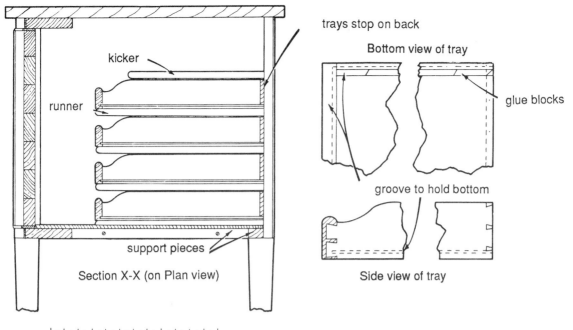

trays stop on back

Bottom view of tray

glue blocks

groove to hold bottom

Side view of tray

Section X-X (on Plan view)

kicker

runner

support pieces

Fig. 4.6

sheets glued to both inside faces. Five pieces of 4 mm ply are glued together, the outer grain of each running the opposite way to the next and placed into the jig, which is then put under pressure with G-cramps. There is, of course, more work entailed in making the ply doors but shrinkage will not occur later; also you will not have the shaping and cleaning off to do as with the solid method.

Let's presume that the solid obeche fronts are being made. Patterns are made from stout card or thin ply to the shape of the doors and centre drawer, the latter being used for the spandrel shape also. The shapes are marked off from the top rail of the carcase. The pattern for the doors need not be full-length as cleats will be fitted later. The correct number of shapes are drawn on to the obeche and then cut out on a bandsaw. These pieces are then glued and cramped, making sure to test with a straightedge to keep them in alignment. When these are dry cleats are fitted to each side

of the doors with a loose-tongue joint – care must be taken not to lose the shape of the doors at this stage, so check the shape of these on the top rail before gluing together. Use carpenter's dogs at top and bottom to pull the joint together when finally gluing up. This is shown in Fig. 4.9. Door, drawer and spandrel are then fitted and care must be taken to make a good fit of all these.

Next, commence work on levelling the backs on each of these with a spokeshave and toothing iron. Fig. 4.11 shows the method you can use to finish the shaped inside surfaces after they have been spokeshaved. A toothing iron is clamped between two pieces of timber (preferably hardwood) using screws with wing-nuts, thus making it easy to tighten and release the iron. One face is concave and the other convex, so all that's needed to shape the opposite curves is to reverse the iron.

Satisfy yourself that these surfaces are smooth and

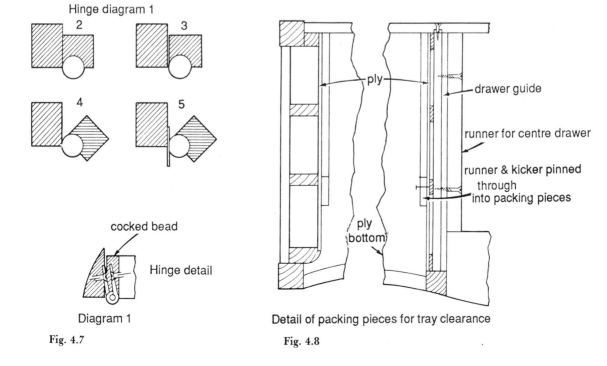

Hinge diagram 1

2 3

4 5

cocked bead

Hinge detail

Diagram 1

Fig. 4.7

ply

ply bottom

drawer guide

runner for centre drawer

runner & kicker pinned through into packing pieces

Detail of packing pieces for tray clearance

Fig. 4.8

15

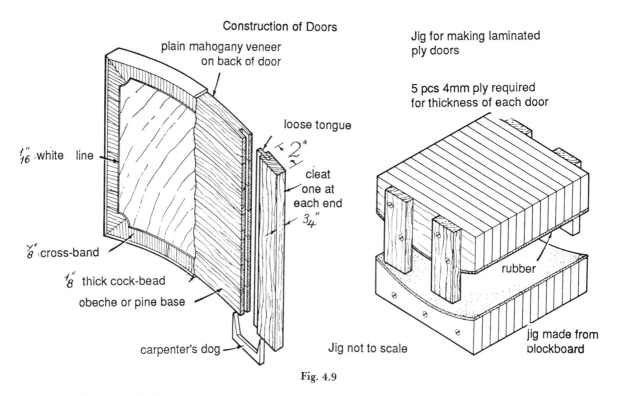

Construction of Doors

plain mahogany veneer
on back of door

$\frac{1}{16}$" white line

loose tongue

2"

cleat
one at
each end

$\frac{3}{4}$"

$\frac{1}{8}$" cross-band

$\frac{1}{8}$" thick cock-bead

obeche or pine base

carpenter's dog

Jig for making laminated
ply doors

5 pcs 4mm ply required
for thickness of each door

rubber

Jig not to scale

jig made from
blockboard

Fig. 4.9

any imperfections and also by using a straightedge. Size the faces with thin Scotch glue, and when dry, veneer the inside surfaces with a straight-grain mahogany veneer. The grain on all the inside surfaces should run from top to bottom. Leave to dry for 24 hours before cleaning off.

Cut a groove in the back of the centre drawer-front to take a ply bottom later. Then make up the centre drawer and fit into the carcase. The drawer stops are fitted on the drawer runners against the back, shown in Fig. 4.1 (plan). The spandrel is then temporarily screwed in position and the doors are also panel-pinned through the top and bottom rails. Do not make the mistake of driving the pins right home or they will be difficult to remove later. By fitting all the fronts in position they can all be spokeshaved in the carcase and this will maintain the shapes of the fronts to correspond with the rails.

After this operation these are removed and given a thin coat of Scotch glue size. Veneer the fronts with a good quality figured or "flare" veneer. The leaves should be from the same batch and reversed so that a good match is obtained. One leaf is used on each door and reversed so that the flare slopes to the centre of the sideboard. Two leaves can be used for the drawer and spandrel, reversed and cut to the correct widths for each. The joint made by the two leaves comes to the centre.

Note that the two extra pieces of veneer are mitred on to each side of the spandrel as shows in Fig. 4.1. Just after you have veneered the doors and drawer fronts, set a cutting gauge to $\frac{1}{16}$ in and mark around the outside of both. The waste veneer can then be easily removed while the glue is still wet ready for the white line and crossbanding. The corners are cut out at this stage using a pair of dividers with one point sharp-

DRAWER FRONT AND SPANDREL

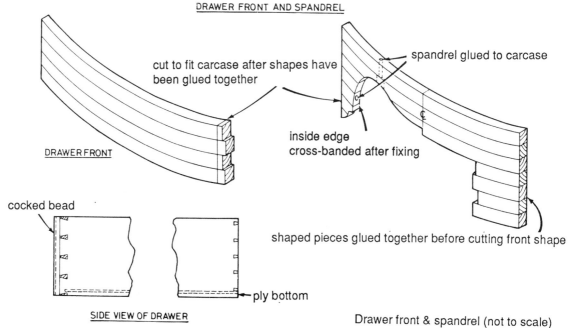

cut to fit carcase after shapes have
been glued together

spandrel glued to carcase

DRAWER FRONT

inside edge
cross-banded after fixing

cocked bead

ply bottom

shaped pieces glued together before cutting front shape

SIDE VIEW OF DRAWER

Drawer front & spandrel (not to scale)

Fig. 4.10.

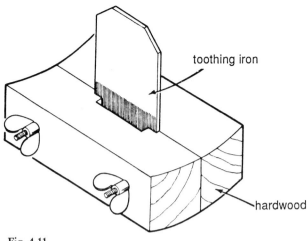

Fig. 4.11.

ened. These dividers will also be used again to cut the crossbanding to fit these corners.

The spandrel can now be glued and screwed in position; note that it is set in $\frac{1}{16}$ in from the front legs and rail to form a break. The screw holes are then plugged and the under edge veneered with a straightgrain mahogany. After this has been allowed to dry, trim off the surplus veneer. A cutting gauge with a round face is set to the thickness of $\frac{1}{8}$ in and then this is taken around the outside edge of the spandrel.

Using a $\frac{1}{4}$ in chisel, preferably a bevel edge, cut out the waste to take the $\frac{1}{8}$ in white line. This is then glued into place using a PVA or resin glue and a clear adhesive tape is used to hold the line in place while the glue is drying. The $\frac{1}{16}$ in white line can now be glued into place around both the doors and drawers, being held in place by the use of small $\frac{1}{2}$ in tacks while drying.

After this operation the crossbanding can be glued in place. Note the mitre joints in each corner.

All the fronts can now be cleaned off, using a fine glasspaper to finish. The $\frac{1}{8}$ in cocked bead is fitted at this stage. First gauge the bead's thickness on to all fronts and reduce doors and drawers to take it. Care must be taken to leave just enough clearance to allow the doors and drawer to work properly. Mitre the cocked bead in each corner. Hinge the doors next, using $1\frac{1}{2}$ in solid drawn brass hinges. The hinges are fitted as shown in the hinge diagram Fig. 4.7(1), so that the knuckle of the hinge coincides with the bead. If the door is hinged as in diagram 2, the bead would grind against the leg, as in 4. However, if the door is hinged as in 3 so that a thin piece of veneer can be placed between the door and the leg, it will be able to open the close without grinding. Diagram 5 shows this clearly.

Now the three locks and escutcheons are fitted into the doors and drawer. To mark the position of the bolts when cutting the mortises into the top rail, coat the tops of the bolts with spirit black; close the door or drawer and turn the key and the position of the bolt will be marked clearly on the rail. To cut this mortise out in order to take the lock bolt, simply drill through the top rail and finish cutting with a chisel. You will be able to see how the bolt is engaging the mortise if you do it this way. Temporarily fit the four brass ring handles.

The top is made from $\frac{3}{4}$ in thick mahogany. You may have to joint two pieces of timber for this. The top is then shaped to leave a $\frac{3}{4}$ in overhang. A rebate is cut to take $\frac{1}{8}$ in thick crossbanding and the outside edge

crossbanded, again $\frac{1}{8}$ in thick. Here again, this can be held in place with clear adhesive tape while the glue dries.

Next a $\frac{1}{16}$ in white line is glued in place; the plan view, Fig. 4.1, shows this, using $\frac{1}{2}$ in tacks to hold this in place temporarily. When dry, crossband against this $\frac{1}{16}$ in line, working around the top with pieces of banding not more than 3 in wide; aim to keep the grain at right angles to the white line. Use G-cramps and odd pieces of wood placed between the crossbanding and cramps to hold this in place till the glue is dry. An easy way of working the banding around the shaped front is to cut the banding roughly to the shape required. Place this in the rebate and with a pair of dividers with one point held against the $\frac{1}{16}$ in line and the other on the banding, the shape can be transferred to the banding. This will give you a clear line to spokeshave down to. Mitre the crossbanding at the corners as shown in plan view, Fig. 4.1. Finally the outer edge is rebated to take a $\frac{1}{8}$ in square white line and the same procedure as was used to insert the $\frac{1}{8}$ in white line into the spandrel is repeated.

Lastly, the whole top can be cleaned off in one operation and finally screwed to the carcase. Pocket-screw through the back and screw through the front rail to secure the top.

Now the sideboard has been completed you will want to give it the best possible finish, and some experience in French polishing is necessary. The whole job is first glasspapered, starting with a medium paper and working down to a fine flour paper. A damp rag can be wiped over the top to raise the grain before glasspapering to give a better finish.

A water stain is preferred by many French polishers. Test the stain out on bits of difficult offcut timber until the right shade is obtained. You can stain the work twice, and after the first application the whole sideboard can be flour-papered and then faked or 'distressed'.

This will give a good antique effect to the finish but take care not to overdo it. The surface is faked with the aid of a stiff wire brush, a piece of clinker, and grit. Afterwards, the job is papered again and given the final coat of stain. If you do not fake your work the stain can be applied in one operation. If the grain is open it may be necessary to fill in, using a wood filler.

Button polish is now built-up using a rubber lubricated with linseed oil in the usual way. Rub down between coats with a fine grade wire wool. If you find the finish patchy in places it may be necessary to use colouring, for example spirit black or Bismarck brown, to bring the patches to a uniform shade. After the last coat of polish has been allowed to dry (the number of coats depending on individual choice), rub down with 000-grade wire wool and wax. A good bit of elbow grease will finish the job off.

In fact, French polish was not used in England until about 1820, some years after Sheraton's death in 1806. It is more appropriate, therefore, that the sideboard should be polished according to Sheraton's own methods as given in his *Cabinet Dictionary (1803)* as follows: (a) by rubbing on a soft wax mixture (turps and beeswax) to which may be added a little red (alkanet root) oil and polishing off with a cloth; or (b) applying linseed oil (with or without the additional of red oil) and brick dust and spreading the paste over the work-this makes a kind of abrasive putty which should not be discarded but rubbed continually until the surface assumes a fine polish; (c) for inside work, unsoftened wax (i.e. without the addition of white spirit) is rubbed on with a cork pad and the 'clemmings' are cleared away by rubbing on powdered brick dust with a cloth.

CUTTING LIST

Part	L	W	T	L	W	T
	INCHES			*MM*		
1 Top (HM)	60½	22¼	¾	1537	565	19
6 Legs (HM)	36½	2	1¾	927	51	45
2 Ends (MP)	18½	16¼	⅝	470	413	16
2 Centre divisions (MP)	18½	16¼	⅝	470	413	16
1 Back (MP)	58½	16¼	⅝	1485	413	16
2 Front rails (AM)	58½	6¼	¾	1485	159	19
2 Cupboard bottoms (MP)	17½	17¼	¼	445	439	6
2 Left side cupbd pcking pcs (MP)	17½	15¼	¼	445	388	6
1 Left side cupbd pcking pcs (HM)	14½	2¼	1	368	58	25
2 Left side cupbd pcking pcs (AM)	15½	2¼	¾	394	58	19
1 Left side cupbd pcking pcs (AM)	15½	1¼	1	394	32	25
4 Left side cupbd pcking pcs (AM)	15½	1¼	½	394	32	12
4 Supports for cupbd bottoms (AM)	14½	1¼	¾	368	32	19
2 Supports for cupbd bottoms (AM)	16½	1¼	¾	419	32	19
4 Drawer runners & kickers (AM)	14½	1¾	¾	368	45	19
2 Drawer sides (HM)	17½	6¼	¼	445	159	6
1 Drawer back (HM)	21½	6¼	¼	546	159	6
8 Drawer blocks (HM)	5½	½	¼	140	12	6
1 Drawer bottom (MP)	21½	21¼	¼	546	540	6
10 Tray runners & kickers (AM)	12½	¾	½	318	19	12
8 Tray runners & kickers sides (HM)	12½	2¼	¼	318	58	6
4 Tray runners & kickers backs (HM)	14½	2¼	¼	368	58	6
4 Tray runners & kickers fronts (HM)	14½	1¾	½	368	45	12
4 Tray runners & kickers bottoms (MP)	14½	1¼	¼	368	32	6
32 Tray runners & kickers blocks (HM)	3½	½	¼	89	12	6
14 Pieces to cut door shapes (OB)	12½	2	2	318	51	51

CUTTING LIST (continued)

Part	L	W	T	L	W	T
	INCHES			*MM*		
4 Door cleats (OB)	14½	2¼	1	368	58	25
7 Pieces to shape drawer front & spandrel (OB)	22½	2¼	1¼	572	58	32
4 Extra pieces for spandrel (OB)	6½	2¼	1¼	165	58	32
To cut shapes for cocked beads on drawer and doors						
2 Pieces for drawer (HM)	22½	2¼	⅛	572	58	3
4 Pieces for doors (HM)	15½	3¼	⅛	394	83	3
5 Pieces for drawer & doors (HM)	14½	1¼	⅛	368	32	3
2 Drawer guides (AM)	17	1¼	⅝	432	32	16
Veneers and cross-banding required (widths are net)						
Total required for crossbanding the top (HM)	108	2	⅛	2742	51	3
Total required for top edge (HM)	108	¾	⅛	2742	19	3
Total required for veneering ends (HM)	36	16	—	914	407	—
Total required for door, drawer & spandrel backing (HM)	42	21	—	1067	533	—
Total required for crossbanding drawer & doors	144	1	—	3656	25	—
Total required for crossbanding drawer & doors (HM)	60	2	—	1524	51	—
Total required for crossbanding front rails (HM)	108	¾	⅛	2742	19	3
4 Leaves mahogany curl veneer for drawer & door fronts & spandrel, each	13	13	—	330	330	—

ALSO REQUIRED:
A 13 ft length of white line for inlay, ⅛ in (3 mm) square, for top and spandrel edges; 49 ft in 39 in lengths of white line for inlay, ³⁄₁₆ in (5 mm) square for top inside inlay, legs, and door and drawer inlay; three 2 in (51 mm) brass cut drawer locks with escutcheons; four 1½ in (38 mm) solid drawn brass hinges; four brass ring handles, 2 in (51 mm) dia; steel screws and panel pins.
KEY TO RECOMMENDED TIMBERS: (HM) Honduras mahogany; (AM) African mahogany; (MP) mahogany ply; (OB) obeche.
Except where otherwise stated working allowances have been made to lengths and widths; thicknesses are net.

MEDIEVAL AUMBRY

The aumbry was the original food cupboard of medieval times and the precursor of the modern refrigerator; the pierced 'windows' served to keep food fresh for as long as possible.

Today the aumbry would not be used for its original purpose, but it is ideally suited for the storage of books, drinks or china, and it would certainly fit well into the decor of a house where the surroundings are

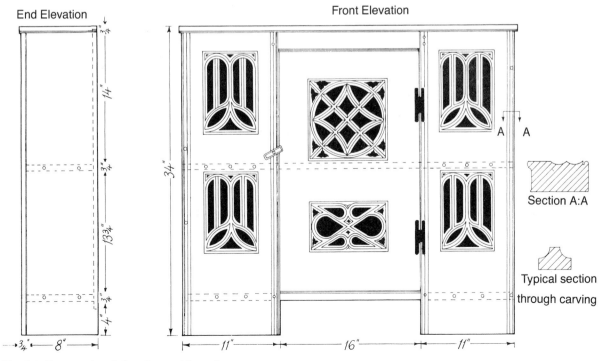

Fig. 5.1. Front and end elevations, with sections.

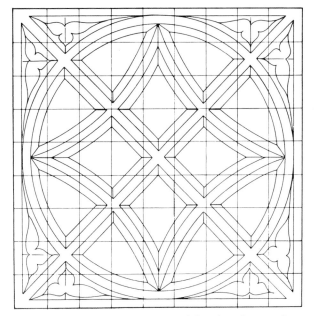

Fig. 5.2. One-inch (25 mm) squared drawing of upper door carving.

Fig. 5.3. One-inch (25 mm) squared drawing of lower door carving.

traditional. With its simple natural surfaces and pierced ornamentation it is an attractive piece of furniture and one which employs a variety of processes and skills.

As the piece is made from solid stuff throughout (even the back) there are no framing problems, and you should start with the door. After cutting to size, mark out the Gothic traceries in accordance with the details shown in the drawings, Figs, 5.2, 5.3 and 5.4.

The pierced areas should be removed by drilling and their edges cleaned up with a chisel or a gouge, as required. Next, a small gouge is used to fillet the ribs, and you can see the profile from the section drawing. Note that the back of the door is reduced in thickness locally behind the windows to improve the delicacy of the tracery, and this is best achieved with a flat gouge.

Do not try to be too fussy or precise with the carving. Remember the originals were made centuries ago when tools were cruder than they are today, and much of the appeal of the carving is due to this. The main aims, therefore, should be crisp edges and delicacy of proportion – all tool marks should be left to contribute to the general effect and glasspaper should never be used in any circumstances.

The side fronts should be tackled next and you can proceed with these on the same lines as for the door.

Fig. 5.4. One-inch (25 mm) squared drawing of side front carvings.

The edges of the fronts are fluted as shown, and the extreme edges are lipped with a small moulding, as detailed. If you do not have a moulding plane or electric router to do the job make up a simple scratch tool by grinding a small blade of steel to the required shape. Sandwich this between two wooden blocks which can be held together with bolts and wing-nuts, and scratch the oak sides to the required depth.

Now you can connect the side fronts to the side pieces by dowelling in the conventional manner. You could cheat a little here and use screws well recessed into the fronts – then fill the recesses with oak pegs, leaving them slightly proud of the surface to act as decoration.

The top rail above the door is tenoned into the two side fronts and sides and pegged. The bottom is fitted next after it has been recessed to take the side fronts; it is then screwed and pegged in place.

Shelves are fitted in the positions required to suit whatever storage arrangements you have in mind. Fit the top next, screwing it and pegging it with the pegs cut off flush or as it is solid, use the buttoning method to allow for movement.

The back, which should also be solid timber of a type in keeping with the period, could be made up from elm boards for economy, rub-jointing the pieces to get the width.

Next you can fit and hang the door, using good quality wrought iron hinges as shown, or something similar. The door is secured by a simple wooden turn-button.

A natural finish would be the authentic one. Use linseed oil, well rubbed in and left for a few days to penetrate the oak; then a good quality wax polish applied with a lint-free cloth, bringing it to a polish with a soft, short-haired brush.

CUTTING LIST

		INCHES			MM		
		L	W	T	L	W	T
2	Side fronts	34½	11¼	¾	876	286	19
1	Door	27½	16¼	¾	698	413	19
1	Top	39	9	¾	990	228	19
2	Ends	34½	8¼	¾	876	209	19
1	Rail at top of door	18½	2¼	¾	470	58	19
1	Bottom piece	38½	8¼	¾	978	209	19
1	Shelf	38½	8¼	¾	978	209	19
5	Back pieces, each	38½	8¼	½	978	209	12

All parts in oak except the back pieces, which are in elm. Working allowances have been made to lengths and widths; thicknesses are net.

SOUTHERN HUNTBOARD

Gentlemen of the American South in the first half of the 19th century were the inspiration for the development of a tall sideboard, referred to as a 'huntboard', and designed along simple lines. They were usually found in hallways where they were loaded with food and drink for hungry huntsmen returning from the fields.

This huntboard is an adapted design and is constructed entirely of walnut. For economy and ease of construction, the back and the bottom can be constructed of $\frac{1}{2}$ in walnut-faced plywood, and the drawer bottoms and sides can be constructed of poplar.

Construction begins with the six legs. These are made from $1\frac{3}{4}$ in square walnut stock, $40\frac{1}{4}$ in long. The taper of these legs is a double taper, beginning $19\frac{1}{4}$ in from the upper end of each leg. The first taper reduces the size of the leg $1\frac{1}{2}$ in, 14 in lower on the leg, and the second taper, beginning at this point, further reduces the size of the leg to 1 in square at the end.

The taper can be made on a circular saw or jointer. If the latter is used, set it for a $\frac{1}{8}$ in cut, and the leg is carefully pulled through with the cutting begun $19\frac{1}{4}$ in from the top end of the leg. For the lower part of the taper, each side of the leg must be pulled through twice to reduce the size further from $1\frac{1}{2}$ in to 1 in at the lower end.

The back legs are then mortised for both the back panel and the side panel. These mortises may be cut on the circular saw using a dado blade, although one must be careful to stop the saw cut at the proper length and to square up the otherwise rounded mortises at each end. Since the grain direction of the sides is the same as that of the legs, expansion and contraction should be no problem, and the appropriate tenons for the sides can be of the same length as the mortises ($17\frac{1}{4}$ in).

If the back is made of dimensioned lumber glued up into a panel, the tenons should be only 4 in long with approximately a $2\frac{1}{2}$ in separation between each of the tenons to allow for some expansion and correction, although the mortises may be $17\frac{1}{4}$ in long. As mentioned, this back piece may be made of walnut-faced plywood.

Before gluing the back piece in place, it would be wise to dado two grooves $\frac{1}{2}$ in by approximately $\frac{1}{4}$ in deep on the inside of the back, as shown for the interior cabinet panels and to rabbet $\frac{1}{4}$ in 6 1 in along the lower edge of the back. After thorough sanding, the back may be glued to the two back legs and set aside temporarily.

The upper and lower front rails are constructed of walnut $2\frac{1}{2} \times 1$ in $\times 59$ in. The dovetails are cut as shown in Fig. 6.2. Note there is a dado cut in the back surface of the central leg to receive the central partition to be placed on each side of the drawer section.

After the upper and lower front rails are satisfactorily fitted to the four front legs and before gluing them, the serving board runner and the drawer runner should be made as in the detailed drawing (Fig. 6.3).

The front portion of this drawer runner must be made of walnut 1 in thick. Similarly, the front rail of the serving board runner must also be of walnut $\frac{3}{16}$ in thick. The remainder of the drawer runner can be of poplar of matching thickness, and as noted in Fig. 6.3 a dust panel is included in the drawer runner. The dimension shown in the drawing is 26 in between the two central legs, and if there is any variation in this dimension, appropriate adjustment of the drawer and serving board runner front rails must be made. After the drawer runner and serving board runner are constructed, the $\frac{1}{2}$ in square drawer guide may be screwed to the respective runners.

After appropriate preliminary fitting, the upper front rail, the serving board runner, the drawer

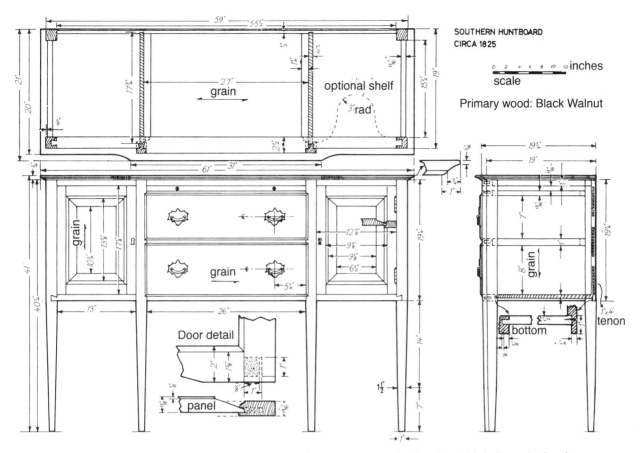

Fig. 6.1. Plan and elevations. Note the shelf with a shaped front to accommodate bottles which is shown in the plan. Also illustrated are the door and panel details, and how the carcase bottom is fixed.

runner, and the lower front rail may be assembled as a unit. Before the final gluing, be sure that a groove is cut with a dado saw along the entire back surface of the lower front rail in Fig. 6.2. This is for acceptance of a tongue made on the bottom piece later. In addition, make sure that mortises are cut in the back portion of

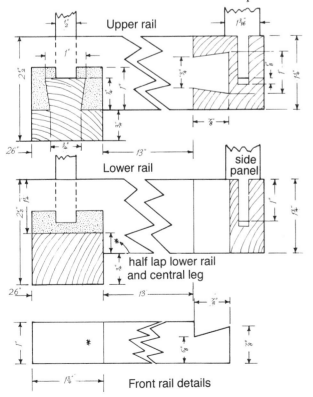

Fig. 6.2. Plans of the fixing of the upper and lower rails, with details of half-lap.

the upper front rail to accommodate $1 \times 1\frac{1}{4}$ in piece which acts as a top runner for the serving board when it is inserted.

The serving board runner assembly and the drawer runner assembly may be glued in their respective mortises before the assembly of the upper and lower rails to the legs.

The sides are constructed of a glued-up panel of walnut $19\frac{1}{4} \times 17\frac{1}{2}$ in wide, and as mentioned, $1 \times \frac{1}{4}$ in tenons are cut on each side of the outer side panels for assembly into the appropriate mortises in the two back legs and the two outer front legs. A dado $\frac{1}{2} \times \frac{1}{4}$ in deep can be cut on the inside lower edge of the side pieces to receive the $\frac{1}{2}$ in thick bottom. Again, this fit should be a little on the loose side to allow for expansion and contraction.

The bottom is constructed of $\frac{1}{2}$ in walnut-faced plywood rebated along the front edge to fit with slight play in the back edge of the lower front rail. The lower inside lip of the back piece has been rebated as shown in the end elevation in Fig. 6.1 to receive the bottom piece. The bottom is fastened to the back with 1 in screws as shown and it should be noted that no glue is used in assembly of the bottom so that expansion and contraction can occur without splitting or warping.

After a satisfactory preliminary fitting of both sides and the bottom, the tenons of the top runners for the serving board can be placed in the mortises on the back part of the upper rail. The bottom piece can be loosely inserted, the two inner panels placed without glue and the two sides placed in their respective mortises. The entire assembly is then glued. At this stage, the six legs should be resting on a perfectly flat surface, preferably a $\frac{3}{4}$ in plywood board, so that no unevenness will occur in the finished piece.

23

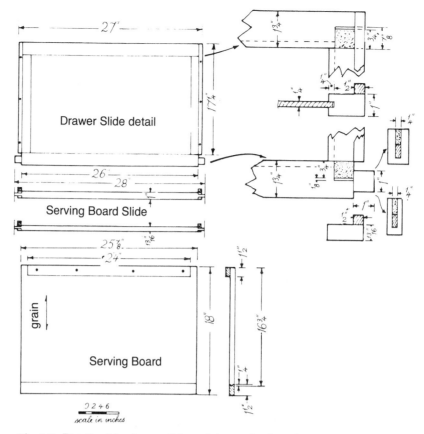

Drawer Slide detail

Serving Board Slide

grain

Serving Board

0 2 4 6
scale in inches

Fig. 6.3. Details of the drawer slide and the serving board.

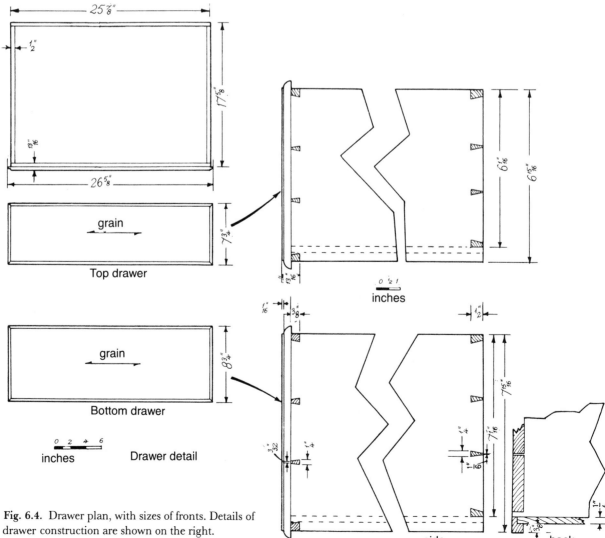

grain

Top drawer

grain

Bottom drawer

0 2 4 6
inches

Drawer detail

inches

side

back

Fig. 6.4. Drawer plan, with sizes of fronts. Details of drawer construction are shown on the right.

24

After the glue has set 1 in brass screws can be used to fasten the back securely to the bottom, the drawer runner, the serving board runner, and the two top runners for the serving board. This completes the basic assembly.

The top is a large panel constructed of $^{13}/_{16}$ in walnut boards measuring 61 × 21 in. The basic front shape is bandsawn or jigsawn as shown in Fig. 6.1 (plan), and the edge is moulded as shown in the detail, using a spindle moulder or router as appropriate. Several screws drilled through the upper front rail and diagonally from the inside of the two sides will fix the top satisfactorily to the cabinet.

After preliminary fitting of the top, attention can be given to the construction of the two side doors and the two central drawers, as well as the serving board. For strength, the serving board is made of a built-up panel of walnut $25^7/_8$ in wide and 18 in long. A front, longitudinally-placed piece finishes off the end grain and is glued in place with a tongue-and-groove joint. A back stop 24 in long serves not only as a stop but helps prevent warping of the serving board. This is screwed in place. The serving board can be finished completely except for the back stop and this can be inserted just before finally placing the top in place.

Although measurements are given for the panel doors, the final dimension should be gauged after construction of the cabinet itself to allow for slight variations in wood thickness, etc. The panel of each door is not glued in place but is placed in the groove cut along the inside of the door rails during construction.

An alternate method of construction would be to place the panel in the door frame after assembly, much as one would place a picture in a frame, using a bead to hold the panel in place.

The drawers may be constructed using a solid walnut front and poplar sides and back. The bottom of the drawers may be $^1/_4$ in plywood, and standard dovetail construction is used. A variation in the dovetails will allow for individuality in construction of this piece of furniture, although the small dovetails Fig. 6.4 are traditional. The dimensions as shown allow for approximately $^1/_{16}$ in clearance on each side of the drawers, and a $^1/_{16}$ in clearance top and bottom. Drawer stops are unnecessary because of the over-lapping moulded edge flange on the front of each drawer. Shelves may be placed in each side cabinet, and one shelf is shown in Fig. 6.1. Shelf supports may be screwed to the inside of the back and sides of the cabinets on each side of the huntboard as desired.

Small locks are inserted in each cabinet. Most sanding should precede final assembly, since working into blind corners is quite difficult with glasspaper. After initial sanding with 3/0 garnet paper, the wood is dampened and subsequent sanding removes the raised grain. Final sanding with 6/0 glasspaper is advisable, and this is followed by an appropriate paste wood filler. A Danish Oil finish provides most satisfactory results for completion of this piece, followed by a good grade carnauba wax. The rich, brown tones of walnut in this huntboard will enhance any dining or living room.

CUTTING LIST

		INCHES			*MM*	
	L	*W*	*T*	*L*	*W*	*T*
6 Legs (W)	40¾	2	1¾	1035	51	45
2 Front rails (W)	59½	2¾	1	1511	70	25
1 Front drawer slide (W)	28¹/₂₀	2	1	724	51	25
1 Front board slide (W)	28½	2	$^{13}/_{16}$	724	51	21
2 Side panels (W)*	19¾	17¾	$^{13}/_{16}$	502	451	21
1 Drawer front (W)	27½	9	$^{13}/_{16}$	699	229	21
1 Drawer front (W)	27½	8	$^{13}/_{16}$	699	203	21
1 Top (W)*	61½	21¼	$^{13}/_{16}$	1562	540	21
4 Side doors (W)	17⅜	2¼	$^{13}/_{16}$	442	58	21
4 Side doors (W)	12⅜	2¼	$^{13}/_{16}$	315	58	21
2 Panels (W)*	14½	10⅛	$^{13}/_{16}$	368	257	21
1 Serving board (W)*	26⅜	18¼	$^{13}/_{16}$	670	464	21
1 Serving board (W)*	26⅜	2¼	$^{13}/_{16}$	670	58	21
1 Serving board (W)*	24½	2¼	$^{13}/_{16}$	623	58	21
1 Piece for drawer slides (P)	73½	2¼	1	1866	58	25
1 Piece for Serving board slides (P)	73½	2¼	$^{13}/_{16}$	1866	58	21
1 Piece for drawer sides (P)	approx. 10 sq.ft		½	approx 0.93 sq.m		12
1 Top serving board rail (P)	17½	1½	1	445	38	25
2 Drawer bottoms (Ply)	26½	18¼	¼	673	464	6
1 Dust panel (Ply)	26½	18¼	¼	674	464	6
1 Back (Ply)	56	19½	½	1422	495	12
1 Bottom (Ply)	19½	17¾	½	495	451	12
2 Inside panels (Ply)	18¾	18	½	476	457	12

Working allowances have been made to lengths and widths; thicknesses are net. (W) = walnut; (P) = poplar; (Ply) = plywood. * indicates glued-up boards of varying widths.

GATE-LEG TABLE WITH BOW FRONT

In the eyes of the purist the design may be judged a hybrid – hybrids, though, are often more vigorous than the pure stock! Apart from the usual setting out and cutting the various parts, turning, veneering, inlaying, laminboard construction, some metalwork, and perhaps carving are all called for.

For the table shown in the illustration all the show wood is walnut, using nicely figured veneers for the tops and rather heavier figured stuff for veneering the rails, which are mahogany. The groundwork for the tops is shown in laminboard.

Undoubtedly, the table would look well made in mahogany (perhaps even better than in walnut), choosing nicely figured stuff for the tops and curl veneers for the rails. Whatever timber is used, only prime quality well seasoned material should be chosen. Incidentally, the finished weight of the table is only 13 lb and it is surprisingly rigid for its light weight.

COPYING THE LEG
The leg is copied from a small drawing in a book. Nothing very complicated or scientific is used; in addition to a drawing board and a sheet of cartridge paper, only tee and set squares, a rule and a pair of dividers are needed.

Draw out the leg as in Fig. 7.2 to an assumed full size, scaling off the drawing with dividers. Take off first the front rail depth and next the centre height of the stretcher rails from the floor. Next comes the neck part between the top square and the fluted part and then the fluted part itself. The various beads and hollows are then put in and adjusted to look right. The drawing was inked in and the dimensions put on. To scale down to 20 in high, reduce at first all sizes to two thirds, adjusting the vertical measurements slightly to come within the 20 inches. These are all marked on the drawing. Next a specimen leg is turned, adjusting slightly here and there the diameters and beads and hollows until it seems correct. In doing a job like this

you cannot be too literal; you cannot scale nature! Most of the diameters finally come out rather over than under the calculated ones, which is to be expected – the main thing is to get it right visually.

TURNING THE LEGS
These are the heart of the job and the most tricky part, so they are done first. The six squares are prepared to finished size before turning. If you have a planer with a thicknesser it is a good plan to do them on it, making the final light sizing cuts with the thicknesser in position. Before doing the initial cuts, check that the fence is set exactly at 90 degrees as it is important that the ends carrying the mortises are dead square.

Details of the turning are shown in Fig. 7.2, with and enlarged section at Fig. 7.3 showing how the stretcher rails are incorporated.

Getting a nicely finished straight taper on the middle portion may prove the biggest problem. Briefly, the method consists of mounting a pair of profile boards on the lathe bed on which the straight taper can be planed with a low angle block plane after bringing it nearly to size with the gouge. The top edges of the profile boards are at lathe centre height plus half the diameter of the finished taper at any given point. The plane is worked slightly obliquely across the top edges of the boards until it ceases to cut – the taper is then to size and all six will come out exactly alike.

The set-up for this job is shown in Fig. 7.12. Note that a chuck jaw guard is needed to avoid catching your knuckles when working close to the chuck. It is quite practical to use the top edge of the near board as a tool rest when doing the various beads and hollows. This saves a considerable amount of time in exchanging the profile unit for the usual tool rest. After completing the turning of the first leg, take it out of the lathe and take a good long look at it; ask yourself 'Does it look right?' A small difference in the diameter or thickness of a part can make a big difference to the final appearance, and now is the time to put it right.

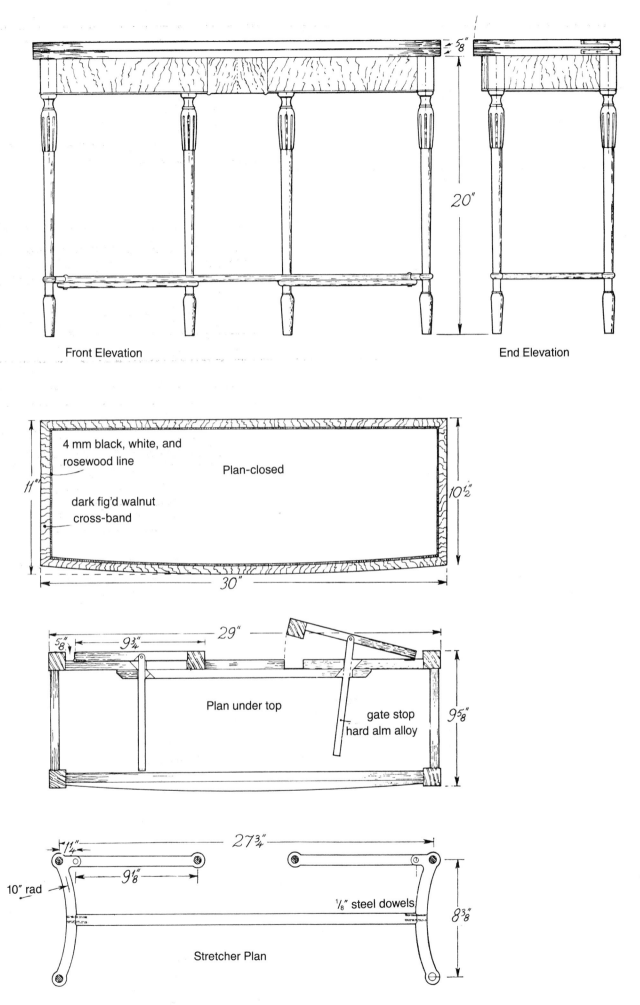

Front Elevation

End Elevation

4 mm black, white, and
rosewood line

Plan-closed

dark fig'd walnut
cross-band

Plan under top

gate stop
hard alm alloy

$\frac{1}{8}$" steel dowels

Stretcher Plan

Fig. 7.1.

27

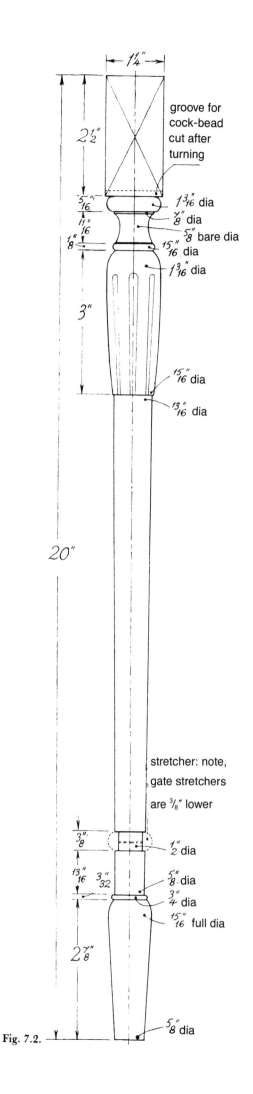

Fig. 7.2.

1¼"

groove for
cock-bead
cut after
turning

2½"

5/16"

1³⁄₁₆" dia
⅞" dia
5/8" bare dia
15/16" dia
1³⁄₁₆" dia

11/16"

⅛"

3"

15/16" dia

1³⁄₁₆" dia

20"

stretcher: note,
gate stretchers
are ⅜" lower

3/8"

½" dia

13/16" 3/32"

5/8" dia
¾" dia
15/16" full dia

2⅞"

5/8" dia

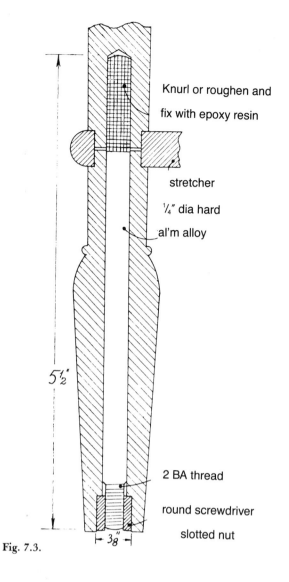

Fig. 7.3.

Knurl or roughen and
fix with epoxy resin

stretcher

¼" dia hard

al'm alloy

5½"

2 BA thread

round screwdriver

slotted nut

⅜"

CUTTING THE FLUTES

Workers used to carving will have no difficulty here.
For those who are no use with a carving gouge, here is
a good method. In the absence of a dividing head on
the lathe, all that is needed is some simple method of
locking the mandrel together with eight equal divisions marked on the chuck body and an index pointer
fitted in a suitable position. An easy way to get the
eight divisions is to cut a strip of paper in length the
circumference of the chuck body, marking it off into
eight equal parts and sticking it around the chuck.

For the actual cutting of the flutes, mount (if you
have one), a vertical milling attachment on the lathe
top-slide, setting it over to suit the taper needed (about
2 degrees). The depth of cut is then controlled by the
cross-slide with the cut traversed by the top-slide
screw. The set over of the top-slide is adjusted so that
the flute just runs out at the bottom when the depth is
correct at the bulbous portion. When the setting is correct both for depth and run-out it is possible to do each
flute at one pass of the cutter, leaving a flute that needs
practically no cleaning up. The cutter height is
adjusted to lathe centre height on the milling attachment itself. The cutter spindle is driven from a shaft
running behind the lathe (actually an extension of the
lathe motor shaft), the belt coming over a pair of over-
head jockey pulleys. The cutter can be made from a
centre drill from which the drill point has been broken

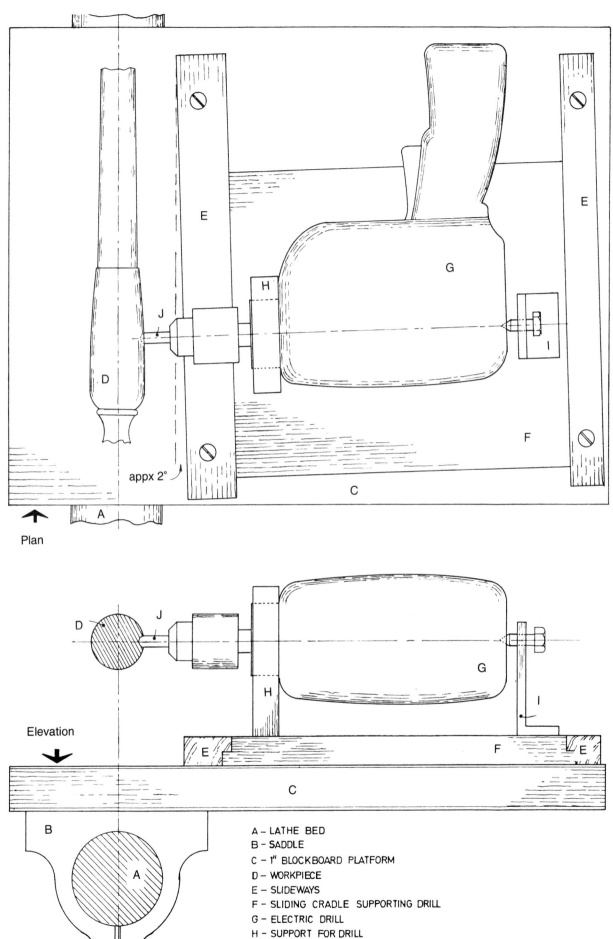

Plan

Elevation

A – LATHE BED
B – SADDLE
C – 1" BLOCKBOARD PLATFORM
D – WORKPIECE
E – SLIDEWAYS
F – SLIDING CRADLE SUPPORTING DRILL
G – ELECTRIC DRILL
H – SUPPORT FOR DRILL
I – REAR SUPPORT FOR DRILL
J – CUTTER

appx 2°

Fig. 7.4.

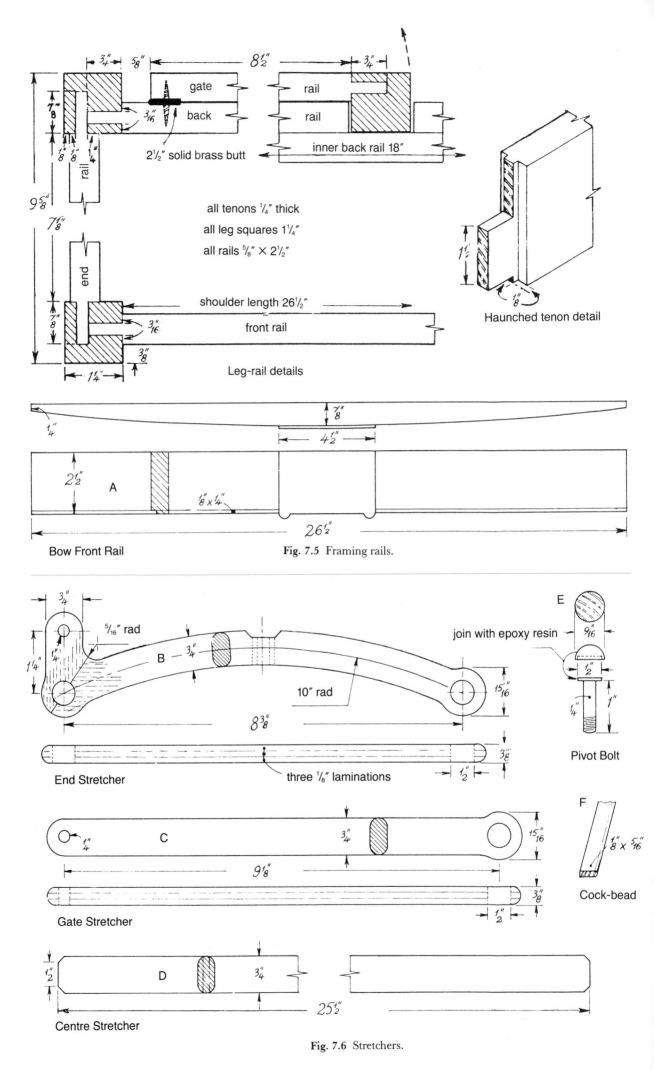

all tenons ¼" thick

all leg squares 1¼"

all rails ⅝" × 2½"

2½" solid brass butt

inner back rail 18"

shoulder length 26½"

front rail

Leg-rail details

Haunched tenon detail

Bow Front Rail

Fig. 7.5 Framing rails.

End Stretcher

three ⅛" laminations

Pivot Bolt

join with epoxy resin

Gate Stretcher

Centre Stretcher

Cock-bead

Fig. 7.6 Stretchers.

30

off, leaving the 60 degree centre portion with its two flutes intact. The end is shaped freehand on the grinder to a half-round, taking care to grind it with a small clearance to the cutting edges. The cutter spindle is driven at the top speed available, probably around 4000 to 5000 rpm.

AN ALTERNATIVE WAY

In the absence of a lathe with the usual metal turning equipment (cross and top-slides and a vertical milling attachment), the job can be done on the more usual woodturning lathes with round beds. A suitable set-up is shown in Fig 7.4. A platform is bolted to the saddle, on which slides a cradle guided by slideways, carrying an electric drill to drive the cutter. The depth adjustment of the cutter will not be quite so easy, but a small adjustment can be made by altering the projection of the cutter in the chuck.

The turned parts of the legs are sealed with polish at this stage, saving time later.

Drilling the holes in the lower part of the legs for the metal dowels is done with a long $\frac{1}{4}$ in twist drill. Care has to be taken to avoid wandering of the drill in this relatively deep hole. Have the drill sharp and aligned correctly and as you get deeper keep clearing away the chips.

MORTISING THE LEGS

Details of these are given in Fig. 7.10. They can be cut with a hollow chisel in a drilling machine or in the lathe if you have a mortising attachment, either by the hollow chisel or slot mill method. Following this, the cockbead grooves at the bottom of the squares are cut – they should be $\frac{1}{4}$ in deep.

FRAMING RAILS

These are next prepared and cut to dead length, leaving the rebate for the cockbeads until after the tenons had been cut. The tenon details are given in Fig 7.5. Note that the front rail is straight, the bow being obtained by planting on a shaped piece after assembly. The main back rail is at first in one continuous piece. Before assembly the inner back rail is glued and screwed on, glue not being applied where the recesses for the gate squares come later. These recesses are not cut until after the gates have been hung. This part of the assembly can also be seen in Fig. 7.5.

½" dia
Shank
2BA
3/8" dia
9/16" dia
Guide Collar
3/8"
3/16" rad
15/16"
Cutter
7/32"

Fig. 7.8.

Router
A- BLOCKBOARD BASE
B- PACKING STRIPS
C- WORKPIECE
D- TEMPLATE
E- PACKING
F- ROUTER CUTTER
G- GUIDE COLLAR
H- SUB-BASE FIXED TO ROUTER
H
X
D
E
C
G
F
B
A
Plan on X X
Elevation
F

Fig. 7.7.

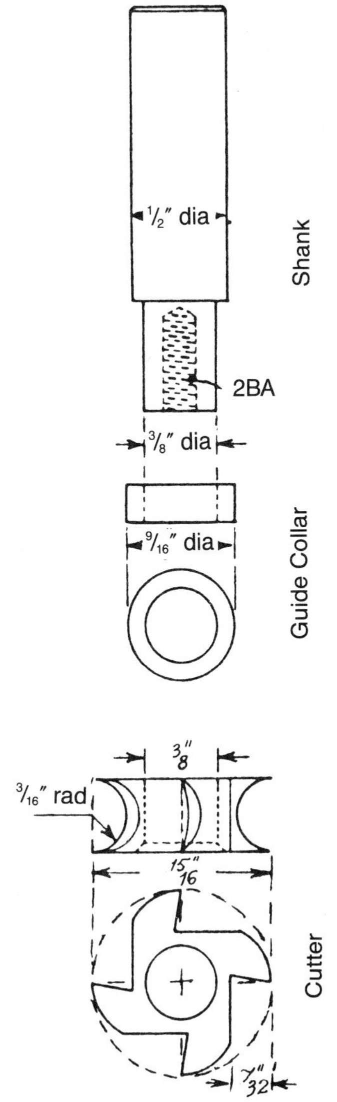

The rebates for the cockbeads are next cut, and following this the two end rails are vertically veneered with some well figured stuff. After a trial assembly the frame is glued together taking particular care to get everything square before putting aside to dry. The front bow piece, A, Fig. 7.5, follows, and again veneering is done before fixing, not forgetting the cockbead rebate.

GATES

At this stage the gate rails are glued to their respective legs. Note that as these rails, unlike the others, finish flush with the leg squares, the outer faces of the rails should be thinned down by the thickness of the veneer to be applied before gluing to the legs. The gates are then hinged to the back rail with $2\frac{1}{2}$ in solid brass butts. The position of these hinges is important; the centre of the hinge pin is $1\frac{1}{4}$ in from the centre of the rear leg and exactly in line with the rear edge of the back rail. Later it will come in line with the stretcher

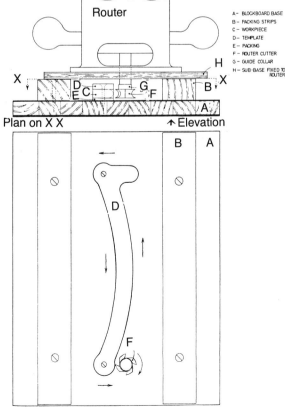

pivot below. Use steel screws initially, as the gates later have to be removed to fit the stretcher rails. The button tongues for fixing the top should already have been cut. These can easily be forgotten until after the frame has been glued up, and are then not so easily done.

STRETCHER FIXING

Before starting on the stretchers, the six metal dowels and nuts for fixing them (Fig. 7.3) are made. These are straightforward turning, drilling, and threading jobs, using $\frac{1}{4}$ in diameter hard aluminium alloy for the dowels and $\frac{3}{8}$ in diameter brass for the nuts. Next the legs are sawn through on the stretcher centre line, numbering each piece so that it can be later returned to its own leg. The dowels are then cemented in the legs with epoxy resin leaving them at least 24 hours for the resin to cure. In the meantime, the gate pivot bolts E, Fig. 7.6, are made up from $\frac{1}{2}$ in diameter aluminium alloy. Wooden heads are stuck to these, again using epoxy. To make the heads a scrap of walnut is chucked in the lathe, the recess for the head turned and the piece parted off. After cementing to the bolt it is rechucked on the shank and the head finish-turned and polished. Four $\frac{3}{32}$ in thick locknuts are also made from suitable hexagon stock.

Fig. 7.3 shows in detail how the stretchers are built into the legs, a neat and strong way of doing the job.

STRETCHER CONSTRUCTION

Producing the half-round moulding all round the stretchers poses quite a problem. It could of course be done entirely by hand methods, but the radiusing of the ends in particular would be a tedious and lengthy job, entailing a lot of careful spokeshaving, rasping, filing, and glasspapering to produce a neat accurate job.

Obviously, what is needed is a high-speed electric router using a cutter with a guide collar in conjunction with a template attached to the workpiece. If you don't have one you can use a drilling machine as shown in Fig. 7.9. This method, though, brings with it the ques-

tion of safety as, although a guard (not shown in the drawing for reasons of clarity) is fixed behind the cutter, this is necessarily limited in its shielding effect owing to the fact that sufficient clearance has to be left to allow the cutter to work into the inner angle of the gate pivot projection. So, although the method produces a satisfactory job it is not recommended, especially in inexperienced hands.

As the workpiece has to be fed to the cutter instead of the cutter to the workpiece, without great care the workpiece can, if the cutter grabs, be snatched out of the hands resulting in the fingers being in danger of contacting the rotating cutter. It should be noted that with cutters only cutting on one side of their periphery (as opposed to groove or channel cutting) the feed must always be against the rotation of the cutter and never must the feed be with the rotation of the cutter or a snatch will surely result.

There is also the question of the speed of the drilling spindle. Few drilling machines or electric drills will run at over 2500 rpm, which is not fast enough for a really sweet cut when routing. 15 to 20,000 rpm is nearer the correct speed. Figs. 7.7 and 7.9 show a method of doing the job with a standard electric router, where the workpiece is fixed and the router worked around it using a template as before – a much safer and better way of tackling the job.

From Fig. 7.6, B, C and D, it will be seen that all the stretchers are, in the interests of strength, laminated from three layers of $\frac{1}{8}$ in stuff, laying the three pieces with the grain running lengthwise, except at the pivot projections of B. Here, as shown, the outer layers are crossed plywood fashion, having the mitre join running through where eventually the leg hole will come. This construction is very much more rigid than the equivalent section of solid wood.

TEMPLATES

Make the templates from some firm hard ply, say $\frac{1}{4}$ in birch, to the outlines of B and C, Fig. 7.6. Set these out accurately and cut out, keeping the saw in the waste and clean up dead to the line, remembering that any inaccuracy in the finished template will be faithfully reproduced in the finished stretcher, Fig. 7.11. The templates can now be used to mark out the stretchers, again keeping the saw in the waste. Drill clearance holes for No. 8 screws on the leg hole centres and from these drill the same size holes in the stretchers.

Now screw down to the baseboard a stretcher with its template, Fig. 7.7. There is some advantage in

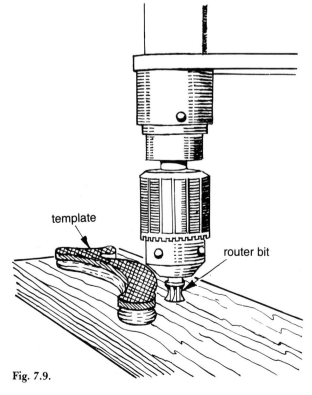

template

router bit

Fig. 7.9.

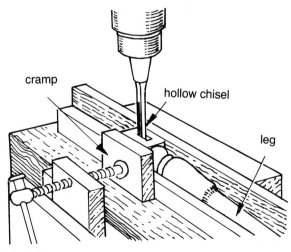

cramp

hollow chisel

leg

Fig. 7.10.

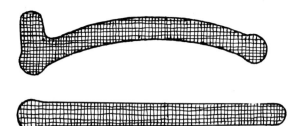

Fig. 7.11.

having the template and guide collar above the stretcher and cutter as shown in Fig. 7.9; in this way there is less likelihood of chips getting between the collar and template, which can cause a rough finish. If the guide collar is below the cutter it may be necessary to make the templates rather thicker to give chip clearance.

CUTTER
The cutter is separate from the shank, as is the collar which can therefore be assembled either above or below the cutter. Suitable cutters can be obtained commercially, but for those who like a little tool making and have the equipment, details are shown in Fig. 7.8. It is made of carbon (tool) steel, hardened and tempered to just on blue. The shank is made of mild steel.

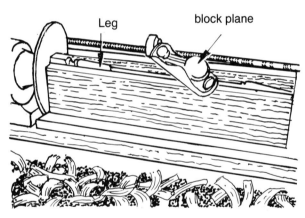

Fig. 7.12.

ROUTING
Before switching on the router, see that everything is firmly fixed and that the cutter is adjusted to the correct height, also that the guide collar will follow the edge of the template. Make certain, too, that the router base will bridge the packing pieces A, fig 7.7, at all positions of its travel. If this is your first time at this kind of job, do a practice run or two on some waste stuff to get the feel of the thing. Providing the guide collar is kept in contact with the template, one complete circuit will complete the job.

After satisfactorily completing the short stretchers, making the long one D, Fig 7.6, will pose no problem. Like the others it is built up of three laminations.

After drilling out the holes for the legs and gate pivots the stretchers are assembled on the legs, using a little glue, the lower part of the leg replaced and the forked screwdriver nuts tightened up – this is all the cramping that is necessary. When tightening up the nuts on the gate legs the stretcher must be dead in line with the rail above.

The long stretcher comes next. This is mitre housed

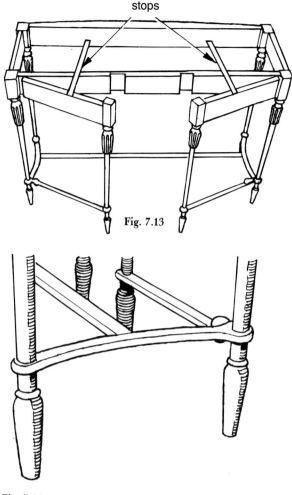

Fig. 7.13

Fig. 7.14.

to a depth of $\frac{3}{16}$ in into the end stretchers, glued, and lightly cramped. After the glue has set, $\frac{1}{8}$ in dowel holes are drilled to a depth of $1\frac{1}{2}$ in and stainless steel dowels inserted with a little epoxy resin. These are pushed below the surface and the holes pelleted. Fig. 7.14 is a close-up of this part of the assembly.

COCK BEADING, ETC.
Next, fix the central panel to the bow front. This consists of a piece of 4 mm ply veneered with matching halves of figured black walnut. Then follow the cock beads around the lower edges of the rails. Although these are rather a fiddling job fitting around the leg squares, this detail adds much to the final appearance and should not be omitted.

The gates are next hung and the two limiting stops made and fitted. These are made from $\frac{1}{2} \times \frac{1}{8}$ in aluminium alloy and are clearly seen in the 'aerial' view in Fig. 7.13. To avoid any scratching of the top, green baize is glued to the top edges of the gates, the thickness of which should have been provided for when hanging the gates. This completes the framework part of the table.

MAKING THE TOPS
The tops are $\frac{5}{8}$ in laminboard, which you can make yourself if you are inclined and equipped for it. A good quality blockboard or ply will also do.

The tops cut to size, allowing $\frac{5}{8}$ in for lippings on the ends and hinge edges. On the front edges $1\frac{1}{4}$ in should be allowed to accommodate the bow-front curve. To take the lippings, $\frac{3}{16} \times \frac{3}{16}$ in grooves are next ploughed on all edges. Lippings with matching tongues are prepared from straight-grained walnut and mitred, glued, and cramped on. The bow-frong edges are then shaped, using a compass plane for cleaning up; both halves are clamped together for doing this.

The lippings should be prepared slightly full in thickness to allow for cleaning off flush with the surface, working obliquely outwards with a sharp finely set plane. In this way it is easier to sense when you are down to the surface, and there will then be no bevelling of the lippings in relation to the top as a whole.

VENEERING

First the underside of the fixed top is done with sapele. This is followed by the insides of each leaf, done with matching leaves of figured walnut. Finally comes the top of the hinged leaf, which matches the inside ones if possible. As this top is to have an inlaid line and be cross-banded, it is best to cut this leaf of veneer a little within the margins of the top before laying. A cutting gauge can then be run round easily to provide the margin for the line and cross-banding. The waste is eased up with the point of the hot iron and lifted away. Once the end is started it is possible to work slowly along the length lifting the waste as the iron goes along.

As most of the glue on the margins disappears they should be re-coated with glue before laying the 4 mm black, white, and rosewood line. Cross-banding the remainder of the margin is done with dark figured walnut cut from waste ends of leaves. This method, using the hot iron has the distinct merit of carrying out the job at one session.

The rosewood line is now scraped down to the level of the veneer — these lines are always slightly over standard veneer thickness. After that, only careful sanding should be needed. Be careful if you use a belt sander on veneers; it is fatally easy to go through the veneer at the edges or corners.

FINISHING

After the usual cleaning up and garnet papering, the following finishing method proves a great success. Wipe on a coat of matt polyurethene, rubbing it really well into the grain and then wiping off any surplus. This is then left 24 hours, after which four or five further coats, at 24 hour intervals are put on in the same manner, using the lacquer much more sparingly — only enough to see where you've been — not enough to leave a 'wet' look. This method finally builds up to a very pleasing matt finish in the modern idiom. Finally, rub down with 000 grade steel wool lubricated with wax polish.

CUTTING LIST

		INCHES			MM		
		L	W	T	L	W	T
6	Legs turned	20½	—	1¼	521	—	32
2	End rails	9¼	2¾	⅝	235	70	16
1	Front rail	28½	2¾	⅝	724	70	16
1	Back rail	28½	2¾	⅝	724	70	16
1	Inner back rail	18½	2¾	⅝	470	70	16
2	Gate rails	9¼	2¾	⅝	235	70	16
1	Front bow piece	26½	2¾	⅞	673	70	23
6	Stretcher laminae (laminate in layers of three)	10	2½	⅛	254	63	3
6	Stretcher laminae (laminate in layers of three)	10½	1¼	⅛	267	32	3
3	Stretcher laminae (laminate in layers of three)	26	1	⅛	660	25	3
2	Tops (laminboard)	29¼	9½	⅝	743	241	16
4	Lippings, cut full on thickness	11	1 1/16	⅝	279	27	16
2	Lippings, cut full on thickness	30½	1 1/16	⅝	775	27	16
2	Lippings, cut full on thickness	30½	1 11/16	⅝	775	43	16
	Cock beading	78½	9/16	⅛	1987	15	3

Also required —7 ft (2132 mm) walnut inlay line; veneer for tops, rails, and crossbandings.

Working allowances have been made to lengths and widths; thicknesses are net.

Farmhouse Kitchen Chair

The type of chair shown here was at one time common in Lincolnshire farmhouse kitchens. It was usually accompanied by up to half a dozen matching brothers of the armless type. Although perhaps not particularly elegant by some standards, they were certainly functional and looked right in their setting. With the seat and back furnished with suitable cushioning they were surprisingly comfortable, serving the double purpose of a carving chair, and one in which the farmer would take his ease.

Generally these chairs were made of elm and beech, and stained a mahogany colour, often at some time in their life freshened up with varnish stain – usually with dire results! This chair has the seat legs, and arms in elm, with the leg stretchers and back parts in beech.

Reproducing the chair is not a difficult job if you have a lathe that will take 24 in between centres. Some simple steaming and bending of the top back rail and

splats is required; this, though, would not be difficult to improvise successfully in the garden or back-yard.

The seat, being the main part around which the chair is built, could be termed the heart of the job. You may have to do a little searching to find just the right piece for this. What you should look for is a 20 in length of 1½ in thick wood, 20 in wide. It must be without wind, have no sapwood in it, and preferably be completely knot-free (although the odd small tight knot can be disregarded); above all it should be free from even any slight cracks.

Little need be said about the construction; no difficulties should be encountered that a little thought and commonsense will not solve. Take it in stages, starting with the seat and legs, and completing the under-framing first. If the seat is squared off before any shaping is done it will be much easier to first mark out the positions of all the holes required in it.

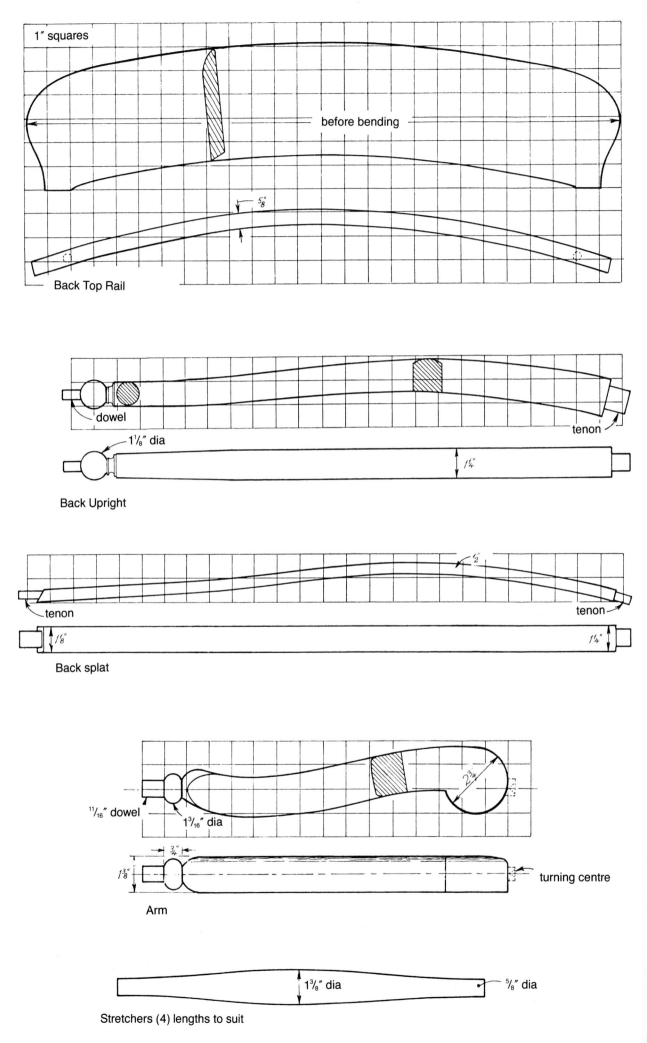

1" squares

before bending

$\frac{5}{8}''$

Back Top Rail

dowel

tenon

$1\frac{1}{8}''$ dia

$1\frac{1}{4}''$

Back Upright

tenon

tenon

$\frac{1}{2}''$

$1\frac{1}{8}''$

$1\frac{1}{4}''$

Back splat

$\frac{11}{16}''$ dowel

$1\frac{3}{16}''$ dia

$2\frac{3}{4}''$

$\frac{3}{4}''$

$1\frac{3}{8}''$

turning centre

Arm

$1\frac{3}{8}''$ dia

$\frac{5}{8}''$ dia

Stretchers (4) lengths to suit

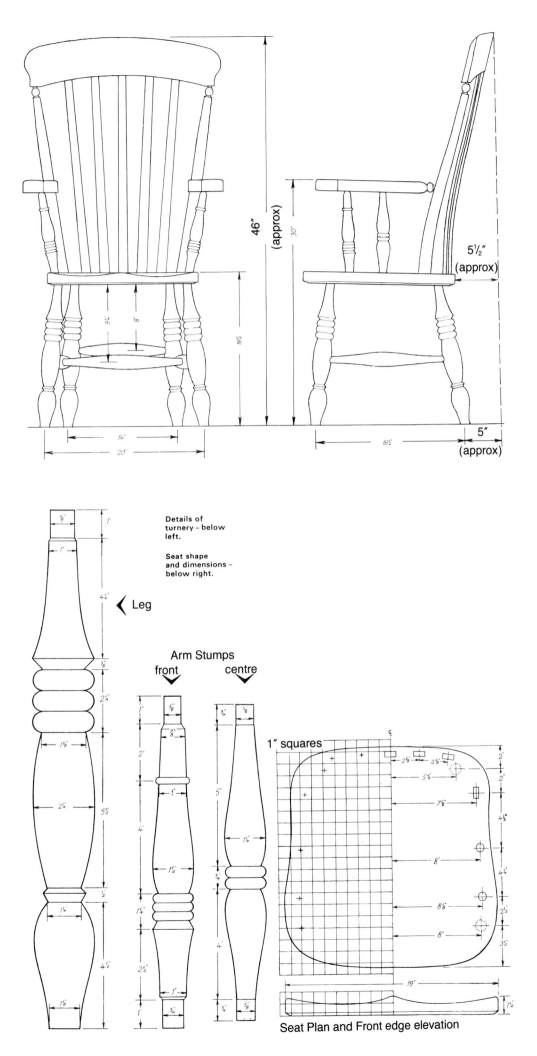

Details of
turnery – below
left.

Seat shape
and dimensions –
below right.

Leg

Arm Stumps
front   centre

1″ squares

Seat Plan and Front edge elevation

46″ (approx)

30′

5½″ (approx)

18½

14″

20′

18½

5″ (approx)

37

For the legs some good dry sound wood not less than $2\frac{3}{8}$ in square will be needed. The arms can be taken from $3 \times 1\frac{1}{2}$ in wood. The back parts and stretchers need not necessarily be of beech; ash would be suitable and is a good 'bender' too.

The outer back uprights are cut from the solid, laying the grain to favour the curve. It is difficult to give the exact lengths of the splats, and lengths are best taken individually from the job after the outer frame has been knocked up dry. A generous length has been shown on the drawing which will doubtless need reducing when fitting. A good firm fit of all dowels and tenons should be aimed at, but lasting success with these joints depends very largely on the moisture content at the time of fitting – so have your timber dry!

Staining is up to you. If you intend to stain, use a water stain after first dampening all over to raise the grain and then papering down. A durable final finish would be three or four thin coats of matt polyurethane which is finally rubbed down with fine steel wool and wax and then well burnished with a dry cloth.

CUTTING LIST

		INCHES			MM		
		L	W	T	L	W	T
1	Seat	20	20	$1\frac{1}{2}$	508	508	38
4	Legs	19	$2\frac{1}{2}$	Turned	483	64	Turned
2	Arms	$16\frac{1}{2}$	$3\frac{1}{4}$	$1\frac{3}{8}$	419	83	35
1	Top back rail	$26\frac{1}{2}$	$6\frac{1}{2}$	$\frac{5}{8}$	673	165	16
5	Back splats	28	$1\frac{3}{8}$	$\frac{1}{2}$	711	35	12
2	Front arm stumps	$12\frac{1}{4}$	$1\frac{3}{4}$	Turned	311	45	Turned
2	Side arm stumps	$11\frac{3}{4}$	$1\frac{1}{2}$	Turned	298	38	Turned
1	Front cross stretcher*	$18\frac{1}{2}$	$1\frac{5}{8}$	Turned	470	42	Turned
1	Back cross stretcher*	$12\frac{1}{4}$	$1\frac{5}{8}$	Turned	311	42	Turned
2	Side cross stretcher*	18	$1\frac{5}{8}$	Turned	457	42	Turned

Working allowances have been made to lengths and widths; thicknesses are net. On items marked * the lengths are generous and final measurements should be checked from the job.

SIDE TABLE IN WALNUT

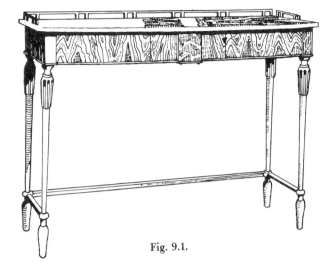

Fig. 9.1.

This small side-table is complementary to the small gate-leg table described on pages 26–34.

The main dimensions are shown in Fig. 9.2. Although not at first obvious, three drawers are incorporated below the top. A slight bow is given to the front which can add much to the visual appearance; but if it's overdone it can be positively ugly. The bowing causes some complication in the construction of the drawers, calling for careful and precise workmanship. A low gallery is fixed along the back edge of the top and returned approximately half-way across the ends, and a 4 mm black and boxwood ladder banding is laid along the front edge and returned at the ends to meet the gallery. Walnut is the best timber, solid for the legs, stretchers, gallery, cockbeading and top lippings. The remainder of the framework is mahogany, veneered with figured walnut on the show faces. For the top, blockboard is best, lipped and veneered. The gate-legged table referred to above, will, when closed stand quite happily underneath.

If you have made up the gate-legged table successfully you need have no fears in tackling this one. Although the workmanship required is of the same high standard this job has rather less detail and on the whole is easier.

TURNING THE LEGS

The methods are exactly the same as with the gate-leg table with the exception that the leg-to-stretcher joints are orthodox mortise and tenon. This is possible due to the increased section of the leg, allowing a satisfactory joint to be made without the complication of the metal dowelled joint. See Fig. 9.2.

After the turning is completed the various mortises can be set out and cut. Fig. 9.6 shows exploded views of the left-hand front and back joints respectively. For clarity on these drawings dimensioning has been kept to the minimum, only those absolutely necessary being shown; dimensions for the mortises can be obtained from the respective tenon dimensions given for the rails in Fig. 9.5. Rail tenons on B and C all have

1/8 in haunches. Cut the mortises on a light mortise machine with a hollow chisel, which saves a good deal of time, or by hand.

In the case of the stretcher rails, the shoulders are cut first by hand, taking particular care that they are truly in line with the square, then cut the mortise; on the machine, use a wooden vee block clamped to the table to support the leg. Finish this part of the job by cutting the dovetail housings in the tops of the front legs for rail D, and then the two rebates at the bottom of each square for the cockbeads.

END AND BACK RAILS

These are shown in detail at C and B, Fig. 9.5, and are a straightforward job. Here, again, for the tenons a machine is an advantage.

The dovetail housings in C will have to be done by hand unless you have an electric router. Planing the rebates on all three rails for the cockbeads and cutting the small mortises for the top fixing-button tongues in C only, completes the work on these parts prior to a trial assembly. At this stage the show faces of the rails can be vertically veneered.

FRONT RAILS

D and E, Fig. 9.5 give details of these. Take care that the shoulder length of each is exactly alike and spot-on with that of the back rail C, and also that the positions of the housings for the drawer divisions (F) are truly in line with the dovetail housings in C, or there will be difficulty when fitting the drawers. Note that the inner tenon on E does not enter the leg but goes into the drawer guide, I. This is shown in the exploded drawing Fig. 9.4.

STRETCHERS

These are shown at K/L, Fig. 9.5. In the interests of strength, use only good straight-grained woods. Note that the radius of the half-round edges must be exactly the same section as the collar or bead on the legs to which the stretchers join or there will be difficulty in

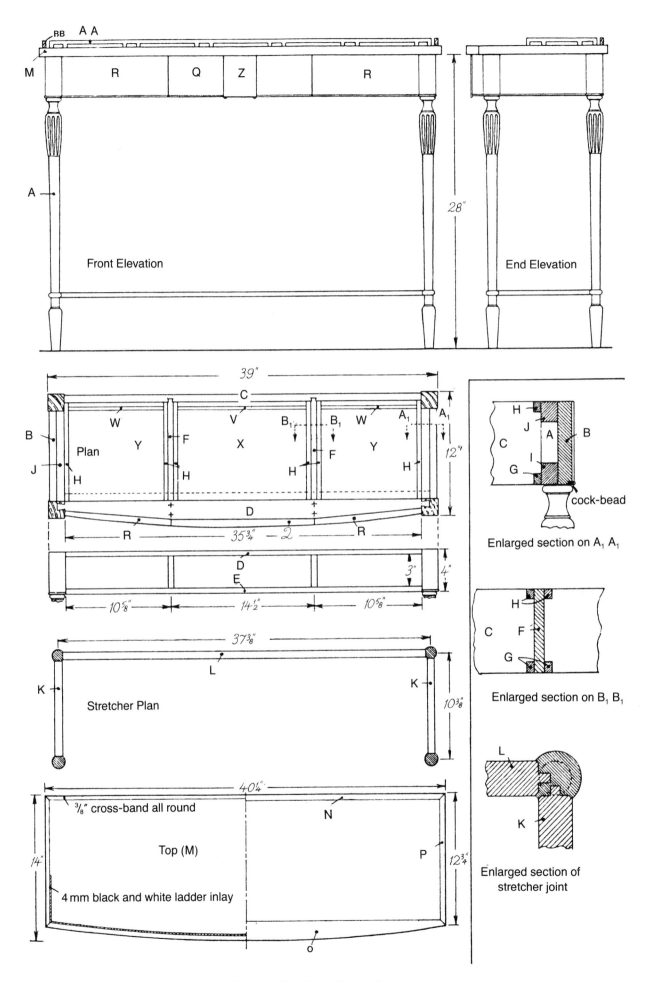

Fig. 9.2. Elevations, plans and sections.

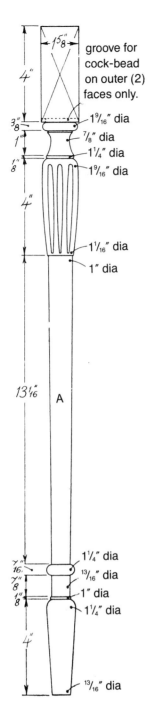

groove for
cock-bead
on outer (2)
faces only.

1⅝"

4"

3⅜"
1"
1⅛"

1⁹⁄₁₆" dia
⅞" dia
1¼" dia
1⁹⁄₁₆" dia

4"

1¹⁄₁₆" dia
1" dia

13¹⁄₁₆"   A

7⁄₁₆"
⅞"
1⅛"

1¼" dia
1³⁄₁₆" dia
1" dia
1¼" dia

4"

1³⁄₁₆" dia

Fig. 9.3. Details of leg.

rail dovetails dry, as this rail will need to be removed when fitting the drawer divisions F, Fig. 9.5. These can be tackled next and glued and screwed through rails D and E.

DRAWER GUIDES, RUNNERS AND KICKERS
The top drawer guides J can now be glued and screwed to the end rails, followed by the runners G and the kickers H, which are likewise glued and screwed.

COCKBEADS
Now is the time to fix these. Although they are rather a fiddling job fitting around the leg squares, they should on no account be omitted as they add greatly to the finish appearance of the job. The correct section is shown at CC, Fig. 9.7. Choose mild, straight-grained wood. The easiest way to make them is to start with a pre-thicknessed 'board', work the half-round on one edge and saw off to the correct width; repeating this until sufficient footage has been obtained. Rout or use a moulding plane, or clamp the square-edged piece between two boards and shape the nose with a finely set block plane, finishing with a hollow felt-lined sanding block.

DRAWERS
Details of the parts for these are given at Q to W, Fig. 9.7. For the front to show a continuous unbroken line, it's necessary for the drawer fronts to overlap the ends of the drawer divisions; consequently, normal lap dovetail construction isn't suitable here, and stub tenons should be used, blind-mortised into the fronts.

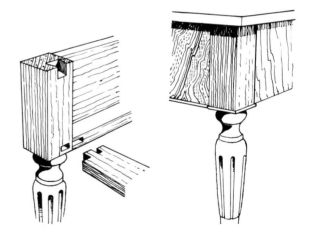

getting a good fit with them. The small tenons with mitred shoulders can next be cut. Cut the tenons first with a square shoulder, then pare the mitres with a sharp chisel to fit each leg individually, marking each part for reference on final assembly.

ASSEMBLY
Glue up the two end frames first, check for squareness and put aside to dry. Use softening blocks for cramping on the squares, as these are, or should be, in a near finished condition. Use thick felt pads under the cramp faces for the stretchers. Only light pressure should be needed here to bring the joint up closely.

At this stage its best to fix the bottom drawer guide I to the end rails. Take care that the mortise in the end taking the inner tenon on the front bottom rail E is dead in line with the mortise in the leg for the outer tenon in this rail.

When bringing the two ends together, leave the top

Fig. 9.4. Front corner jointing ready for gluing up. Finished front corner showing cocked beading detail around the base of the leg square. Left-hand end of framework glued up.

41

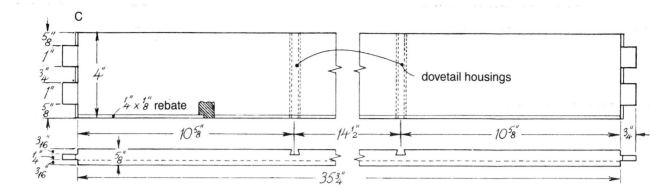

C

$\frac{5}{8}''$ 1" $\frac{3}{4}''$ 1" $\frac{5}{8}''$

4"

$\frac{1}{4}'' \times \frac{1}{8}''$ rebate

dovetail housings

$\frac{3}{16}$ $\frac{1}{4}''$ $\frac{3}{16}$ $\frac{5}{8}''$

$10\frac{5}{8}''$ — $14\frac{1}{2}''$ — $10\frac{5}{8}''$ — $\frac{3}{4}''$

$35\frac{3}{4}''$

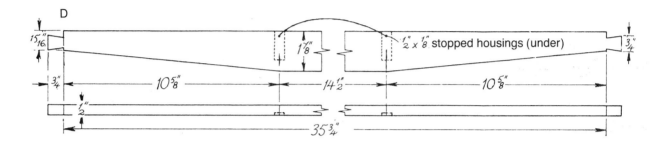

D

$15\frac{1}{16}''$ $1\frac{1}{8}''$ $\frac{1}{2}'' \times \frac{1}{8}''$ stopped housings (under) $\frac{3}{4}''$

$\frac{3}{4}''$ $10\frac{5}{8}''$ — $14\frac{1}{2}''$ — $10\frac{5}{8}''$

$\frac{1}{2}''$

$35\frac{3}{4}''$

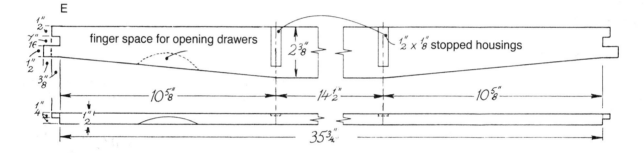

E

$\frac{1}{2}''$ $\frac{7}{16}$ $\frac{1}{2}''$ $\frac{3}{8}''$

finger space for opening drawers

$2\frac{3}{8}''$ $\frac{1}{2}'' \times \frac{1}{8}''$ stopped housings

$10\frac{5}{8}''$ — $14\frac{1}{2}''$ — $10\frac{5}{8}''$

$\frac{1}{4}''$ $\frac{1}{2}''$

$35\frac{3}{4}''$

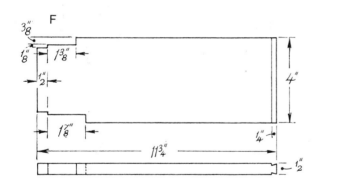

F

$\frac{3}{8}''$ $1\frac{1}{8}''$ $1\frac{3}{8}''$ $\frac{1}{2}''$

4"

$1\frac{7}{8}''$

$1\frac{3}{8}''$ $11\frac{3}{4}''$ $\frac{1}{4}''$ $\frac{1}{2}''$

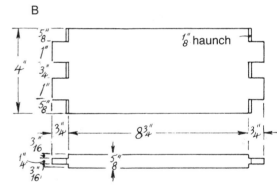

B

$\frac{5}{8}''$ 1" $\frac{3}{4}''$ 1" $\frac{5}{8}''$

$\frac{1}{8}''$ haunch

4"

$\frac{3}{4}''$ $8\frac{3}{4}''$ $\frac{3}{4}''$

$\frac{3}{16}''$ $\frac{1}{4}''$ $\frac{3}{16}'$ $\frac{5}{8}''$

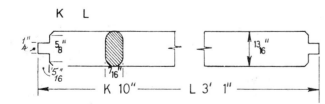

K   L

$\frac{1}{4}''$ $\frac{5}{8}''$

$\frac{15}{16}''$ $\frac{1}{16}''$

K 10" — L 3' 1"

$\frac{13}{16}''$

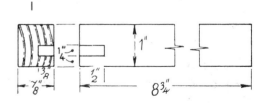

I

1"

$\frac{1}{4}''$ $\frac{3}{8}''$ $\frac{7}{8}''$ $\frac{1}{2}''$ $8\frac{3}{4}''$

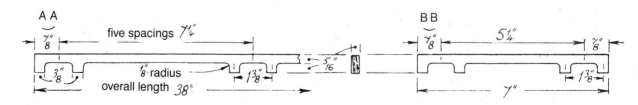

A A

$\frac{7}{8}''$ five spacings $7\frac{1}{4}''$

$\frac{3}{8}''$ $\frac{1}{8}''$ radius $1\frac{3}{8}''$ $\frac{5}{16}''$

overall length $38'$

B B

$\frac{7}{8}''$ $5\frac{1}{4}''$ $\frac{7}{8}''$

$1\frac{3}{8}''$

7"

Fig. 9.5. Shapes and dimensions of parts which are lettered to correspond to the cutting list.

42

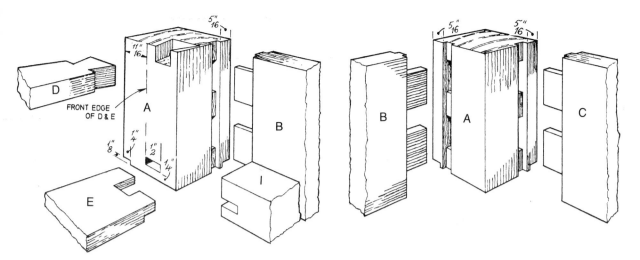

Fig. 9.6. (Left) 'exploded' view of front and end leg/rail joints: (right) 'exploded' view of back and end leg/rail joints.

Notice that although the drawer sides are $\frac{5}{16}$ in thick, the tenons are only $\frac{1}{4}$ in thick, the $\frac{1}{16}$ in shoulder on the outer side. This is to allow for taking off the odd shaving when fitting the drawer to the carcase without affecting the fit of the tenons in the front. Ordinary lap dovetails are used for the outer sides of the end drawers. Note, when cutting these and the mortises in the end drawer fronts, that due to their cant the angle is approximately $5\frac{1}{2}$ in degrees off the true right angle. The mortises in the centre front are, of course, at 90 degrees. Through dovetail construction is used for the backside joints.

In the interests of ease in working, the shaping of the bow on the fronts is not done until after the joints are cut. To mark out the curve, cramp a length of timber under the bottom drawer rail to form a ledge on which

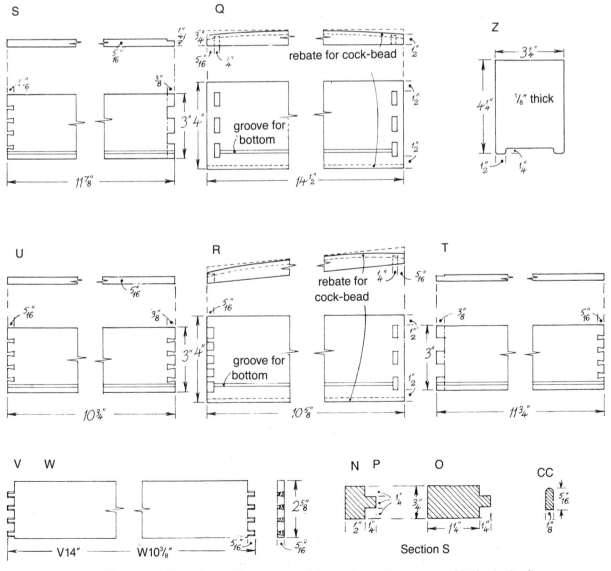

Fig. 9.7. Shapes and dimensions of drawer parts which are lettered to correspond to the cutting list.

the fronts can be set *in situ* for marking the curve. Using a spline, mark this out on the top edges, and carry the line down the ends and repeat the curve on the bottom edges. The waste can now be planed away, taking care to get a continuous unbroken curve along all three fronts when in position. The thickness at the ends of the fronts should not be less than $\frac{1}{2}$ in. The rebate for the cockbeads can now be worked along the lower edges.

The drawers can next be glued up and fitted to the carcase. The fronts are then veneered and the cockbeads glued in, the veneer being laid vertically. To get a matching effect with the grain cut pieces off consecutive leaves, starting veneering with the centre drawer and working outwards to get a balanced effect. Finally the small overlay panel is glued to the centre drawer.

TOP

This is a straightforward job. Use a piece of good quality blockboard and plough $\frac{1}{4}$ in grooves along all edges. The lippings are made with integral matching tongues, and the front lipping is left full width until after gluing up. The curve ($1\frac{1}{4}$ in bow) is again marked with a spline, the waste sawn away and the edge cleaned up.

VENEERING THE TOP

To get a matching effect, use two 14 in wide consecutive leaves of figured walnut with the joint through the centre from front to back. Care is needed here to get a really close fitting butt joint on the end grain – not quite so easy as a joint along the grain. After matching up the two halves, clamp them between boards, shoot the joint dead straight and then tape the two halves together with gummed paper tape and leave it to dry out before laying. The shrinkage of the damp tape on drying will tend to pull the joint tighter. This method works well – with care a practically invisible joint can be obtained.

After laying the veneer trim off any overhang and then, using a sharp cutting gauge set to $\frac{1}{2}$ in cut the margin all round for the inlay line and crossbanding. The waste can be lifted using the point of a warm electric iron to soften the glue. Before laying the line and crossbanding it will be necessary to re-coat the margin with glue. The inlay line is not taken under the gallery and the margin here is cross-banded only.

GALLERY

Details for setting these parts out are given at AA and BB, Fig 9.5. Set the parts out accurately; how you do the cut-outs will depend on the equipment available. Starting with strips thicknessed to $\frac{5}{8} \times \frac{1}{16}$ in rough out most of the waste with a $\frac{1}{4}$ in blade in a jigsaw or bandsaw, keeping well in the waste; then clean the pieces up with a fixed router, using a guide fixed to the table to give the correct size of the top rail. This leaves very little cleaning up to be done by hand. Slightly round off the top corners and round the ends. Failing a router the cut-outs can quite successfully be done with a coping saw and cleaned up with files and garnet paper.

The gallery is attached to the top by screwing up from under, using 1 in × no. 4 screws. Using the gallery pieces for reference, mark out the hole centres on the top on the joint line of the crossbanding. Lightly centre-punch and drill through $\frac{7}{64}$ in, and countersink under. Next clamp the pieces in position and prick through the holes, remove and drill $\frac{5}{64}$ in

pilot holes not more than $\frac{1}{2}$ in deep. Pilot holes must be drilled, or there will be a danger of the pillars splitting when the screws are driven in.

FINISHING

After the usual fine papering down, the framework and drawer fronts should be given four coats (at daily intervals) of matt polyurethane applied with a pad. The first coat is applied fairly generously and well rubbed in; successive coats more sparingly. Finally, after allowing a few days to harden right out, apply a light coat of wax polish with 000 grade wire wool, and then burnish it with a dry cloth.

For the top (after removing the galleries) you can use two-part hard lacquer, which gives a very hard wearing finish. After very careful cleaning up, apply four brush coats, rubbing down lightly between each. Intervals between coats with these lacquers can be quite short, depending on the temperature and humidity of the workshop. The final coat, after a day or two to harden right out, should be rubbed down with 9/0 garnet paper to give a matt surface and then lightly waxed and burnished with a dry cloth. With walnut veneer, four coats can give a completely grain-filled surface. More open-grained veneers might need filling first; consult the instructions on the finish before using a filler, as some fillers are not suitable to use with finishes. Note that before attempting to matt down, the grain must be completely full. Unless this condition is met, matting will leave the lacquer lying low and bright in the grain – a most unpleasant effect.

CUTTING LIST

Part				INCHES			MM		
				L	W	T	L	W	T
A	4	Legs (W)		$28\frac{1}{2}$	$1\frac{7}{8}$	$1\frac{5}{8}$	724	48	42
B	2	End rails (M)		$10\frac{3}{4}$	$4\frac{1}{4}$	$\frac{5}{8}$	273	108	16
C	1	Back rail (M)		$37\frac{3}{4}$	$4\frac{1}{4}$	$\frac{5}{8}$	959	108	16
D	1	Front rail, top (M)		$37\frac{3}{4}$	$2\frac{1}{8}$	$\frac{1}{2}$	959	54	13
E	1	Front rail, bottom (M)		$37\frac{3}{4}$	$2\frac{5}{8}$	$\frac{1}{2}$	959	67	13
F	2	Drawer divisions (M)		$12\frac{1}{4}$	$4\frac{1}{4}$	$\frac{1}{2}$	311	108	13
G	6	Drawer runners (M)		$9\frac{5}{8}$	$\frac{3}{4}$	$\frac{1}{2}$	245	19	13
H	6	Drawer kickers (M)		$10\frac{1}{8}$	$\frac{3}{4}$	$\frac{1}{2}$	245	19	13
I	2	Drawer guides, bottom (M)		$9\frac{1}{4}$	$1\frac{1}{4}$	$\frac{7}{8}$	235	32	23
J	2	Drawer guides, top (M)		$9\frac{1}{4}$	$1\frac{1}{4}$	$\frac{7}{8}$	235	32	23
K	2	Stretchers (W)		$10\frac{1}{2}$	$1\frac{1}{16}$	$\frac{7}{16}$	267	27	12
L	1	Stretcher (W)		$37\frac{1}{2}$	$1\frac{1}{16}$	$\frac{7}{16}$	953	27	12
M	1	Top (BB)		$39\frac{3}{4}$	$12\frac{1}{4}$	$\frac{3}{4}$	1009	311	19
N	1	Lipping, back (W)		$40\frac{3}{4}$	1	$\frac{3}{4}$	1035	25	19
O	1	Lipping, front (W)		$40\frac{3}{4}$	$1\frac{3}{4}$	$\frac{3}{4}$	1035	45	19
P	2	Lippings, ends (W)		$13\frac{1}{4}$	1	$\frac{3}{4}$	337	25	19
Q	1	Drawer front, centre (M)		15	$4\frac{1}{4}$	$\frac{3}{4}$	381	108	19
R	2	Drawer fronts, side (M)		$11\frac{1}{8}$	$4\frac{1}{4}$	$\frac{3}{4}$	283	108	19

CUTTING LIST (continued)

Part			INCHES L	W	T	MM L	W	T
S	2	Drawer sides, centre (M)	12³⁄₈	3¹⁄₄	⁵⁄₁₆	315	83	8
T	2	Drawer sides, inner (M)	12¹⁄₄	3¹⁄₄	⁵⁄₁₆	311	83	8
U	2	Drawer sides, outer (M)	11¹⁄₄	3¹⁄₄	⁵⁄₁₆	286	83	8
V	1	Drawer back, centre (M)	14¹⁄₂	2⁷⁄₈	⁵⁄₁₆	369	73	8
W	2	Drawer backs, side (M)	10⁷⁄₈	2⁷⁄₈	⁵⁄₁₆	277	73	8
X	1	Drawer bottom, centre (P)	14¹⁄₈	11³⁄₄	4 mm	359	299	4
Y	2	Drawer bottoms, side (P)	10¹⁄₂	11³⁄₄	4 mm	267	299	4

CUTTING LIST (continued)

Part			INCHES L	W	T	MM L	W	T
Z	1	Centre drawer front overlay (W)	4³⁄₄	3¹⁄₂	¹⁄₈	121	89	3
AA	1	Gallery, back (W)	38¹⁄₂	⁷⁄₈	⁵⁄₁₆	978	23	8
BB	2	Galleries, ends (W)	7¹⁄₂	⁷⁄₈	⁵⁄₁₆	191	23	8
CC		Cockbeading from	120¹⁄₂	1¹⁄₁₆	¹⁄₈	3059	27	3

Key to timbers: BB = blockboard, M = mahogany, P = plywood, and W = walnut.

Also required: figured walnut veneer; black inlay banding; and black-and-white 'ladder' inlay banding.

Working allowances have been made to lengths and widths; thicknesses are net.

LINEN CHEST

The linen-fold effect is common in furniture of the seventeenth and eighteenth centuries; there is no reason why you should not devise your own version. Quartered oak is a good choice because of its aesthetic value; also it carves well and is relatively free from movement under varying humid conditions.

The carved panels are too wide to be cut from one board, so select two boards that match as near as possible and edge joint them, with a butt joint and glue. When jointing, ensure that the annual rings on each board are concentric so that shrinkage will cause both panels to bow in the same direction. If they are not, they could assume an S shape when viewed end-on and this condition is very difficult to correct. A 'G'-cramp placed across each end of the joint keeps the faces level and saves time dressing up later. After gluing up, set the panels aside to find their equilibrium.

STOOL

The stool is a fairly straightforward construction. The front elevation of one leg and part of a rail are set out full size on a piece of plywood to determine the bevel of the shoulder on rails. To mark out the shape of legs make a template from hardboard or cardboard. The

curves on the rails are sprung with the aid of a thin piece of wood and a helping hand.

After working the joints and cutting and spokes-shaving the curved parts to the correct shape, assemble the long rails and legs dry and place one on top of the other to check the splay on the legs.

Having ascertained the alignment of the legs, assemble the other two short rails and check the stool for size and squareness. The assembly is then knocked down and cleaned up on the inside and given a coat of polish before final assembly. The outside is dressed up and treated similarly and then the stool is put into store with the panels for a few weeks.

FRAMES

The four frames that contain the six linenfold panels employ stopped and haunched mortises and tenons at the ends of the top and bottom rails, and a common stopped mortise and tenon on the muntins. After the setting out, which is quite straightforward, the mortises are chopped to the required depth and the tenons are cut.

Before the tenons can be fitted it is necessary to work the grooves into which the haunches fit. The chamfers are only partly set out in the early stages. In

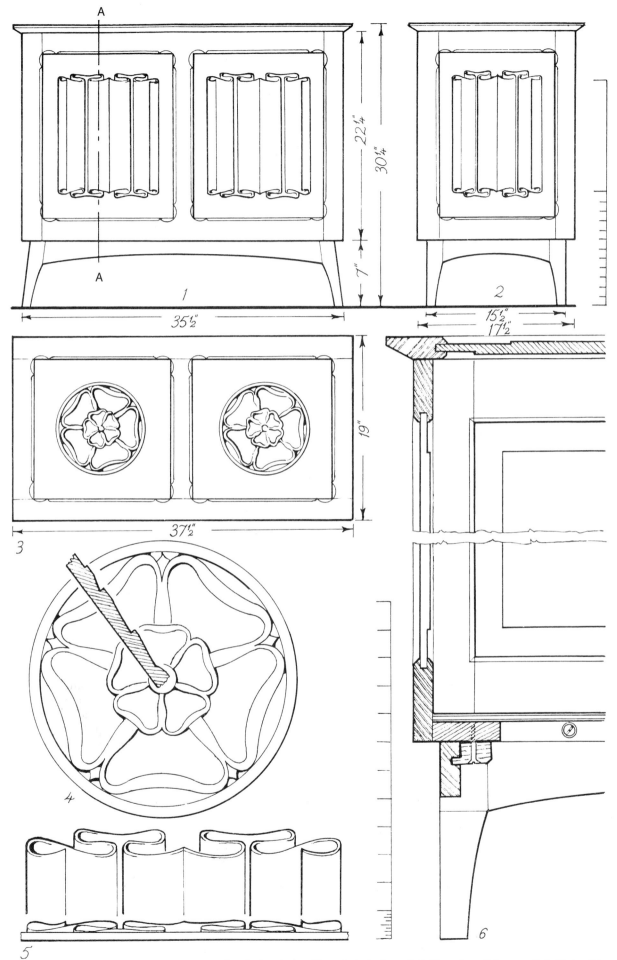

Figs. 10.1 to 10.6. 10.1 and 10.2 Front and end elevations with scale in inches. **10.3** Plan view of the top. **10.4** Tudor Rose detail: the outer circle is 10 inches (254 mm) diameter. **10.5** Detail of linenfold panels; the carved detail is 11½ in (293 mm) wide. **10.6** Enlarged section (with scale) on line A–A in Fig. 10.1.

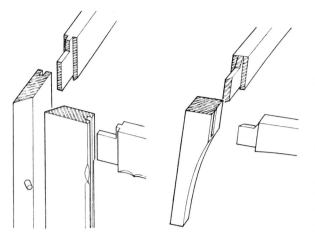

Fig. 10.7. (Left) Mortise and tenon joints between top rails and stiles; also dowelled mitre joining front and end frames. (Right) Joints between stool rails and legs.

the pursuit of greater accuracy, the setting out of the stopping at the corners is done when the frames are initially assembled. The mason's mitre on the inside chamfer is also accomplished when the frame is assembled.

Use a pencil gauge, not a marking gauge, for marking the line of the chamfers. A pencil gauge is quickly made from any small scrap of wood as it only requires a corner cutting out the size of the chamfer.

The stopping of the chamfers is accomplished with a ³⁄₄ in chisel, using a scooping action and with the bevel face down. The frame for the lid is made similarly. The frame for the bottom of the chest is ¹⁄₄ in oversize to allow for fitting. This frame is very straightforward to make and may be glued up after checking for size and then put into store with the other items. The plywood covering for this frame is fitted later.

JIG
Before starting work on the panels it's advisable to make a cradle to hold them. A thick piece of manufactured board approximately 3 in larger than the largest panel is required. To this are glued two 3 in wide strips of plywood, positioned flush with two edges of the board to form an L shape. The edges are placed on the cradle to be dressed up and carved. Begin dressing up the panels by traversing them at forty-five degrees to the grain with a foreplane, and finish by planing parallel with the grain. They may then be squared off to the required size.

ROSE CARVING
The two panels for the lid are fielded on the back the required amount and on the face they must be rebated to leave a square in the middle slightly larger than a circle containing the carving. A tracing of a rose is made and a similar size piece of carbon paper is placed underneath the tracing. Both are positioned on the panel by piercing the centre of the tracing with a drawing pin and pressing it firmly into the centre marked on the panel. They are then sticky-taped round the edges to prevent any movement. A better transfer is produced if the circles are drawn with a compass. Make sure that none of the points of the pentagon line up with the corners of the quadrilateral frame that contain it.

Tenon saw and chisel the corners of the square to the circular shape, working right up to the line by vertical paring with a sharp ³⁄₄ in bevel-edged chisel, and trimming the horizontal ground with an open mouthed rebate plane.

Before starting work on the actual carving, sharpen up a ¹⁄₄ in as well as the ³⁄₄ in bevel-edged chisel, plus a ¹⁄₂ in shallow inside-bevelled gouge for hollowing the petals and a larger outside-bevelled gouge for the vertical cuts round the outer edges of the large petals.

When you are making the vertical cuts on the outer edges of the large petals, it must be borne in mind that the depth varies from about ¹⁄₈ in in the middle to ¹⁄₁₆ in where it curves sharply. The outer edges of the small petals are cut to a uniform depth except where they meet the edges of the large petal, and here the cut is about ¹⁄₁₆ in deep.

Pare a very shallow bevel on the centre to give it a convex appearance and then go over it with a background punch. This punch may be made out of a piece of square section mild steel, and a pattern is made on the end by parallel saw cuts dividing it up into small squares.

LINENFOLD
The linenfold panels are likewise fielded on the back and rebated on the face up to the edge of the moulding. To work the moulding by hand, a plough plane and two convex moulding planes are required; one of these must be a very shallow curve. (It would also be possible to devise a series of jigs so this job could be done with a power router.) The sole of an old wooden smoothing plane for instance could be rounded and the cutting iron ground to match. If the corners of the back iron protrude beyond the cutting iron when it is set back as far as practically possible, simply grind them off.

Four grooves are worked in a panel first. Two of these are part of the finished moulding and two simply determine the depth of the moulding where the fold turns back and finishes. A strip of wood fastened across the panel will act as a guide for the plough plane and prevent any skid marks across the panel occuring. Finish the moulding with a scraper ground to the appropriate shape and then rub down with glasspaper wrapped around a shaped wooden block.

The next stage is to make a tracing of the carving and sticky-tape it to the panel, and then lightly prick through. Cut away the outline shape of the folds right down to the groundwork. The first step-down is then cut away and the shape of the second step-down is pencilled in before it too is cut away. Try to avoid a feather edge occurring at the places marked on the drawing, and do not overdo the undercutting. A ¹⁄₄ in bevel-edged chisel is very useful for getting right into awkward corners. Try to finish the carving without recourse to glasspaper as the resulting scratch marks will show up badly against the corners of the carving that you cannot get into with glasspaper.

All the panels are then polished before assembly, as this eliminates a white edge showing if the panels shrink slightly. The panels are not glued into the frame, which allows for possible movement under varying conditions of humidity.

When dressing up the assembled frames it is advisable to cover the bench top with an old soft woollen blanket or something similar, to prevent the bench scratching the finished job.

ASSEMBLY

The four frames are mitred and dowelled at the corners. You can strengthen the corners with glue blocks, but the job should be strong enough without.

The mitre may be worked with the frame held in the vice and a block of wood on the floor supporting the heel of the frame. Wrap something soft round the part of the frame held in the vice. A depth stop is required when drilling for the $\frac{3}{8}$ in dowel and your helping hand to sight the angle of the bit, which is at right angles to the mitre.

The task of gluing up the carcase frames is a difficult one, definitely requiring a helping hand again! You will also require eight sash cramps and eight cramping strips.

Assemble the chest in its normal upright position and place four cramps around the base where they can rest on the bench and use just one cramp to twitch up the top of the chest, twitching up each side in turn. When the mitres are all closed, the remaining cramps may be added to the top where they will hold themselves in position. Don't forget to check the diagonals for squareness.

When the cramps are taken off, the feather edges of the mitres are cleaned up and the base frame fitted. As soon as the buttons are made the stool may be screwed on, and the legs scribed down to a perfectly flat surface. The top edge of the chest is planed free of any slight winding and then the lid is fixed with three solid brass hinges and brass cabinet stays. In order to highlight the chamfers they are given two coats of gold paint.

Finally, the framework only is rubbed down and given a finishing coat of polish and then the whole is waxed and given some elbow grease!

CUTTING LIST

	INCHES			MM		
	L	W	T	L	W	T
LID						
2 Stiles (quartered oak)	38	$\frac{1}{2}$	$\frac{3}{4}$	965	12	19
3 Rails (quartered oak)	20	$\frac{1}{2}$	$\frac{3}{4}$	508	12	19

CUTTING LIST (continued)

Part	INCHES			MM		
	L	W	T	L	W	T
2 Panels (quartered oak	$16\frac{1}{2}$	$16\frac{1}{4}$	$1\frac{5}{8}$	419	413	42
CARCASE						
8 Stiles (quartered oak)	$22\frac{3}{4}$	$2\frac{1}{2}$	$\frac{3}{4}$	578	64	19
2 Top rails (quartered oak)	36	$2\frac{3}{4}$	$\frac{3}{4}$	914	70	19
2 Top rails (quartered oak)	18	$2\frac{3}{4}$	$\frac{3}{4}$	457	70	19
2 Bottom rails (quartered oak)	36	$3\frac{1}{4}$	$\frac{3}{4}$	914	83	19
2 Bottom rails (quartered oak)	18	$3\frac{1}{4}$	$\frac{3}{4}$	457	83	19
2 Mutins (quartered oak	$11\frac{1}{2}$	$2\frac{3}{4}$	$\frac{3}{4}$	572	70	19
4 Panels (quartered oak)	$18\frac{1}{2}$	$15\frac{1}{4}$	$\frac{5}{8}$	470	387	16
2 Panels (quartered oak	$18\frac{1}{2}$	$14\frac{1}{4}$	$\frac{5}{8}$	470	362	16
BOTTOM FRAME						
2 Stiles (Scots pine)	35	$2\frac{3}{4}$	$\frac{3}{4}$	889	70	19
3 Rails (Scots pine)	$16\frac{1}{2}$	$2\frac{3}{4}$	$\frac{3}{4}$	419	70	19
1 Floor (oak ven'd ply)	35	$16\frac{1}{4}$	$\frac{1}{4}$	889	413	6
STOOL						
4 Legs (quartered oak)	$7\frac{1}{2}$	2	$1\frac{3}{4}$	191	51	45
2 Rails (quartered oak)	36	$2\frac{3}{4}$	$\frac{3}{4}$	914	70	19
2 Rails (quartered oak)	16	$2\frac{3}{4}$	$\frac{3}{4}$	406	70	19

Also required: one 36 in (927 mm) length of $\frac{3}{8}$ in (10 mm) beech dowel; three 2 in (51 mm) brass hinges; two 7 in (178 mm) brass cabinet stays.
Working allowances have been made to lengths and widths; thicknesses are net.

CHILD'S TURNED ARMCHAIR

This is a basic design in period style, allowing plenty of scope for your own variations to the intended user's specification! Steam-bend or laminate the arm: for added effect, you can use strips of different woods for the lamination. The seat, of course, can be used as a former if you laminate the arm.

SEAT

For this there is nothing better than a piece of sound dry elm. If you have to join two pieces together to get the width, the joint should be double-loose-tongued as shown in the inset drawing, Fig. 11.2, using cross-grained tongues. It seems a moot point which way to have the run of the grain; from the picture it will be seen that it runs from front to back. Often, in Windsor chairs with arms, it runs across the seat, and in ones without arms from front to back. Jointed-up seats usually have grain running front to back. You can take your pick!

Set out the seat shape as shown in Fig. 11.1 first only cutting the main curve and cleaning up, leaving the front and rounded corners until later, as in this state you need the seat as a former for laminating the arm/back rail. Not until after this is done are the front corners and front edge shaped, and the bevel planed on the underside to produce a seen edge thickness of 1 in.

LAMINATING

The laminations for the arm piece should be cut $\frac{7}{8} \times \frac{3}{32}$ in; eight are required. This will produce an arm section of $\frac{3}{4}$ in square after cleaning up the laminated edges. First plane the edge of a piece of $\frac{7}{8}$ in wood, cut off a strip $\frac{1}{8}$ in thick, replane the edge of the stock and repeat until you have enough (an extra one provides a safety factor in case of accidents). Now put them on the thicknesser and bring them down to $\frac{3}{32}$ in. Two passes over the planer may be needed – it's not

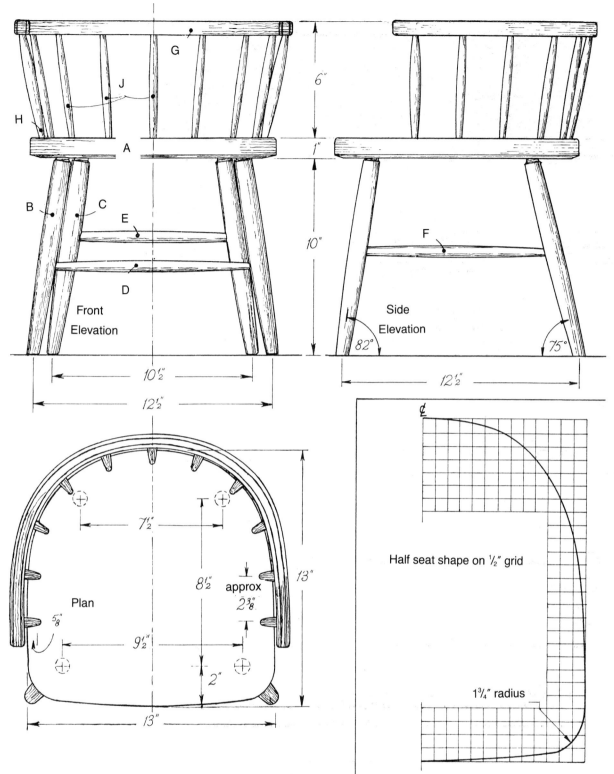

Front Elevation

Side Elevation

6"

1"

10"

10½"

12½"

82°

12½"

75°

Plan

7½"

8½" approx 2⅜"

13"

5⅞"

9½"

2"

13"

$\mathrm{\mathbb{C}}$

Half seat shape on ½" grid

1¾" radius

Fig. 11.1.

wise to take too heavy a cut on light sections like these. If you have a planer blade on your saw in good condition, you should be able to cut the strips finished thickness and use them straight off the saw, but it is essential that they are reasonably smooth and of even thickness, or you may have trouble with gaps when gluing up.

Gluing and cramping, using the partially finished seat as a former, can now be done as shown in Fig. 11.4. Use a synthetic resin glue; if you have a band cramp this could be used instead of the steel band. Put a strip of polythene each side of the complete lamination before cramping to avoid it sticking to the seat-former and possible staining from the steel band.

With strips of this thickness and no sharp bends it should be possible to do the lamination without having to go to the trouble of pre-soaking in water, cramping up and drying right out before doing the gluing up. Leave the job overnight, preferably in a warm room, before releasing and cleaning up.

HOLES FOR LEGS

The seat can now be dressed to its final shape, the under bevel planed and the top edge nicely rounded. The plan view in Fig. 11.1 gives the positions for the holes, and Fig. 11.3 shows the true angles at which they should be bored.

If you have a drilling machine with a canting table

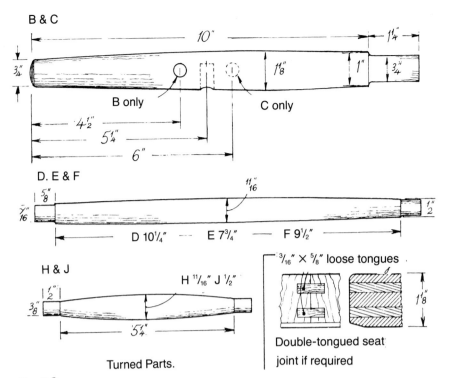

Turned Parts.

Fig. 11.2.

the job is easy; simply set the table with a cant of 12 degrees for the front legs and 16 degrees for the back and put the seat on the table in line with the cant, at the angles to the centre line shown in Fig. 11.3 and away you go. With a fixed table it will be necessary to use tapered packing pieces of 12 and 16 degrees for the front and back holes respectively to bring the angle correct.

Boring by brace and bit can be done by making guide blocks to the necessary angles and placing these on the true angle lines W–X and Y–Z, Fig. 11.3. Whether you drill the holes blind, relying on the glue and a good fit with the leg, or take them right through and kerf the leg and wedge it is a matter of choice. For the former method the leg will need to be turned from

really dry wood to avoid loosening by possible later shrinkage. Also, the holes should be taken as deep as is practicable without breaking through. After boring as far as is safe with an ordinary bit the full depth can be got with a Forstner bit. With this method and care you should be able to get a hole 1 in deep.

If the legs are to be taken right through, don't saw the kerfs for the wedges until the legs have been drilled for the stretchers, as in this way you can make sure that the wedges come across the grain in the seat.

TURNED PARTS
These are fully detailed in Fig. 11.2, and are straight-forward 'between centres' turning. Beech is a very suit-able wood; you can use oak for the legs (B and C) and

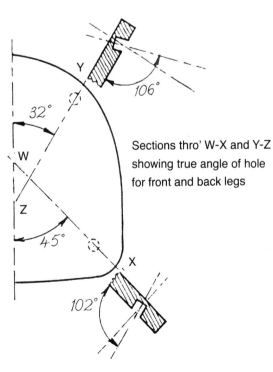

Sections thro' W-X and Y-Z showing true angle of hole for front and back legs

Fig. 11.3.

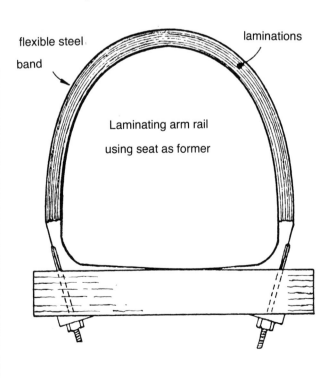

Laminating arm rail using seat as former

Fig. 11.4.

beech for the stretchers (D, E, and F). Yew would, of course be ideal, and it is a lovely wood to turn. Before removing the legs from the lathe, run a light pencil line round them at the heights of the stretcher hole centres.

Now to drilling the holes for the stretchers; this is where you have to concentrate, remembering that when this is done correctly no two legs are alike, being in pairs, front and back, and side and side. Consequently, any one leg has only one correct position in the seat. It's very easy to finish up with two legs alike instead of a pair! Perhaps the best way to avoid confusion is just start each leg in its hole in the seat and mark them lf (left front), rf, lb, rb; you can then mark the exact drilling positions on the height lines which are already there.

The best way to drill the holes is on a drilling machine with a canting table (or with a tapered packing piece) in conjunction with a vee cradle in which to rest the leg. The cradle can be simply made by nailing two triangular-section strips of wood to a piece of ply, cramping this to the table in such a position that the point of the drill comes down into the bottom of the vee. When drilling don't forget a depth stop or you may go right through! Note that the angle for the side stretcher in the back leg is 75 degrees (15 degrees cant of table) instead of 82 degrees (8 degrees cant) which is the angle for the others.

ARMS/BACK
The holes for this can now be set out in the top of the seat and drilled and also those in the arm rail, G, Fig 11.1; these are best marked off by reference to those in the seat. To do this, put the arm piece around the seat edge with the rear centre aligned with the centre line of the seat and mark across, transferring the lines to the underside by squaring round. The true angle for drilling these holes is approximately 12 degrees off the vertical on radial lines from the centre, except for the two arm stumps H, the angle here being on a line drawn directly across the seat.

Drilling can be done on the drilling machine similar to that described for the leg holes. There is a 'freehand' method, using a long bit in the electric drill and an ordinary joiner's bevel set to 102 degrees, putting the stock on the seat and sighting along the blade; a bit

rough-and-ready perhaps, but with care it works. When doing the holes in the arm piece remember that because you are drilling from the underside, the angle slopes inwards in relation to the curve of the arm and not outwards as when drilling the seat.

ASSEMBLY
Glue up the leg-stretcher frame first and straightaway glue and drive the legs progressively into the seat. If the legs are made to come right through the seat the wedges can then be glued and driven home, any projection sawn off, and the leg ends flushed off with the surface of the seat before putting on the top part. Synthetic resin should be used throughout, as at some stage in its life in the chair will doubtless be left out in the rain!

FINISHING
Three coats of satin polyurethane give a good serviceable finish, the first and second coats rubbed down lightly with fine steel wool. Using a clean brush and doing the job in a dust-free atmosphere (is there one?) enables the last coat to be left 'off the brush'. Note: take care to remove all dust before starting and subsequently after rubbing down, as apart from lacquer dust there is a certain amount of steel debris due to the breaking down of the steel wool.

CUTTING LIST

Part			INCHES			MM		
			L	W	T	L	W	T
A	1	Seat	13½	13¼	1⅛	343	336	29
B	2	Front legs	11¾	1½	1¼	299	38	32
C	2	Back legs	11¾	1½	1¼	299	38	32
D	1	Front stretcher	12	1	¾	305	25	19
E	1	Back stretcher	9½	1	¾	241	25	19
F	2	Side stretchers	11¼	1	¾	286	25	19
G	8	Laminations	32	1⅛	3/32	813	29	3
H	2	Arm stumps	6¾	1	¾	172	25	19
J	9	Back uprights	6¾	⅞	⅝	172	22	16

Working allowances have been made to lengths and widths; thicknesses are net.

PERIOD TRIPOD OR 'SNAP' TABLE

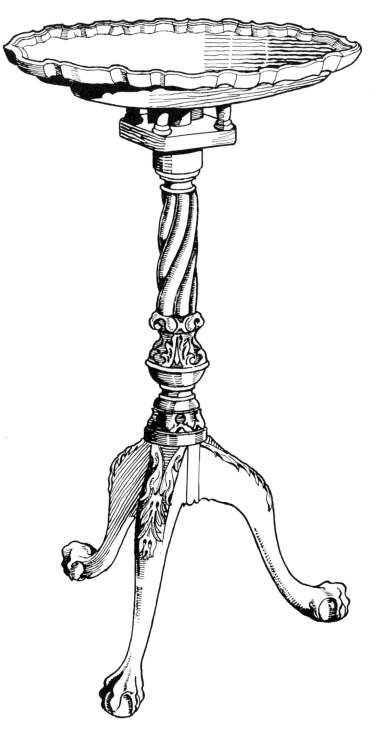

This is based on an eighteenth century model and has the delightful movement frequently incorporated at that period, a revolving and pivoted top known as the 'birdcage'. Whether this is of special practical value is doubtful, but there is a touch of novelty about it that makes it worthwhile. If you find the carving too time-consuming, you could omit it, fitting a plain pillar instead of the twist and acanthus leafage, cutting plain shaped feet rather than the claw-and-ball, and substituting a plain and turned top rather than that with pie-crust edging. Mahogany is used throughout.

PILLAR

A 3 in square is needed for this, and it needs to be carefully centred on the lathe to enable the fullest part of the turning to finish $2\frac{7}{8}$ in diameter. It requires a length of at least 21 in to enable the finished length of $19\frac{1}{2}$ in to be turned. The top spigot is $1\frac{3}{4}$ in diameter to fit into holes in the birdcage (Fig. 12.1D).

If you don't have a bit of the exact size, it would be advisable to bore a hole with whatever is available, and use this as a gauge when turning the spigot. An expansive bit is, of course, the real answer. The fit of the

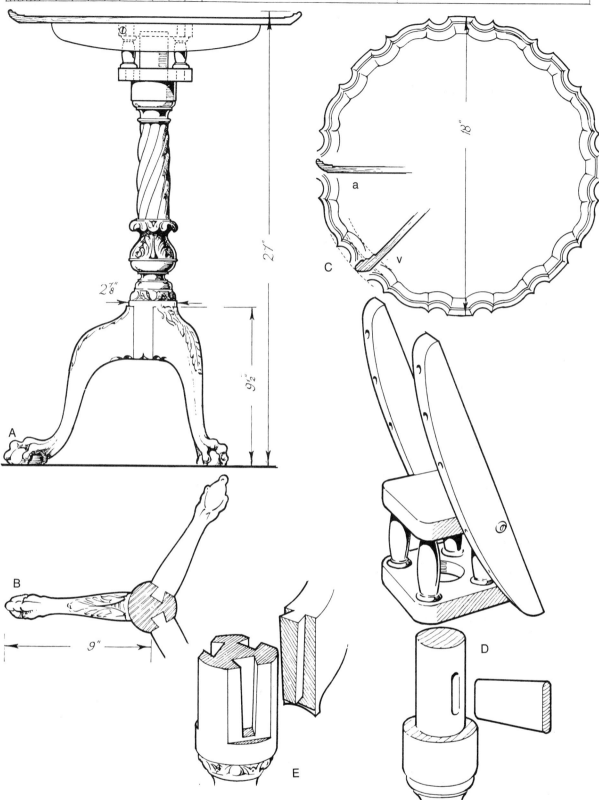

Fig. 12.1 Details of the table. (A) elevation with principal sizes; the scale can be used to determine the sizes of details. (B) plan of legs. (C) shape of top with sections. (D) birdcage movement. (E) dovetails joining legs to pillar.

spigot should be fairly easy without slackness. The whole pillar should first be turned to a cylinder and the various members marked off. An important point to note is that you should leave enough for the turnover of the acanthus leafage to be carved.

Slot dovetails have to be cut at the bottom for the legs, and it is strongly advisable to make them slightly tapered as at (E), Fig. 12.1. The advantage is that when the dovetail is fitted into its slot, it is slack until pressed

finally home. In this way it is easy to detect where the joint is tight and ease it accordingly. If it is made parallel, the joint is tight from the moment of insertion until right home; too tight a joint should be avoided as it is liable to split the wood.

First cut flats on the wood so that square shoulders can be cut on the legs; careful marking out is necessary. After chiselling, they are best trued by drawing a file along them. Saw in the sides of the dovetails as far as you can and then chisel the rest.

To mark the spiral portion of the carving, step round the circumference with dividers. There are 11 bines, though the number could be varied. At the bottom the setting will have to be increased slightly as compared with the top to enable the stepping out to be exact. A piece of card is cut to length and bent round the spindle so that it aligns with the stepped-out marks. At the top, the card is level with a mark about three turns on from the one at the bottom. A parting tool is used for the preliminary cutting, but to use this on a single centre line is almost certain to result in a crooked line. It is better to mark two lines about $\frac{3}{16}$ in apart and use the parting tool midway between them and cut in until both sides of the V-cut line up with the two lines. A flat gouge follows and finally the inevitable facets taken out with glasspaper wrapped around a specially-made rubber. The most awkward parts are the ends.

The acanthus leafage follows, and here there are four repeat patterns (Fig. 12.3). Cut in at the top to free the main leaves, and this will enable the lower lobes to be cut in. It is advisable to sink the triangular recesses between the leaves first; also the bottom circular recess. There is little modelling to the leaves, but it is desirable to go over the entire surface to remove any suggestion of its turned origin.

It is a help when cutting the egg-and-tongue detail below to use the parting tool at each side of the eggs first. This frees the main egg form and enables a gouge to be used in setting in the shape. To finish off the egg, a gouge can be held with the hollow side downwards and used with a rocking movement which follows the contour. If you're doing this kind of work for the first time, it's as well to practise on a spare piece of wood first.

LEGS

The shape should be cut out in card and used as a template for marking out. The finished thickness is $1\frac{5}{8}$ in. The first essential is to plane the bottom part of the foot and the top vertical part of the dovetail at right angles with each other. At the ankle the leg is $\frac{7}{8}$ in thick and the sides should be tapered down to this thickness. The side claws of the foot are the full thickness of $1\frac{5}{8}$ in. At the ankle the leg is approximately circular in section, but above this the shape resolves into an approximate rectangle with the top rounded over to a flat curve, and the lower corners also slightly rounded.

First, however, the top dovetail of the leg should be cut (E, Fig. 12.1). To mark it, the leg should be turned the reverse way up so that the wide part of the dovetail can be marked from the wide part of the socket in the pillar. (You may prefer to work the other way round, cutting the leg dovetails first and marking the pillar sockets from them.)

The claw-and-ball foot can be tricky to carve at the

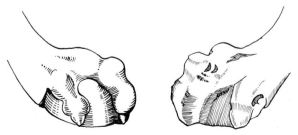

Fig. 12.2 The claw and ball in stages of being carved; bosted-in on the right, the job almost finished on the left.

Fig. 12.3 The first stage in carving the acanthus leafage on the bulb.

first attempt, and those in doubt could model a foot in modelling clay first. In any case the shape can be marked on the underside with a template. The ball itself is elliptical, with the four claws projecting beyond. Cut in the claw shapes first, trying to keep the ball to a rounded shape which is continuous at each side of the claws. The claws are modelled as shown in Fig. 12.2, and are quite deeply undercut where they join the ball.

Detail of the acanthus leafage at the top of one of the legs is shown in Fig. 12.4. It is advisable to cut a

Fig. 12.4 Template of acanthus leaf carving on legs; it is bent around the curve of the knee.

template in thin card to enable the detail to be balanced. In most original tables the detail is the same on all three legs, but it makes it more interesting to vary the legs as long as the same general character is preserved. The carving is quite shallow – not more than say $\frac{1}{16}$ in. Start by running a parting tool round the main outline then set in with gouges of the required curvature. This enables the leg to be cut back from the leaves and thus frees the design.

Owing to the curved shape the grain direction varies throughout, and needs care if chipping out is to be avoided. There is a slight modelling to the leaves, and care must be taken to make the main lines of this flow sweetly from the centre outwards towards the leaf tips (Fig. 12.5).

TOP

Even when the pie-crust edging is to be carved, it is advisable to do the main recessing of the top on the lathe. The whole of the centre can be turned in this way, but clearly the rim itself cannot be finished completely. However, its limits can be turned, and this is a considerable help. Fig. 12.1 C, shows at (a) the finished

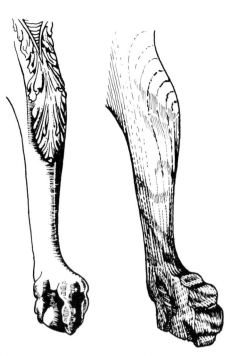

Fig. 12.5 Two views of a leg. On the right, it has been bosted-in; on the left, carving has been finished.

Fig. 12.6 View of the birdcage movement.

section and (b) the extent to which it can be turned.

Having done this, a template of the repeat pattern can be used to mark out. It is necessary to draw in the top in full size to get the shape. The outer shape can be cut in with the coping saw and trimmed with the file. Clearly the inner members of the moulding have to be parallel with this outer shape, and to enable the marking to ride over the contour of the turned section, a form of scratch-stock can be used. This has a pencil fitted in place of a cutter and the notched shoulder of the scratch is rounded to enable it to run round the undulating shape. If the scratch-stock is lifted as it passes over the moulding it will mark lines parallel with the edge.

Cutting the moulding is an exacting task because of the changing direction of the grain, and in places it's necessary to work against the grain. Generally it is advisable to cut in the mitre lines first. Start by cutting in a rebate which aligns with the inner edge of the bead down to the depth of the fillet or square. The simplest way is to go round the line with a small veiner held to the waste side. Then, when cutting down with gouges which approximate to the curve, the waste wood crumbles away easily. The bead shape is then cut in its entirety.

Now cut in the inner line of the hollow member, again cutting in with gouges of suitable curvature, and use a wide chisel to remove the groundwork. A scraper is useful to finish off to ensure a flat surface – in fact it is advisable to scrape the whole of the centre recessed part portion to take out any turning marks. At the back the edge is cut to a slightly rounded chamfer as at (a), Fig. 12.1 (C).

BIRDCAGE MOVEMENT
As shown at (D) Fig. 12.1, this consists of two square pieces held together with four small turned pillars, which have dowels turned at each end to fit into corresponding holes. The lower square piece has a centre hole right through it to fit over the spigot of the pillar. In the top piece, the hole is only about ¼ in deep. A slot cut right through the spigot enables a wedge (D,

Fig. 12.1) to pass through, so securing the whole on the pillar, yet allowing it to be revolved.

Two curved cross pieces are screwed across the grain beneath the top. They are as far apart as the width of the square pieces, and are pivoted to the top pieces with large brass screws. It gives a neat finish if screw cups are used. A circular table catch holds the top in the horizontal position yet leaves it free to be tilted when not in use. Fig. 12.6 shows the movement pictorially.

FINISH
If the mahogany is too light it can be darkened with potassium bichromate made up as a concentrated solution and diluted as required. Alternatively a weakened oil stain can be used which has the advantage of not tending to raise the grain. An excellent finish is with teak oil or by oil polishing. Those who prefer could use either French polish, plastic coating, or a polyurethane lacquer. If the last two give too glossy a finish they can be dulled down with steel wool lubricated with wax polish.

CUTTING LIST

		INCHES			*MM*		
		L	W	T	L	W	T
1	Top	19	1	t'rnd	483	25	t'rnd
1	Pillar	21	3	t'rnd	533	76	t'rnd
3	Legs (from one piece)	20	9½	1⅝	508	242	42
2	Struts	14	1¼	¾	356	45	19
2	Birdcage pcs (top & bottom)	5	4¾	⅝	127	121	16
4	Birdcage pillars	4	1	t'rnd	102	25	t'rnd
1	Wedge from scrap						

Working allowances have been made to lengths and widths; thicknesses are net.

OAK CRADLE

Back in history babies were swaddled in heaps of mattresses and coverings. From this evolved the cot or cradle which gave more protection from the draughts and dirt of the outside world. Various styles have been made since the 15th century, from the wicker basket to the rich decorative types.

The design featured here is a typical 17th century oak cradle mounted on bearers shaped as rockers, and has a hood which was popular in this period (oak was widely used at this time). It comprises a main structure consisting of corner posts connected by top and bottom rails. Intermediate posts divide its length, and the spaces between these and the rails are composed of fielded panels. The basic outside frame size is 36 × 17 in.

FRAME CONSTRUCTION

Begin with the four corner posts. These are made from $1\frac{3}{4}$ in square material, into which are jointed the top and bottom rails. The rails are laid to the outside edge of the posts. Blind mortise and tenons are used at the corners and as the inside edge of the rails and posts are grooved, the width of the joint is reduced by this amount to enable the groove to be carried through. The $\frac{1}{4}$ in grooves for holding the fielded panels in place are shown machined with a milling piece attached to a power drill and suitably jigged (Fig. 13.4). You can, of course, rout or spindle-mould these

grooves and the other machining work. It is possible to carry the grooves right through in the case of the rails and the intermediate posts as just explained.

The top rails are from $2\frac{3}{8} \times \frac{3}{4}$ in material and the bottom from $2\frac{1}{8} \times \frac{3}{4}$ in. The latter is less wide because a decorative trim strip is added beneath it which also serves to hide the edges of the bottom boards.

Having made the corner posts, the intermediate posts, the top and bottom rails, both side and crosswise, it is then possible to make a preliminary assembly of the frame to check dimensional accuracy, squareness, and alignment. Stopped chamfers are finally added to the inside edges of the posts and the rails where the fielded panels fit. No gluing can be done at this stage as the fielded panels have yet to be made and fitted.

FIELDED PANELS

Altogether 10 panels are needed of various sizes, made from $\frac{5}{8}$ in thick material. The three main panels on each side are from approximately 10 × 8 in material, the bottom panel from 14 × 8 in and the head panel from 14 × 14 in. The two small hood panels are from approximately $7\frac{3}{4} \times 5$ in wood, and it is suggested that they are all made up from $4 \times \frac{5}{8}$ in section strip.

The perimeter of each panel consists of a $\frac{1}{4}$ in wide tongue which fits into the grooves cut in the rails and posts. Fielded edges are also cut round each panel and

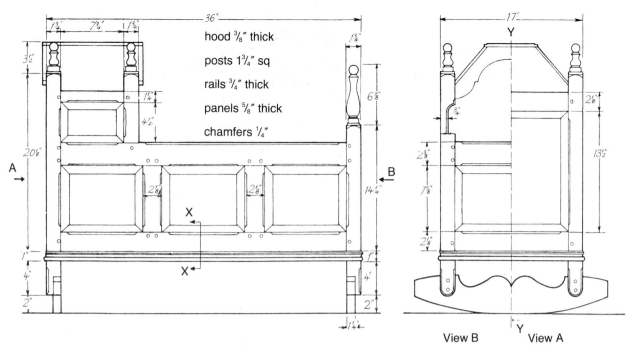

Fig. 13.1 Side and end elevations of cradle; for sections X-X and Y-Y see Fig. 13.2.

on both sides after tonguing. Cutting tongues and fields with the milling attachments is illustrated in Fig. 13.4, a suitable jig being made for this. The profiles are the same, of course, if you are using a router or spindle moulder.

BASIC ASSEMBLY

You can now assemble the cradle frame members and the fielded panels. These can be glued and cramped together. Be sure to include the small side hood panels and their sub-frame post and rail, as otherwise

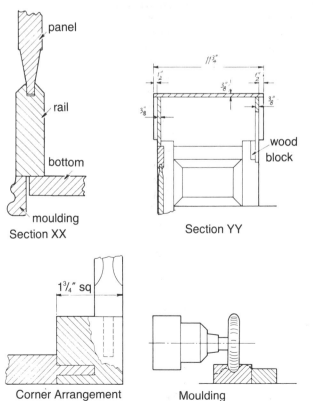

Section XX

Section YY

assembly will not be possible at a later stage because of the arrangement of joints.

All the mortise and tenon joints are then pegged, preferably with dowels in the same material as the frame.

HOOD

This is made from $\frac{3}{8}$ in thick material and it is suggested it is built up from 4 in wide strips. The front and back frame mouldings are marked out on squared paper and the design transferred to the wood (Fig. 13.3). They are then cut out and glued to the posts with the help of small blocks of wood in the corners. The hood is then covered, applying the sloping sides first and finally the top.

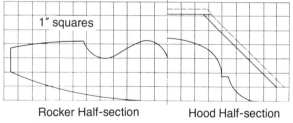

Rocker Half-section   Hood Half-section

Fig. 13.3 Half shapes of rocker and hood drawn on 1 in grid.

DECORATIVE MOULDING STRIP

A moulding strip is run round the cradle beneath the bottom rail. As explained earlier, its purpose is both decorative and to cover the edge of the bottom boards of the cradle. The moulding profile is shown using milling cutters again, but with moulding plane, router or spindle moulder you could get nearer the finished profile quicker. You can alter the shape to your own ideas or equipment. Finishing was completed by sanding with a block of wood shaped to the mould required.

Corner Arrangement   Moulding

Fig. 13.2 Sections X-X and Y-Y; Fig. 13.1 refers. Plus corner construction and method of shaping moulding.

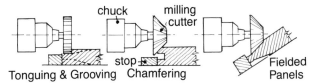

Tonguing & Grooving Chamfering Fielded Panels

chuck   milling cutter   stop

Fig. 13.4 Method of forming fielded panels using milling cutters.

BOTTOM

This is constructed from boards of 6 × ¾ in elm but any other suitable width can be used. Boards are laid across the cradle, and screwed and glued.

ROCKER BEARERS

These are made from 4¼ × 1¼ in wood, the curved form being first marked up on squared paper as for the hood (Fig. 13.3). After cutting out and cleaning up, rebates are cut in the foot of each corner post and the rocker bearers glued and dowelled into place.

FINISHING

A water stain will raise the grain unless precautions are taken. The remedy is first to brush the cradle with water which will raise the grain, and rub this down with glasspaper. Then the stain should be applied and you will find the grain will not be raised this time. Take care to apply the stain evenly. Oil or spirit stains are also suitable.

Matt polyurethane gives a good finish, the surface being wire-woolled smooth, taking care not to penetrate the stain. Finally, beeswax the surface.

CUTTING LIST

		INCHES			MM		
		L	W	T	L	W	T
2	Side top rails	35	2⅝	¾	889	67	19
2	End top rails	16	2⅝	¾	407	67	19
2	Side bottom rails	35	2⅜	¾	889	61	19
2	End bottom rails	16	2⅜	¾	407	61	19
2	Main posts (cuts two)	72½	2	1¾	1842	51	45
4	Intermediate side posts	10½	2⅜	¾	267	61	19
6	Side panels	10½	8¼	⅝	267	210	16
1	Bottom panel	14½	8¼	⅝	368	210	16
1	Head panel	14½	14¼	⅝	368	362	16
2	Hood panels	8¼	5¼	⅝	210	134	16
2	Hood rails	9½	1½	¾	241	38	19
1	Hood cover frame from strips	126	4¼	⅜	3200	108	10
2	Rockers	23½	4½	1¼	597	115	32
6	Bottom boards from 1 piece	110	6¼	½	2794	159	12
1	Moulding, total length	108	to choice		2742	to choice	

All parts are oak except the botom, which is in elm.

Working allowances have been made to lengths and widths; thicknesses are net.

CUTLERY CABINETS IN MAHOGANY AND OAK

Fig. 14.1 Oak.

Fig. 14.2 Mahogany.

Two different styles are presented for this cutlery cabinet design, both basically the same size. The 'oak' model, Fig. 14.1 has turned legs and fielded drawer fronts. The 'mahogany' style, Fig. 14.2, has square tapered spade foot legs (slightly longer to give a more slender effect), and the drawer fronts are cock-beaded and vertically veneered.

CUTTING LIST

The cutting list shown is for the 'oak' design, but where the parts differ for the 'mahogany' design they are marked with an asterisk and the alternatives are listed at the end. On Figs. 14.2, 14.4, 14.5 and 14.6, the 'oak' parts are shown, but where the equivalent 'mahogany' part differs, it is shown again below and is double lettered for identification, e.g. KK = lower drawer front for the mahogany design.

With the oak model, the timber for the main carcase and drawer fronts should be quarter-sawn. With the mahogany style, solid is best throughout for all the show parts, with oak for the drawer sides, backs and runners. For the carcase backs, drawer bottoms and dust boards, plywood is used.

The 'mahogany' design would look quite good in European or English walnut, but here, if you have difficulty in getting suitable wood wide enough for the top and sides of the carcase, laminboard (lipped on the

edges with solid), and then veneered would be a good alternative.

CARCASE

First prepare the four main parts, A, B and C. Note that the bottom (C) is 10 mm narrower than the other three parts, to allow for the ply back to slide in. Shoot all the ends to length and dead square. To prevent accidental damage to the mitred ends while working on the pieces, leave the mitring until all the other work on them has been done. It only needs one slip to damage the 45 degree edges and spoil the appearance of the finished job. Start by ploughing the groove for the ply back in A and B. Next set out and cut the housings for the drawer runners in A. Note that these are stopped at both ends. The ideal tool for this job is a high-speed electric router, leaving only the ends to be squared out with a chisel. You can also use a circular saw, making two cuts only for each housing and then routing out the waste with a routing plane. As the pieces have to be 'dropped on' to the saw table, limiting stops should be fixed to the table for the start and finish of the cut. The groove to take the tongue on the bottom (c), is cut next, using the same limiting stops. Note that this groove is deeper, and being narrow, it can be done with two or at most three cuts and will then need no routing to finish it, only the ends squaring out with a chisel.

Oak Style

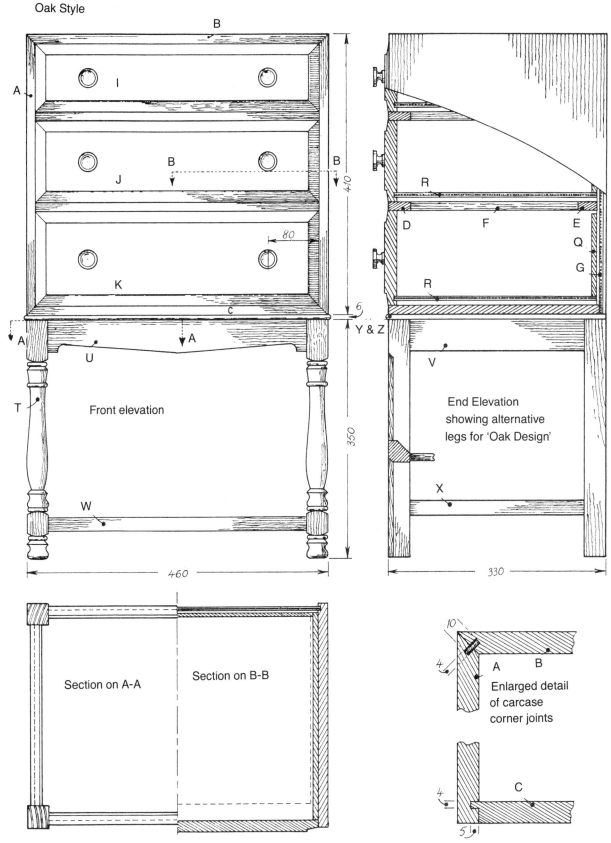

Fig. 14.1.

Next the 45 degree mitres are cut on the top end of A, and also on each end of B. With a table saw, first saw them slightly over-size, using the tilt arbor. Then after setting over the fence on the planer to 45 degrees and checking on some waste that the angle is 'spot on', plane the mitres to size, taking only light cuts.

The grooves for the loose tongues are then cut on the saw bench at one pass, using the tilt arbor and a wobble-saw blade. Again limiting stops are necessary for both ends of the cut, as, while the grooves run out at the back edge, this edge is the leading edge on two of the cuts, and on the other two cuts it is the trailing edge, owing to the parts being 'handed'. Note that in this case the wood cannot be 'dropped on' due to the cant of the blade, but they must be put in position for the start of the cut, and then the blade raised while running a pre-determined amount to give the correct depth of groove.

62

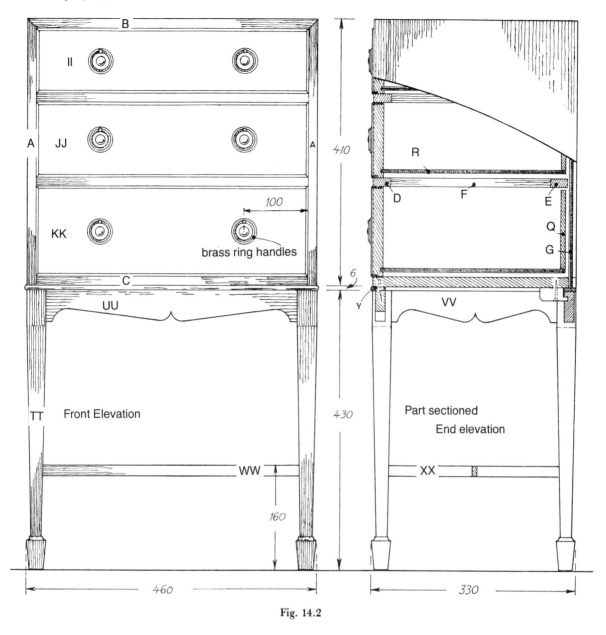

Fig. 14.2

A trial run on waste should be done first. This method of cutting the grooves can only be used if you have a screw control to the rise and fall of the saw-blade. Other methods for cutting these grooves can of course be used, including by hand. If you have an electric router, this is undoubtedly the tool to use, preferably with the router mounted under a table with the cutter projecting through the top, and using a 45

degree angled fence. With a set-up of this kind, cutting time would only be a matter of some minutes; all the other grooves on these parts could be cut in the same way, too.

If you like cutting dovetails, these corner joints could of course be made in this way, preferably using the secret mitre dovetail on the top corners and lap dovetails on the bottom. The secret mitre variety needs

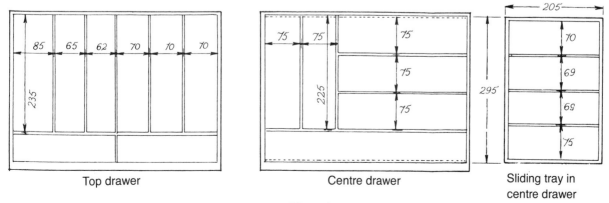

Top drawer   Centre drawer   Sliding tray in centre drawer

Fig. 14.3

63

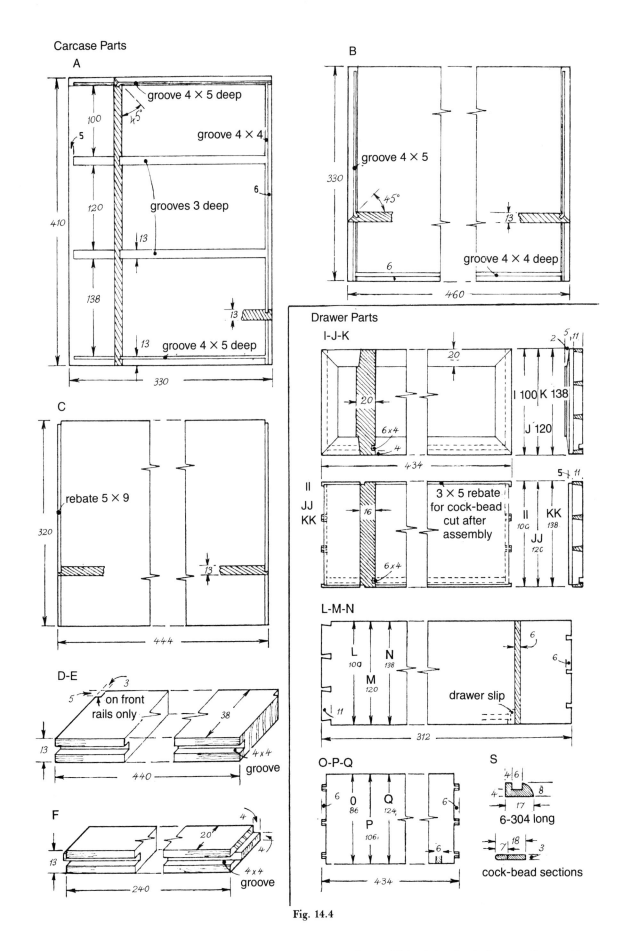

Fig. 14.4

both patience and practice to make a good job. The splined mitre joint used here is quite adequate for a carcase of this size and weight.

After preparing the bottom (C), a trial assembly can be made dry and then if everything is in order the carcase can be glued up. It's a good idea to make two operations of this gluing in the bottom first and leaving it overnight for the glue to dry. As it is necessary, doing it this way, to 'spring' the sides slightly when fitting in the top, keep a couple of cramps on the bottom joint while getting the top in place to avoid any chance of the bottom joint breaking. Cut the loose tongues from

64

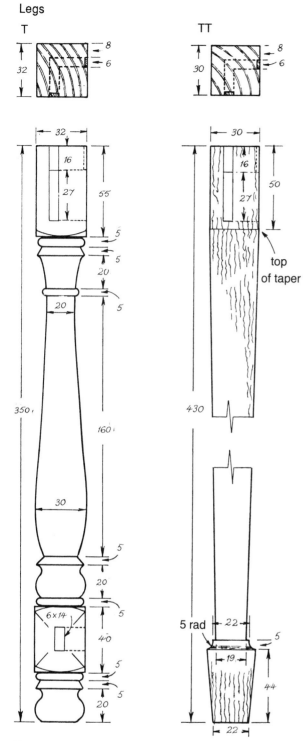

Legs

Fig. 14.5

the bottoms directly, slips are used to take these, (S, Fig 14.4).

The fronts I, J and K, Fig. 14.4 for the oak design should be quarter-sawn, if possible from the same board. They should be fitted in their respective openings just on the tight side, as this will allow for taking off a final shaving or so to get a perfect fit after making up. There is some advantage in leaving the fielding of the fronts until after the drawers are made up and fitted. For this the bulk of the waste can be removed on the planer/jointer by cutting a rebate of the correct depth and width, leaving the slight bevel to be worked by hand with a rebate plane.

When making the mahogany design, the rebates for the cockbeads are not cut until after the drawers are made up and the fronts veneered. The rebates can be worked by hand, or much more quickly on the planer. In either case the depth of the rebate on the veneered face should be incised deeply with a cutting gauge first; this will avoid any splintering of the veneer when doing the rebates. Note that the cockbead along the top edge of the drawers extends the full thickness of the drawer front, while those along the bottoms and sides only go to the dovetails.

STAND
Taking the legs for the oak design first; with these there are some advantages in chopping the mortises for all the rails first, before doing the turning. Likewise the tenons on the rails should be cut and fitted before doing the shaping of the top rails. When assembling, glue and cramp up the two end frames first, and complete the assembly at a second operation.

With the tapered spade foot legs of the mahogany design, here too, the mortises for the top rails should be done first — however, the mortises for the side stretcher rails will have to be cut after the shaping has been done. The final shoulder length of these two rails XX, Fig. 14.6, is best checked from the job after assembling a pair of legs with a side top rail, lightly cramping, and checking that the legs are parallel. The same method can be used for the centre stretcher, WW, Fig 14.6, after the two end frames have been glued up — it's very annoying to find that a prepared rail is a couple of mm or so short when assembly time comes!

SPADE TOE LEG
Making these successfully needs time and patience and as the description of the method is rather complicated, we have give it as an appendix to this design.

FIXING CARCASE TO STAND
After the stand has been glued up the nosing parting bead, Y and Z, Fig. 14.6 between the stand and carcase can be glued and pinned in position. The fixing of the carcase and stand together is done by screwing the carcase bottom into the front top rail of the stand. This gives a permanent location of the carcase front with the front of the stand, then, to allow for any movement in the width of the carcase, buttons are used at the back, engaging with the back top rail. This is shown in the sectional elevation, Fig. 14.2

cross-grained wood or ply. Have the width just a fraction less than the double depth of the grooves and just a push fit — not tight.

The front drawer rails D, Fig. 14. 4 can now be prepared and glued in place, followed by the drawer runners, F, dustboards H, and the back drawer rails E, in that order. Note that while the runner tenons are glued into the rails, these and the back rails are not glued in the housings, this is to allow for any movement in the carcase sides. At this stage the back can be fitted; it is fixed along the bottom edge with screws.

DRAWERS
Normal dovetail construction should be used here. As the thickness of the sides hardly allows for grooving in

DRAWER DIVISIONS
Up to this stage, no mention has been made of dividing the drawers into cutlery compartments; you

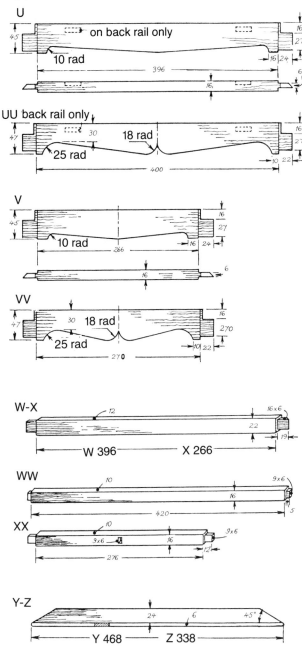

Stand Parts

Fig. 14.6

may prefer to lay them out to suit your own requirements. Suggested layouts for the top and centre drawers are shown in Fig. 14.3. The depth of the division should be $1\frac{3}{4}$ in, and $\frac{1}{8}$ in thick in both cases; the centre drawer is fitted with a half-width sliding tray above the divisions. For this layout about 13 ft of material will be needed.

The layout should be decided upon before the drawers are glued up, so that the necessary grooved housings in the sides, fronts and backs can be cut. The interior divisions should be covered with green baize.

HANDLES — KNOBS

For the oak design, nicely turned knobs will look well. Alternatively suitable drop handles can be used if preferred. For the mahogany design, small ring handles are a must. Those shown are $1\frac{1}{2}$ in diameter.

FINISHING

For the oak cabinet a suitable finish can be obtained by sealing with a couple or three thin coats of french polish and rubbing down with fine wire wool and waxing.

For the mahogany design the same finish would also be suitable if you want an open grain finish, or it could of course be polished to a full bright finish. Do not attempt this way of finishing, though, unless you are prepared to put in some time on the job and carry the process right through to the end — nothing looks worse than a badly completed french polished job!

If you want a darker finish on mahogany, the best stain is still the time-honoured potassium bichromate one. This is a chemical stain and the colour obtained will not be seen until it is dry and some polish is put on. Some varieties of mahogany are more affected by it than others, so always try it out on some scrap pieces of the same wood. The stain is made up by dissolving potassium bichromate crystals in water to a near saturated solution — about 1 oz to $\frac{1}{2}$ pint of water. At this strength it will most likely be too strong but can be diluted with water to give lighter tones.

Before staining dampen the wood with water to raise the grain and then sand smooth; this will avoid heavy sanding after staining (although it will need a light rub down) thereby avoiding cutting through the raised grain and exposing unstained wood. You can then proceed with whatever finish you have chosen.

MAKING SPADE-TOE LEGS
(Appendix to 'Cutlery Cabinets')

This type of leg is most commonly associated with the late 18th century. A plain square tapered leg presents no problems; it is just a matter of planning the taper. When there is a spade toe, however, it is more awkward because the plane can only be used to a limited extent. You can use an overhand machine planer to cut the taper, but the result isn't very good if left from the machine, and the spade toe needs to be completed by hand methods.

SETTING OUT
There are no rigid rules for this. It is merely a matter of what looks well. The following can be taken as a general guide, however. Draw a rectangle the same size as the square from which the leg is to be worked on the blank. Across it square lines (a), (b), and (c), Fig 14.7(a), giving the point at which the taper begins, and the hollow member at the top of the toe. Draw in the slope of the taper, and from where these lines cut the line (b) continue to (d) with lines parallel with the sides, marking positions (e) (e).

Set a gauge to (d) (e) and mark round the bottom of the leg. This marking out is given at A, Fig. 14.7. For clarity the taper is shown as though marked on all four sides. In practice only the two opposite sides would be so marked because the tapering itself would remove the marks on two faces.

CUTTING THE TAPER
A saw cut is made at line (b) down to the depth of the taper, the two opposite sides being so cut. It also helps to make a few saw cuts across the grain at various points along the leg, care being taken to stop short of the line of the taper. The advantage of this is that it cuts up the grain and prevents a split from developing if the grain happens to run awkwardly. A notch is cut with a wide chisel immediately above line (b) as shown at B finishing in line with the taper. The opposite side is also notched as shown, and the leg then turned so that the remaining two sides can also be notched as at C.

The chisel can be used to an extent to cut the rest of the taper, but a smoothing plane is advisable for the top portion, though it will probably be necessary to hold it askew, and in any case to stop short of the toe. A bullnose plane is handy to finish off where the taper terminates at the toe. The scraper can be used to take out plane marks, but to finish off a piece of glasspaper is wrapped around a wood block and used with fair pressure along the length. Use a medium coarse grade first, then finish with fine – 1½ or 1. The end of the wood block should be cut at an angle so that its corner reaches close up to line (b). The two opposite faces having been cut in this way lines marking the taper on the two remaining faces can be drawn in as at D. These tapers are then worked in the same way as the first two.

THE SPADE TOE
It will be seen from Fig 14.8 that the widest part of the toe (c) stands in from the outer surface of the square. A gauge is set to the extent of this set-in and the two opposite faces marked (Fig. 14.7D). The wood is

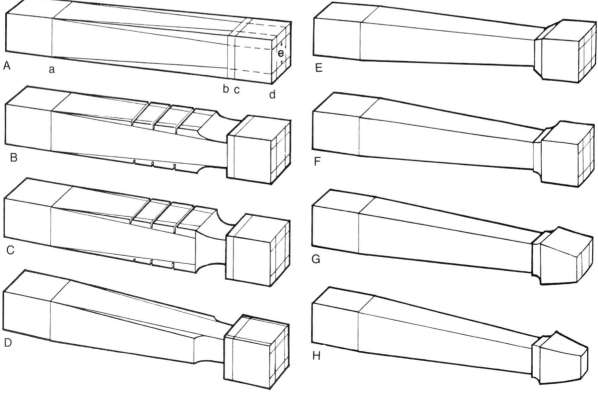

Fig. 14.7

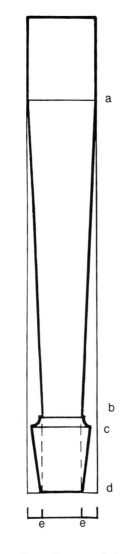

Fig. 14.8

The cutting list shown above is for the oak design and where parts differ for the mahogany design they are marked with an asterisk* and given below; also, oak parts are shown on the drawing and where a mahogany part differs, it is double-lettered for identification.

ALTERNATIVE PARTS FOR MAHOGANY DESIGN

Also required: for oak design, material for turned knobs; for mahogany design, veneer for drawer fronts plus 6 ring handles. For both designs, material for drawer divisions and sliding tray.

Working allowances have been made to lengths and widths; thicknesses are net.

planed down to these lines, and the two remaining faces marked in the same way.

One effect of planing the first two opposite faces is to remove the lines (c) on these faces. It is therefore advisable to square in the lines afresh from those on the adjoining faces before planing the latter.

The small hollow member around the top of the toe is now worked, and it is helpful to cut a plain chamfer first as at Fig. 14.7E. The hollow itself can be cut with a small gouge, taken in from each side to avoid splintering out the grain. A rat-tail file is also handy, and finally glass-paper wrapped around a shaped wood rubber.

It now remains to work only the taper of the toe, and here again it is helpful to plane down the two opposite faces first as at G. The bulk of the waste can be removed with the smoothing plane, but a block plane used with a slicing action is invaluable to finish off.

PART-PROCESSING DETAILS
CARCASE
Part

A	Cut groove for part G. Cut housings to match parts D, E, and F. Cut groove to match tongue in part C. Mitre top ends to 45 degrees and cut groove on face of mitre, as shown.
B	Cut 45 degree mitre on ends and groove on face of mitre, as shown.
C	Work tongue on ends.
D	Plough groove to match part H. Cut notch in ends as shown.
E	Plough groove to match part H.
F	Plough groove to match part H and cut tongue to match tongue in parts D and E.
G & H	Cut to size.

DRAWERS

I, J, & K.	Cut lap dovetail pins (I, J, and K) to match tails on parts L, M, and N respectively.
L	Cut dovetails to match pins on parts I and O.
M	Cut dovetails to match pins on parts J and P.
N	Cut dovetails to match pins on parts K and Q.
O	Cut dovetail pins to match dovetails on part L.
P	Cut dovetail pins to match dovetails on part M.
Q	Cut dovetail pins to match dovetails on part N
R	Cut to size.
S	Plough groove to match part R. Work quarter-round as shown.

STAND

T	Cut mortises to match tenons on parts U, V, W, and X. Turn to shape shown.
U, V, W, X	Cut tenons to match mortises on parts T.
Y & Z	Work half-round on one edge. Mitre ends to 45 degrees.
II, JJ, KK	Cut lap dovetail pins to match tails on parts L, M, and N respectively. Cut groove for R on each.
TT	Cut mortises to match tenons on parts UU and VV. Shape foot as shown. Plane tapers. Cut mortises to match tenons on part XX.
UU, VV WW	Cut tenons to match mortices on parts TT. Cut tenons to match mortices on parts XX.
XX	Cut tenons to match mortises on parts TT and mortises to match tenons on part WW.

MAHOGANY CORNER CUPBOARD

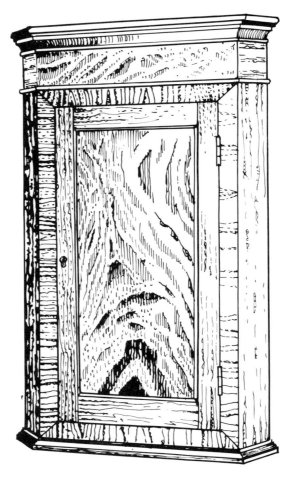

This rather nice old mahogany corner cupboard shown in the illustration is veneered with some excellent curls. The frame surrounding the door is cross-banded with mitred corners. Around the door opening is an ⅛ in flush bead covering the thickness of the frame, which is pine. The pilasters, again, are in pine, with the veneer laid vertically up to the astragal above the door (C, Fig. 15.2). Above this the veneer is laid horizontally on the pilasters as well as along the front. These pilasters and the adjoining vertical front members run right through to just below the top of the cornice moulding. The front flat part of the cornice is well glue-blocked behind, and is best tongued-and-grooved into the verticals. This suggested construction is shown at E, Fig. 15.1. The joint between the pilasters and the front uprights is just butted and glued but grooving and tonguing would be suitable. This is also shown at E, Fig. 15.1

The frame of the door is solid, with haunched mortise-and-tenon joints. The panel is veneered on solid mahogany, with the moulding D (Fig. 15.2) planted in the angle. The panel is grooved into the rails, and there is no bead on the inside.

The backs are pine, with rebated front edges entering grooves in the pilasters (E, Fig. 15.1). Note that the backs are set in ½ in from the edge of the pilasters, to allow them to fit the walls and also, no doubt, for hanging in a corner with the walls at an angle of

rather more than 90 degrees – a condition not unknown in old houses!

The top is fitted between the backs and the top front rail and glued and nailed in position. There is a similar construction at the bottom. You could, of course,

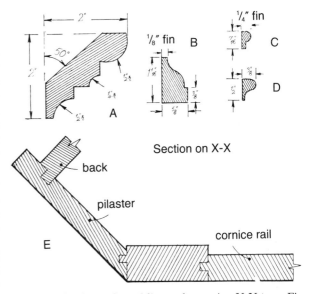

Fig. 15.1. Sections of mouldings; also section X-X from Fig. 15.2.

70

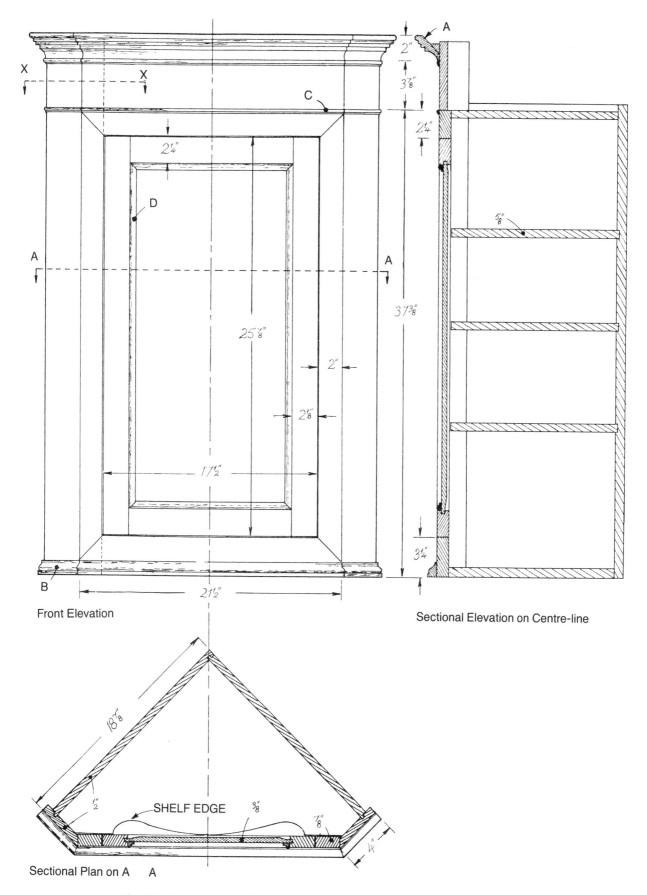

Front Elevation

Sectional Elevation on Centre-line

SHELF EDGE

Sectional Plan on A   A

Fig. 15.2. Front and end elevations of cupboard, together with plan section A-A.

use a more usual dovetail construction. Butting, gluing and nailing is also employed at the back corner joint. In Fig. 15.2, the shelves are also of pine, and are shown as grooved into the backs. The front edges are shaped as shown in the plan view, Fig. 15.2.

Note that the small astragal C, (Figs. 15.1 and 15.2, is separate from the cornice moulding proper and is

planted in the angle formed between the lower edge of this and the front. This moulding is the same size and section as the lower one above the door.

In working the mouldings B, C and D, moulding planes, a scratch-stock, spindle moulder or router could be used. They are best worked on the edge of a board and then sawn off afterwards. The cornice moulding A may prove a little more difficult. Working by hand, the bulk of the waste can be removed by rebating and the final shape worked with a scratch stock.

It's unlikely that mahogany dark enough to finish with the genuine rich colour will be available without some form of staining. For this the use of potassium bichromate is suggested. Start with a 5% solution, which can be diluted further if it proves too dark, this it may well be. Tests must be made on scrap pieces, particularly as the depth obtained on pieces from different sources or trees may vary considerably. Even then some slight colouring up may have to be done at the polishing stage. Before doing the staining, dampen the surfaces and when dry, paper down the raised grain. This will avoid much of the lifting of the grain when doing the staining proper.

For the final finish in this class of work, there seems nothing to beat french polish with a fully filled grain. Even if some dulling down of the brightness is envisaged the process should be carried through to the end before attempting this or it will not be satisfactory — there is no short cut!

CUTTING LIST

		INCHES			MM		
		L	W	T	L	W	T
2	Pilasters	43	$4\frac{1}{2}$	$\frac{1}{2}$	1092	115	13
2	Front vertical posts	43	$2\frac{1}{4}$	$\frac{7}{8}$	1092	58	22
2	Backs	$38\frac{3}{8}$	$19\frac{3}{8}$	$\frac{1}{2}$	974	493	13
1	Front cornice panel	$19\frac{1}{2}$	$5\frac{3}{8}$	$\frac{1}{2}$	495	137	13
2	Corner cornice panel	$4\frac{1}{2}$	$5\frac{3}{8}$	$\frac{1}{2}$	115	137	13
1	Top*	27	17	$\frac{5}{8}$	686	432	16
1	Bottom*	27	17	$\frac{5}{8}$	686	432	16
3	Shelves*	27	17	$\frac{5}{8}$	686	432	16
2	Door stiles	$26\frac{7}{8}$	$2\frac{3}{8}$	$\frac{7}{8}$	683	60	22
2	Door rails	$17\frac{1}{2}$	$2\frac{1}{2}$	$\frac{7}{8}$	445	64	22
1	Door panel	$22\frac{7}{8}$	$13\frac{3}{4}$	$\frac{3}{8}$	581	349	10
1	Cornice rail	19	$2\frac{1}{2}$	$\frac{7}{8}$	483	64	22
1	Bottom front rail	19	$3\frac{1}{2}$	$\frac{7}{8}$	483	89	22
Mouldings							
1	Length (A)	36	$2\frac{1}{4}$	2	914	58	51
1	Length (B)	36	$1\frac{5}{16}$	$\frac{5}{8}$	914	34	16
1	Length (C)	36	$\frac{11}{16}$	$\frac{1}{4}$	914	18	6
1	Length (D)	75	$\frac{3}{4}$	$\frac{3}{8}$	1904	19	10

*Items marked * may be nested and marked out from one piece.*

Working allowances have been made to lengths and widths; thicknesses are net.

CHILD'S HIGH CHAIR

This chair, suitable for a child of from one-and-a-half to four years, is of a height to suit a normal dining table. It would form a useful elementary excursion into chair making on the Windsor principle, and also good practice in 'between-centres' turning. Beech would be a good choice for the beginner in spindle turning.

TURNING THE LEGS

Begin by turning the legs. Endeavour to get a nice flowing curve from the major to minor diameters, placing the major diameter where indicated on the drawing (Fig. 16.3).

THE SEAT

For the seat, select a piece of sound timber without any incipient cracks or shakes. Plywood would probably be stronger, but it would not look so good when finished. Set the seat out as shown in Fig. 16.2. Cut the outline to shape and curve the edges. The holes for the legs can most conveniently be drilled on a machine with a canting table. Set the table over to about 12½ degrees and note the line of cant is diagonal from corner to corner of the seat; this gives the correct splay of the legs in both planes. These holes are drilled from the underside of the seat which is clamped to the

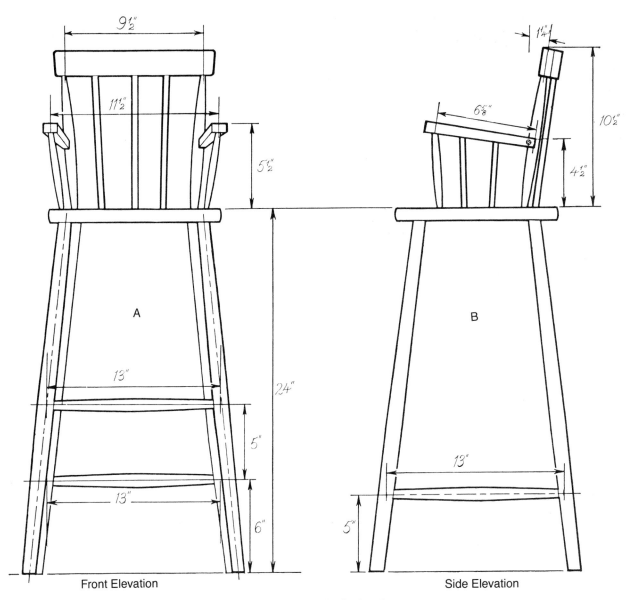

Fig. 16.1 Front and side elevations.

machine table with a waste piece of wood under to get a clean break through. This gives a better finish to the hole on the upper side than drilling from the top. The holes for the back uprights and the arm stumps are drilled from the upper side, with the table cant reduced to about 8 degrees. For these holes the seat is positioned on the machine table diagonally to the cant as before. The holes for the intermediate spindles are left until the top work is ready for assembly.

STRETCHERS

For the stretchers, ⅝ in dowelling is used. If the lathe has a hollow mandrel of ⅝ in bore or over they can best be done in a self-centring chuck. If the lathe mandrel isn't hollow, the stretchers will have to be done between centres. In this case they could be turned out of ¾ in wood and given a fully shaped curve from end to end. With care in centring it should be possible to hold the major diameter up to ¹¹⁄₁₆ in.

Before assembling and gluing up the lower half of the chair, cut the saw kerf in the pins for wedging. Note that this should be positioned in relation to the stretcher holes so that the line of the wedge is at right angles to the grain of the seat; this will avoid any tendency to splitting the seat when driving in the wedges. After assembly and before the glue sets, check the

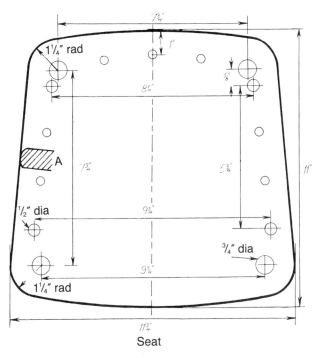

Fig. 16.2 Marking-out details for the seat.

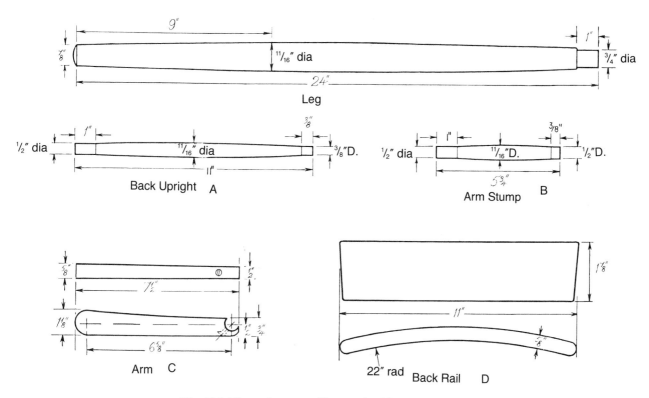

Fig. 16.3 The various parts illustrated, with measurements.

ARMS AND STUMPS

The main back uprights and arm stumps are shaped as shown (Fig. 16.3). The top back rail can be shaped by hand methods, bow saw, spokeshave, scraper and glasspaper; or an easier way is to use a bandsaw, and if carefully sawn, it is finished on a disc and belt sander. Insert (dry) the back uprights and arm stumps as guides to drilling the blind holes in the seat for the intermediate uprights in back and arms. After fitting, the rear ends of the arms are fixed to the back uprights with ¾ in No. 6 raised head brass screws. It is best to insert a steel screw here until final assembly. Time spent in getting a pleasing shape to the arms is well repaid and can add much to the final appearance. Assembly the whole of the top work dry to be sure everything will come together satisfactorily before finally gluing up. The arm stumps and back uprights are wedged from underneath, and the upper ends pegged with ¼ in dowels through the arms and back rail respectively.

FINISHING

After a final clean-up, the chair can be finished with three coats of polyurethane lacquer. The first coat can be thinned down with 10% white spirit, and when dry sanded lightly to remove dust nibs. The second coat should be well rubbed down and all dust removed before applying the final coat which should be applied in as dust-free an atmosphere as possible. This can be left off the brush, or if a satin finish is preferred, rubbed down with fine steel wool and waxed. This finish will stand up well to the kind of wear this type of chair will be subjected to.

CUTTING LIST

		INCHES			MM		
		L	W	T	L	W	T
4	Legs	24½	T'rnd	¹¹/₁₆	622	T'rnd	18
2	Back uprights	11½	T'rnd	¹¹/₁₆	293	T'rnd	18
2	Arm stumps	6	T'rnd	¹¹/₁₆	153	T'rnd	18
2	Arms	7¾	1¼	⅝	197	32	16
1	Back rail	11½	2	1½	293	51	38
1	Seat	12	11½	¾	305	293	19
4	Leg stretchers	13	T'rnd	⅝	330	T'rnd	16
3	Back uprights	11	T'rnd	⅜	279	T'rnd	10
2	Arm uprights	6	T'rnd	⅜	153	T'rnd	10
2	Arm uprights	5½	T'rnd	⅜	140	T'rnd	10

Working allowances have been made to lengths and widths; thicknesses are net.

PERIOD 'HUTCH' CUPBOARD

This piece of improvised period furniture would serve the purpose of a normal modern sideboard, housing drinks glasses, table linen, etc. A mixture of sideboard, court cupboard and tallboy, it is usually called a 'hutch'.

The cupboard has two pairs of doors having altogether 12 panels. Six of these are carved, each with a different motif, and the top and middle rails carry a guilloche carving. Being partly designed to house drinks, the top cupboard will hold bottles and glasses and a leaf pulls out allowing drinks to be served with ease. English oak is the best choice of timber, and the cupboard features wooden catches and antique iron hinges.

CARCASE

The four corner posts are cut to length and the appropriate mortises sunk. It is important to remember that the tenons will not be the full width of the end rails, as the grooves for the panels have to be run through. Matters are simplified if both the groove width and the tenon thickness are the same. A further groove is also run straight down the appropriate face of each post to house the side panels. Rebates are worked on the back face of the rear posts to house the back panels of the cupboard later in construction.

The various rails are prepared, the tenons cut and grooves worked where necessary along the side rails to house the side panels. Rebates are again worked on the four back rails to hold the same back panels.

The floors of the upper and lower cupboards will be tongued into grooves which are now worked on the inside faces of the $1\frac{1}{4}$ in front middle rail, the two 4 in side upper middle rails and the 4 in upper middle back rail for the upper floor, and also on the bottom front, side and back rails for the lower floor (see Fig. 17.4).

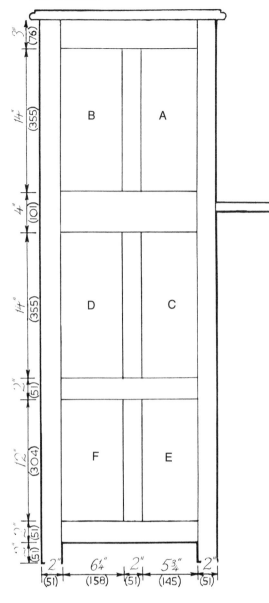

Fig. 17.1 Side elevation with leaf extended. In all illustrations, metric equivalents of dimensions are shown in brackets.

The side muntins are cut and jointed to the side rails, and again grooved to house the side panels. At this stage the twelve side panels are cut and rebated on all four edges to fit these grooves.

The two sides of the cupboard are now assembled dry to see that all is well, and if the front and back rails are added the whole carcase can be checked.

CARVING
The guilloche carving is repeated on the top and middle front rails. To ensure symmetry on a length such as this the first circle to be cut is the one in the middle and the pattern can then be worked outwards in both directions.

LEAF
The leaf must be perfectly flat and square as it has to run smoothly between the four runners which are attached internally to the two sides (Fig. 17.4). A stop is fastened to it to prevent the leaf being drawn out too far, and to ensure that it pulls out square – even if only

one knob is pulled – add two side pieces to the leaf, flush up against the runners, part 3 in Fig. 17.4.

The knobs themselves are turned from scrap oak, and dowel screws are used to fasten them to the leaf.

SHELVING
The floors of the top and bottom cupboards are prepared and a tongue worked round, to fit into the groove previously made on the inside faces of the rails. A middle shelf in the bottom cupboard can be conveniently supported by the lower middle side and back rails, which are purposely left thicker for this reason. Shelving in both cupboards could be arranged to suit individual requirements.

ASSEMBLY
The carcase can now be assembled, starting with the sides. Remember that the panels are not glued in place but must be able to move in the grooves to avoid splitting as a result of shrinkage. Glue the sides, then the front and rear rails are glued across, not forgetting to insert the top and bottom floors and the draw out leaf. When the glue has set the ply back panels are added with the oak face to the inside of the cupboard.

TOP
The top is jointed if necessary, planed flat, and a moulding worked around the edge. It can be fastened to the carcase using either shrinkage plates or buttons.

DOORS
The door frames are jointed with through or haunched tenons. The stiles, rails and muntins all have stopped chamfers worked on them, and are grooved on the appropriate edges to accept the door panels. These twelve panels are all the same size and six of them are carved, each with a different design. Again a rebate is worked around the panels to fit them into the grooved frames. This construction is straightforward but repetitive and when the doors are completed they can be fitted on to the carcase. Surface-fitting antique iron hinges with an armour bright finish are the sort of thing you need. The door catches are made from oak and pivoted on brass screws as shown in Fig. 17.3B.

FINISHING
Fuming suits period oak furniture very well; it is an involved process, and you may prefer ordinary stain and polish.

Oak, especially English oak, contains tannic acid which, when exposed to the fumes of ammonia, changes the colour of the oak to a dull brown. The ammonia used should be of the type known as ' · 880' which is very strong. Treat it with respect, being careful not to spill any or inhale the fumes. If any should be spilt on the skin its effect can be neutralised by liberal washing in water and rubbing with a pad soaked in vinegar.

Depending on the space available, the piece can be fumed either complete or in pieces. If it's complete, the process can be carried out possibly in a garage or even in the open air. The whole thing is covered with a polythene sheet which is supported so it doesn't touch the

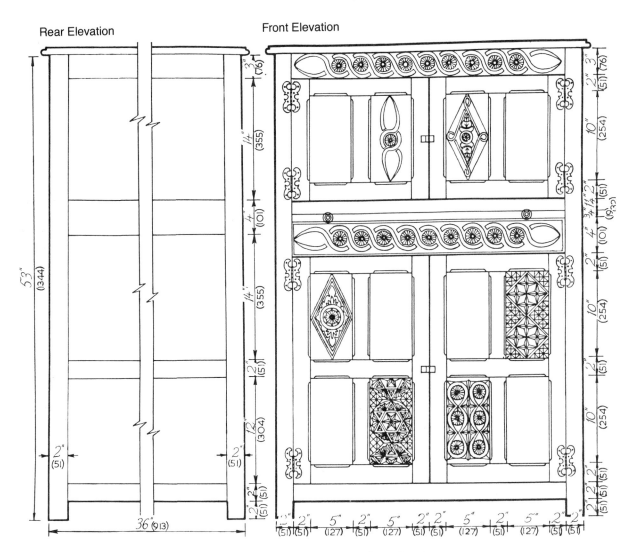

Fig. 17.2 (left) rear elevation; (right) front elevation.

cupboard at any point. If you fume dis-assembled components, the pieces are stacked in a suitable cupboard, care being taken that the fumes can circulate freely. The pieces are supported (with scrap wood) by the tenons or other parts which will not show later.

A saucer full of ammonia is put into the cupboard, the door of which is shut and sealed with adhesive tape. The actual fuming time varies from a couple of hours to half a day, depending upon the depth of colour required.

After assembly, the cupboard is brushed liberally with a 50/50 mixture of pure turpentine and linseed oil, to which a small quantity of Jacobean oil stain has been added. This brings back the warmth and tone of the wood and the piece is now left for a day or so for this to soak in. If it is required to 'antique' the finish a little, darker stain can be put into the deeper parts of the carving with a fine paint brush, and points that would naturally receive wear can be lightened by careful sanding or rubbing with steel wool. After all the oiliness has been absorbed, a sealing coat of white french polish is applied and allowed to dry. Again, steel wool may be used to burnish slightly, and this leaves the piece ready for wax polishing. Add a little lamp-black to the initial coat of wax polish further to age the appearance, followed by repeated applications of pure wax polish.

VARIATIONS

Many variations are possible on this basic cupboard.

The middle carved front rail could form the front of an extremely useful drawer for cutlery, etc. where use as a sideboard is envisaged. The number, design and distribution of the carved panels may be varied and if the hinges leave enough space carved beading could be worked up the front of the front posts.

Finally metal knobs, handles and escutcheons could be added as desired.

CUTTING LIST

Carcase	INCHES			MM		
	L	W	T	L	W	T
4 Corner posts	53½	2¼	2	1358	58	51
2 Top rails	35½	3¼	⅞	902	83	22
1 Front middle rail	35½	1½	⅞	902	38	22
2 Middle rails	35½	4¼	⅞	902	108	22
1 Back lower middle rail	35½	2¼	2	902	58	51
2 Bottom rails	35½	2¼	⅞	902	58	22
2 Top side rails	18	3¼	⅞	457	83	22
2 Upper middle side rails	18	4¼	⅞	457	108	22
2 Lower middle side rails	18	2¼	2	457	58	51
2 Bottom side rails	18	2¼	⅞	457	58	22
2 Side muntins	50½	2¼	⅞	1282	58	22
2 Top front side panels (A)	15½	6¾	½	394	172	12

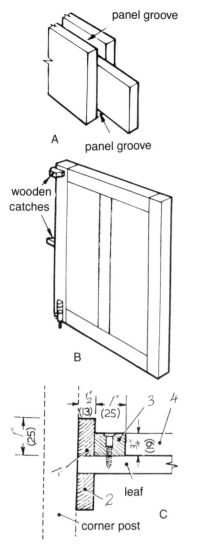

Fig. 17.3 (A) detail of grooving on intermediate door rail; (B) inside view of upper left-hand door; (C) front cross-sectional view.

CUTTING LIST (continued)

Part	INCHES			MM		
	L	W	T	L	W	T
2 Top rear side panels (B)	15½	7¼	½	394	185	12
2 Middle front side panels (C)	15½	6¾	½	394	172	12
2 Middle rear side panels (D)	15½	7¼	½	394	185	12
2 Bottom front side panels (E)	13½	6¾	½	343	172	12
2 Bottom rear side panels (F)	13½	7¼	½	343	185	12
1 Top	38½	19¼	1	978	489	25
1 Upper back panel	33½	15¼	3/16	851	387	4
1 Centre back panel	33½	16¼	3/16	851	413	4
1 Lower back panel	33½	12¾	3/16	851	324	4
2 Upper & lower cupb'd floors	35¼	17¾	½	895	451	12
1 Lower cupb'd middle shelf	35	12¼	½	889	311	12
Leaf and leaf parts						
1 Leaf	32½	17¼	¾	826	438	19
2 Leaf runners (1)	17½	1¼	½	445	32	12
2 Leaf runners (2)	17½	1¼	½	445	32	12
2 Leaf runners (3)	6½	1	1	165	25	25
1 Leaf stop (4)	28½	1	1	724	25	25
Doors						
4 Upper door stiles	14½	2¼	7/8	368	58	22
4 Lower door stiles	26½	2¼	7/8	673	58	22
10 Rails	16½	2¼	7/8	419	58	22
2 Upper door muntins	14½	2¼	7/8	368	58	22
2 Lower door muntins	26½	2¼	7/8	673	58	22
12 Door panels	11½	6¼	½	293	159	12

Working allowances have been made to lengths and widths; thicknesses are net.

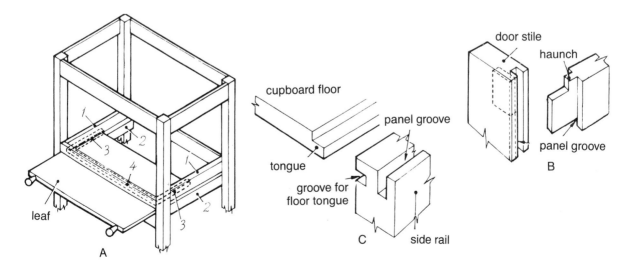

Fig. 17.4 (A) general view of arrangement of leaf. (B) detail of joint in door stile and rail; (C) arrangement of grooves for floor and panel on side rail.

Design No 18

NEST OF TABLES

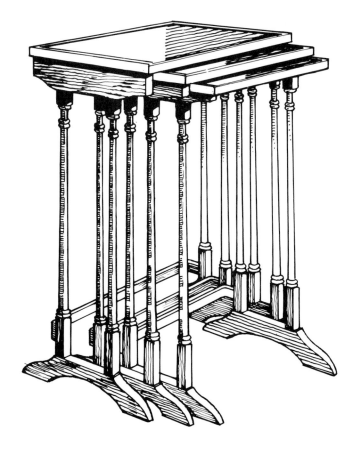

These very delicately made tables are based directly (but not in every detail) on a late 18th century design. They are not 'period reproduction pieces', but rather a useful set of tables suitable for a modern home, yet with the charm of the 18th century design.

TIMBER

Although the tables are lightly made they are surprisingly strong – the complete set weighing only 12 lb. They should be made up in one of the better cabinet woods, strictly speaking mahogany; if you can get hold of some Spanish (Cuban) from old furniture this is the stuff to use, particularly as it turns so well. Walnut is a good alternative.

Whatever timber is chosen it must be dry and well-seasoned; that for the legs should be picked from straight-grained stock or you may have trouble with movement when turning. This can be caused by hidden stresses being released during working – which would be fatal to the leg frames coming together without wind, an essential to getting a nice nesting fit.

CONSTRUCTION

Start by preparing all the framing parts, A, B, and C, (Fig. 18.2). These can be cut in length to the finished sizes and planed up in square-edged form. If you have a small planer with thicknessing attachment this is quickly done without any gauging and laborious hand planing.

FEET AND RAILS

First mark out and chop all the mortises in both rails and feet. Be particularly careful that these are accurately centred. With due care, accuracy in all ways should be automatic. The shaped ends of both rails and feet can then be cut on a narrow bandsaw or with a bowsaw and cleaned up. Cleaning up of the curves is best done on the drum end of a belt sander. Do not at this stage cut out the bottom centre curve on the feet or the rebates in the rails; this is better done after gluing up, making cramping easier.

TURNING THE LEGS

For the novice, turning the long slender legs will perhaps prove the trickiest part of the whole job, so the method will be described in some detail. For the long straight tapered part, the principle is that two profile boards are fixed to the lathe bed, one in front and one behind the part being turned. The top edges of these follow the profile to be planed, in this case the taper from $\frac{3}{4}$ in to $\frac{1}{2}$ in diameter. From this it will be seen that the top edges of the boards at any point will need to be at lathe centre height plus half the finished diameter to be planed. After roughing out with a gouge in the usual way to about $\frac{1}{16}$ in over finished size, a block-plane is used across the edges of the boards until it ceases to cut. Only the straight tapered parts were finished in this way, the beads being turned in the normal way with a long cornered chisel. Using

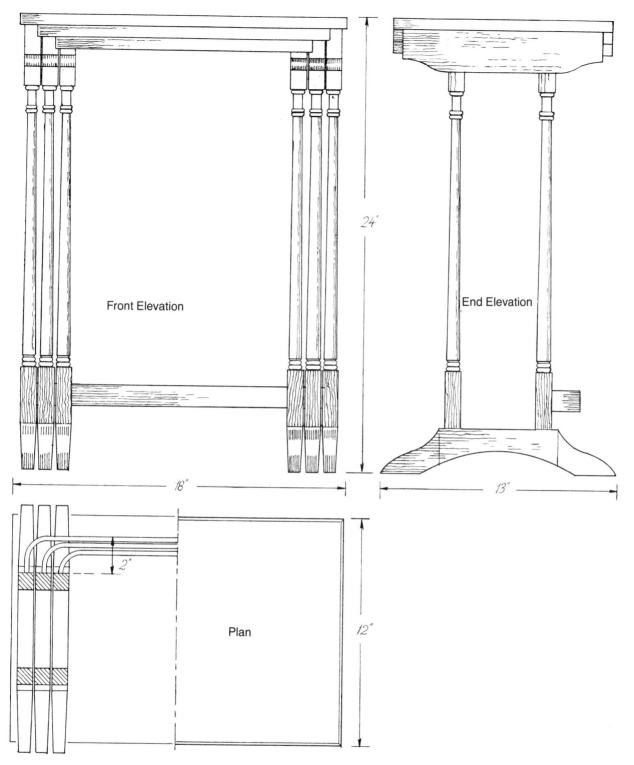

Front Elevation

End Elevation

24"

18"

13"

2"

Plan

12"

Fig. 18.1. Elevations and plan.

this method the tapers will come out identical in diameter without any measuring, which is a distinct advantage seeing that there are 12 legs to be done.

Fig. 18.4 is a cross-section showing how the jig was made up and attached to the lathe, which is a flat-bed engineer's type. An alternative method is also shown which is suitable for a round-bed lathe.

From Fig. 18.4 it will be noted that a four-jaw independent chuck is used for driving, preferable to using a forked centre, giving extra stiffness when turning the tapers. A half-round guard is fixed to the ends of the profile boards, to shield the knuckles when working close to the chuck. The positions of the shoulders and the beads are marked on the front profile board. Fig.

the beads are marked on the front profile board. Fig. 18.4 also shows the small wooden pads glued to the chuck jaws to protect the leg square.

PROCEDURE

After accurately centring the top ends of the squares, put a blank in the lathe, preferably using a ring centre in the tailstock, and adjust the chuck jaws to get true running at the headstock end. Accurate centring is important, as the squares are finished size except for a small cleaning-up allowance on the sides only. This adjustment should only have to be made once, if, when changing over you only slack off jaws 1 and 2, and remember to use only these two jaws when tightening up.

PARTS REQUIRED

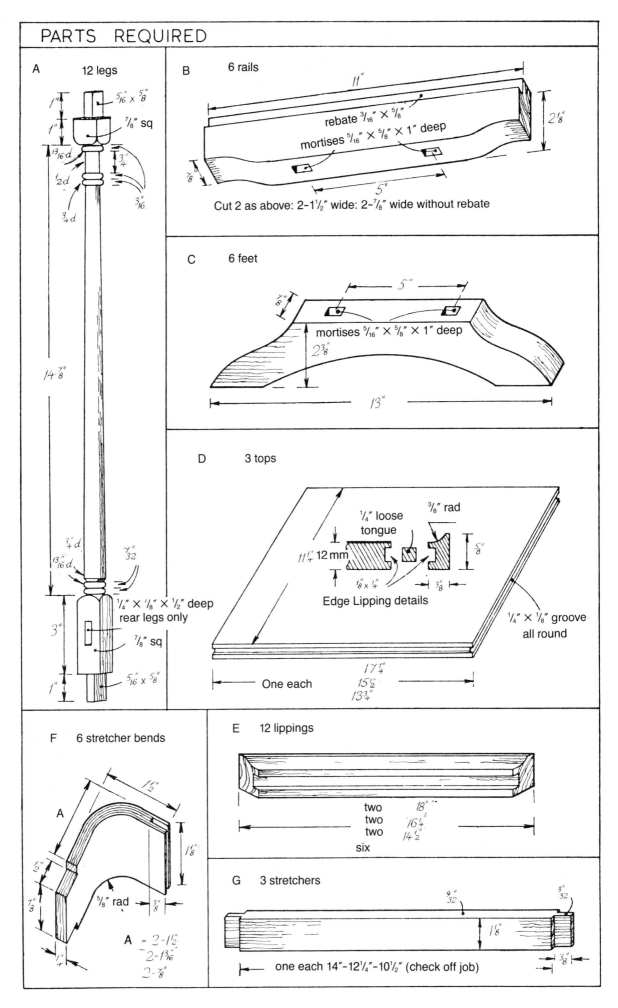

A   12 legs

$\frac{5}{16}" \times \frac{5}{8}"$

1"

1"

$\frac{7}{8}"$ sq

$\frac{13}{16} d$

$\frac{1}{2} d$

$\frac{3}{4}$

$\frac{3}{16}"$

$\frac{3}{4} d$

$14\frac{7}{8}"$

$\frac{3}{4} d$

$\frac{13}{16} d$

$\frac{7}{32}"$

$\frac{1}{4}" \times \frac{1}{8}" \times \frac{1}{2}"$ deep rear legs only

3"

$\frac{7}{8}"$ sq

1"

$\frac{5}{16}" \times \frac{5}{8}"$

B   6 rails

11"

$2\frac{1}{8}"$

rebate $\frac{3}{16}" \times \frac{5}{8}"$

mortises $\frac{5}{16}" \times \frac{5}{8}" \times 1"$ deep

$\frac{7}{8}"$

5"

Cut 2 as above: 2-$1\frac{1}{2}"$ wide: 2-$\frac{7}{8}"$ wide without rebate

C   6 feet

5"

$\frac{7}{8}"$

mortises $\frac{5}{16}" \times \frac{5}{8}" \times 1"$ deep

$2\frac{3}{8}"$

13"

D   3 tops

$\frac{1}{4}"$ loose tongue

$\frac{3}{8}"$ rad

$11\frac{1}{4}"$ 12 mm

$\frac{5}{8}"$

$\frac{1}{8}" \times \frac{1}{4}"$

$\frac{3}{8}"$

Edge Lipping details

$\frac{1}{4}" \times \frac{1}{8}"$ groove all round

One each

$17\frac{1}{4}"$

$15\frac{1}{2}"$

$13\frac{3}{4}"$

F   6 stretcher bends

A

$1\frac{1}{2}"$

$1\frac{1}{8}"$

$\frac{1}{2}"$

$\frac{7}{8}"$

$\frac{5}{8}"$ rad

$\frac{3}{8}"$

$\frac{1}{4}"$

A = 2-$1\frac{1}{2}"$
       2-$1\frac{3}{16}"$
       2-$\frac{7}{8}"$

E   12 lippings

two   18"

two $16\frac{1}{4}"$

two $14\frac{1}{2}"$

six

G   3 stretchers

$\frac{9}{32}"$

$\frac{3}{32}"$

$1\frac{1}{8}"$

$\frac{3}{8}"$

one each 14"-$12\frac{1}{4}"$-$10\frac{1}{2}"$ (check off job)

Fig. 18.2 Showing processing required for parts.

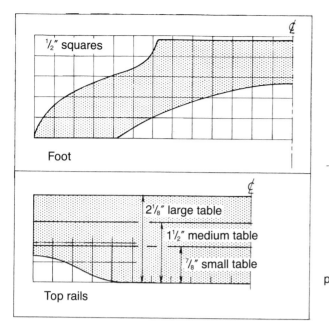

Fig. 18.3 Squared-off shapes for feet and rails.

Although the top edges of the profile boards are above centre height it is quite practicable to use the front board as a tool rest for the chisel and gouge work. This saves a lot of time changing over.

Now nick in and turn the shoulders of the squares, then turn the left-hand end down to $^{13}/_{16}$ in tapering to $^3/_4$ in at the right-hand end. Next turn the five beads, noting that these must be accurately sized and placed otherwise any discrepancy will be painfully obvious when the tables are nested, each group of three legs being side by side.

Do not attempt to scrape the beads or you will surely have trouble with 'picking up' on the periphery. Neither is it possible to use a form tool for the same reasons. Only the closest-grained hardwoods can be successfully turned in this way — boxwood is one of the few.

Small bead turning can be a little tricky if you have done none before, so put in a bit of practice on waste before starting the job proper; use a $^1/_4$ in long cornered chisel for this size of bead.

PLANING THE TAPERS

First, with a gouge, take the tapered parts down to near their finished diameters. For sizing the tapers a low-angled blockplane is suitable, and for working up to the beads and for the top short taper a $^5/_8$ in shoulder rebate plane.

Hold the block plane slightly obliquely so that the middle of the blade is cutting and move it gently along the work. Do not run the lathe too fast, about 800 to 1000 rpm is fast enough. If you get chatter lower the speed and/or alter the angle at which you are applying the plane or work from the other end. If you get persistent chatter (much depends on the wood being used) a $1^1/_2$ in hole drilled near the top edge in the middle of the back profile board can be used to apply a small steady. This could be a short length of $^5/_8$ in square wood with a forked end padded with leather. It would be applied by hand through the hole, supporting the bottom and the back of the turning while the plane is used with the other hand. Only light upward and forward pressure should be given or the

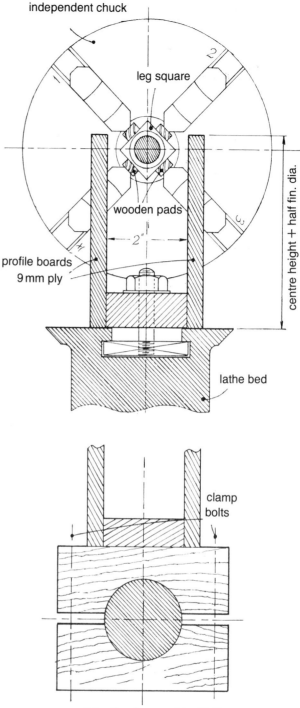

Fig. 18.4 Showing cross-section of profile boards mounted on lathe, and (below) mounting for round-bed lathe.

finished diameter will be too small. When the plane ceases to cut and it beds down on both profile boards the taper is down to size.

The really experienced turner will perhaps smile at all this but for the inexperienced worker these legs are not 'just a piece of cake,' and to turn them with a chisel requires quite some know-how.

All these instructions pre-suppose that your tools are correctly ground and really sharp; no fine turning can be done with incorrectly ground or dull tools. Set your planes to take off only a fine shaving.

Sanding with fine garnet is now done and the turned part polished while still in the lathe. Finish with fine steel wool lubricated with wax.

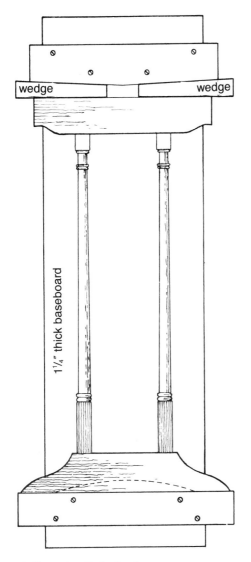

1¼" thick baseboard

wedge   wedge

Fig. 18.5 Cramping jig for leg frames.

LEG FRAMES

The tenons on the legs can now be cut to match the mortises on parts B and C, Fig. 18.2. Here, again, it is important to have them truly central or on cleaning up you will be likely to snip the rounds of the beads if you have much material to remove.

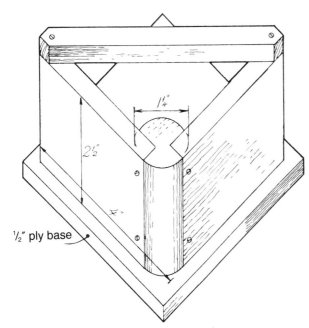

1¼"

2½"

½" ply base

Fig. 18.6 Jig for laminating stretcher ends.

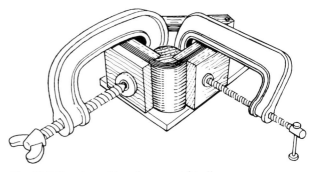

Fig. 18.7 Laminated bends cramped to jig.

Light sash cramps can be used when gluing up, but the jig shown in Fig. 18.5 is an advantage. If all joints have been well cut no great pressure is needed, the main point being that they must come up close and the frame be without any wind when released from the jig.

The central arch can now be sawn in the feet C and the rebates in parts B worked in the four frames for the large and medium tables.

TOPS

Fixing, veneering and lipping the tops is comparatively straightforward, and needs no detailed explanation.

STRETCHERS

As mentioned earlier, the back stretcher rails are made with 90 degree laminated bends. For making these bends, F, Fig. 18.2, make up a jig as shown in Fig. 18.6. The laminations are 1 mm mahogany constructional veneer, and seven will give a thickness of about $\frac{9}{32}$ in which is about right. Cut them 4 in long by 2½ in wide, and this will produce two bends by sawing in half after gluing. Soak the laminations in hot water for a few minutes and cramp to the jig. Put a cramp radially across the bend before pulling down the ends; the

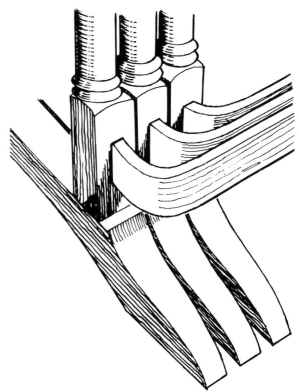

Fig. 18.8 Close-up view of rear feet showing laminated stretcher bends.

radial cramp can then be removed. Fig. 18.7 shows a set of laminations cramped up. Let them dry right out before releasing to glue and re-cramp using a synthetic resin glue. When dry the bend can be sawn in two and the tenons and grooves cut. Now fit the bends (dry) to the small table and temporarily fix the legs the correct distance apart to take the exact shoulder length of the straight stretcher rail, G, Fig. 18.2. The bends can then be glued to the stretcher and when dry, cleaned up and face veneered before gluing in position. A veneer-grade impact adhesive is ideal.

The second and third tables are done in the same way, bearing in mind that when taking the shoulder length of the stretcher a small clearance should be allowed between the legs and those of the adjoining table: this should be about 1 mm.

FINISHING

After a final clean-up and fine garnet papering the tables can then be polished. A brush cellulose or something similar on the frames, finishing with fine steel wool and wax; for the tops a hard two-pack poly-urethane will give a very serviceable finish. This can be matted down with steel wool and wax after allowing sufficient time for the lacquer to harden.

CUTTING LIST

Part		L	W	T	L	W	T
		INCHES			*MM*		
A	12 Legs	$21\frac{3}{8}$	$1\frac{1}{8}$	$\frac{7}{8}$	543	29	22
B	2 Rails	$11\frac{1}{2}$	$2\frac{3}{8}$	$\frac{7}{8}$	292	60	22
	2 Rails	$11\frac{1}{2}$	$1\frac{3}{4}$	$\frac{7}{8}$	292	45	22
	2 Rails	$11\frac{1}{2}$	$1\frac{1}{8}$	$\frac{7}{8}$	292	29	22
C	6 Feet	$13\frac{1}{2}$	$2\frac{5}{8}$	$\frac{7}{8}$	343	67	22
D	1 Top	$17\frac{3}{4}$	$11\frac{3}{4}$	$\frac{1}{2}$	451	298	12
	1 Top	16	$11\frac{3}{4}$	$\frac{1}{2}$	406	298	12
	1 Top	$14\frac{1}{4}$	$11\frac{3}{4}$	$\frac{1}{2}$	362	298	12

CUTTING LIST (continued)

Part		L	W	T	L	W	T
		INCHES			*MM*		
E	2 Lippings	$18\frac{1}{2}$	$\frac{7}{8}$	$\frac{3}{8}$	470	22	10
	2 Lippings	$16\frac{3}{4}$	$\frac{7}{8}$	$\frac{3}{8}$	426	22	10
	2 Lippings	15	$\frac{7}{8}$	$\frac{3}{8}$	381	22	10
	6 Lippings	$12\frac{1}{2}$	$\frac{7}{8}$	$\frac{3}{8}$	318	22	10
F	Laminated bends – see note below						
G	1 Stretcher	$14\frac{1}{2}$	$1\frac{3}{8}$	$\frac{9}{32}$	368	35	7
	1 Stretcher	$12\frac{3}{4}$	$1\frac{3}{8}$	$\frac{9}{32}$	324	35	7
	1 Stretcher	11	$1\frac{3}{8}$	$\frac{9}{32}$	279	35	7
	Loose tonguing	180	$\frac{1}{2}$	$\frac{1}{4}$	4575	12	6

Also required: 1 mm constructional veneer for the laminated bends, approx 6 sq ft; also veneer for the tops.

Working allowances have been made to lengths and widths; thicknesses are net.

PROCESSING DETAILS

Part A To be turned as described in text. Cut tenons to match mortises in parts B and C; cut mortises in 6 legs only to match tenons on parts F.

Part B Shape profile of lower edge. Cut mortises to match tenons on parts A. Do not rebate until after gluing up.

Part C Cut mortises to match tenons on parts A. Shape profile of ends only.

Part D Select material for flatness. Plough grooves on all edges.

Part E Select mild-grained wood. Plane to size, plough groove, and plane hollow on top inner edge. Mitre ends to 45 degrees.

Part G Adjust thickness to match parts F. Cut tongue on ends to match groove on parts E.

LADDERBACK CHAIR

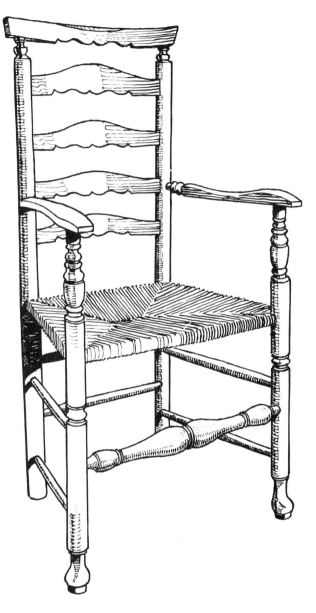

All the main parts of this traditional rustic chair are detailed in Fig. 19.1 which, together with the seat plan Fig. 19.2, should enable prospective constructors to go ahead.

The seat plan, Fig. 19.2 gives the angles at which the holes for the cross-members come, and also shows the approximate angle of the mortises in the back legs for the splats. Apart from these mortises the whole construction is ¾ in dowels turned on the ends of the various rails.

The wood in which such original chairs were made would be ash. Undoubtedly yew, if obtainable, would be the best choice for this job. The seat rails seem to be rather on the light side so it would be well to choose a tough long-grained wood for these.

While reasonably detailed particulars of the decorative turning of the legs is shown, it is obviously impossible to give separate measurements of all the small quirks and beads. Precise sizes of every tiny detail is

hardly necessary – in any case, in the originals, it is doubtful if one leg is exactly like the other to the last fraction of an inch. It is much more a question of the job 'looking right' when it's finished.

For the back legs you will need a minimum of 1⅞ in square wood, and for the front ones (to produce the foot) a section of not less than 2⅛ × 2⁵⁄₁₆ in material will be needed. The inset drawing, Fig. 19.2, shows the position of the main centre and also the secondary offset centre for finish-turning the foot. Only one centre hole is needed at the top end which is positioned on the true centre of the square.

First turn the leg on the main centres, taking care not to reduce the last inch at the foot end below what would have produced a diameter of 2¾ in if the square had been big enough to give a cut all round – the cut here at this stage will still be intermittent. The easiest way to ensure this is to strike off the main centre a part circle of 1⅜ in radius on the end of the square (inset

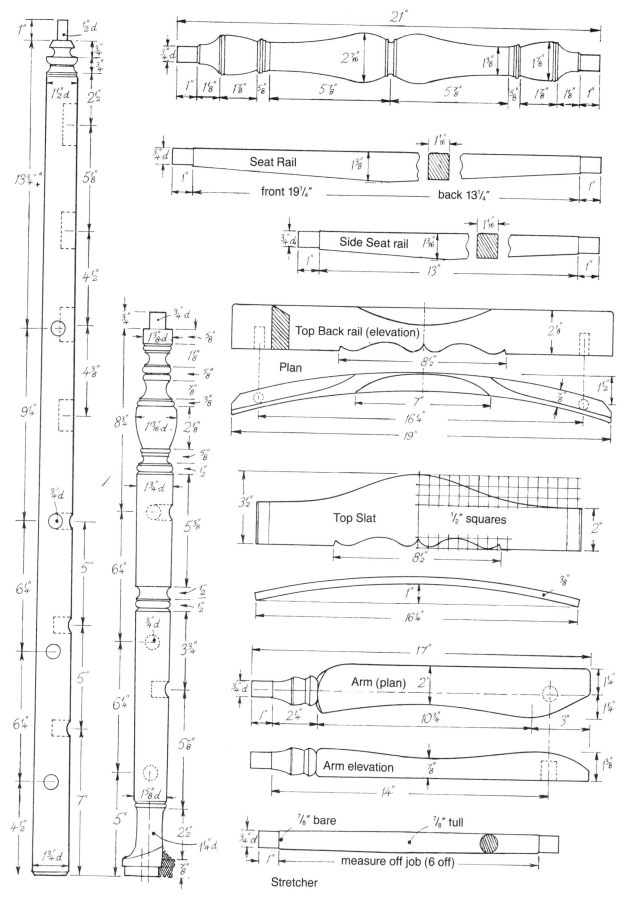

Fig. 19.1

Fig. 19.2 A). To finish the foot move the tailstock centre over to the secondary hole and turn down until you just get a cut all round (inset, Fig. 19.2). This should produce a foot of 2 in diameter. Finally, turn the pad at the extreme end. The square will at first be quite a bit out of balance, so it will be necessary to run the lathe slower than usual until you get rid of some of the waste.

The top back rail and ladder splats in the original are bent work, so this will mean steaming. The top rail

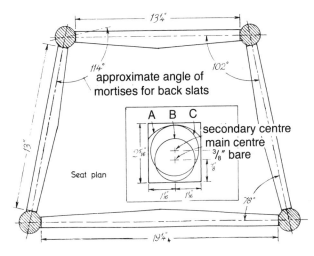

Fig. 19.2

could be bandsawn from the solid, but the splats being only ³⁄₈ in thick, they would be rather weak. So, if you have to steam and bend these it would be little further trouble to make the top rail in the same way.

In Fig. 19.1 only the top slat is shown, the other three reduce in width progressively to the bottom. The centre widths of these are 3¼ in, 2⅞ in and 2½ in respectively, and the end widths where they enter the mortises in the legs are 1¹³⁄₁₆ in, 1⅝ in and 1⁷⁄₁₆ in.

For the arms 2¾ × 1½ in wood will be needed. Do the turned part first and allow a little extra in length to be sure of getting rid of the centre hole at the front end when doing the shaping.

The lower front rail needs no comment – it is just a straightforward turning job, as also are the plain stretcher rails. Lengths for these are not given, as they can be taken off the job.

If you fight shy of doing the rushwork yourself, in many districts there are Blind Institutions which will take on this kind of work, and a good job they do too.

Otherwise it's best to read up a book on the subject. Do not be tempted to do the seat with 'Sea Grass'; while this is a hardwearing material the appearance is not so good nor in keeping as genuine rushwork.

CUTTING LIST

		INCHES			MM		
		L	W	T	L	W	T
2	Back legs	41½	2	1¾	1054	51	45
2	Front legs	27½	1¹⁵⁄₁₆	1¹³⁄₁₆	698	49	47
1	Crest rail (steam-bent)	19½	2⅜	⅞	495	61	22
1	Top slat (steam-bent)	16¾	3¾	⅜	426	95	10
1	Upper middle slat (steam-bent)	16¾	3½	⅜	426	89	10
1	Lower middle slat (steam-bent)	16¾	3⅛	⅜	426	80	10
1	Bottom slat (steam-bent)	16¾	2¾	⅜	426	70	10
2	Arms	17½	2¾	1⅜	445	70	35
1	Front stretcher (check on job)	21½	2¹¹⁄₁₆	2⁷⁄₁₆	546	68	63
2	Back stretcher (check on job)	15¾	1⅛	⅞	400	29	22
4	Side stretcher (check on job)	15½	1⅛	⅞	394	29	22
1	Front seat rail	21¾	1⅝	1¹⁄₁₆	552	42	27
2	Side seat rail	15½	1⁷⁄₁₆	1¹⁄₁₆	394	38	27
1	Back seat rail	15¾	1⅝	1¹⁄₁₆	400	42	27

Working allowances have been made to lengths and widths; thicknesses are net.

ARCHITECTURAL-STYLE MIRROR FRAME

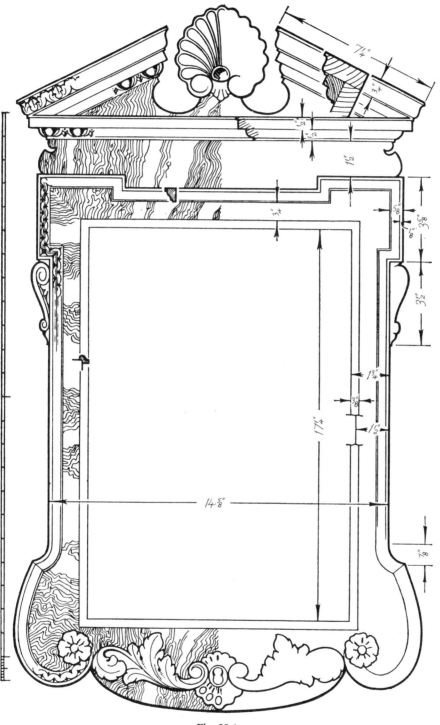

Fig. 20.1

This is a most attractive mirror, and an extremely interesting item to make. The main framework is in softwood veneered with walnut, and the mouldings and decorations are gilt. If you prefer a simpler piece of work, you could follow the suggestion in Fig. 20.3 in which plain mouldings are used, and the decorative carved ornaments omitted.

FRAMEWORK

For the main framework any good-quality softwood can be used, or a plain-grained hardwood. It is a simple square-edged frame, the only unusual feature about it being that, since the top rail is about 7 in wide, there is risk of shrinkage. Consequently an unglued joint is made just above the level of the bottom of the

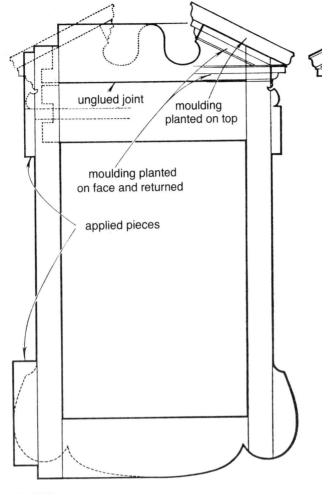

unglued joint

moulding planted on top

moulding planted on face and returned

applied pieces

Fig. 20.2

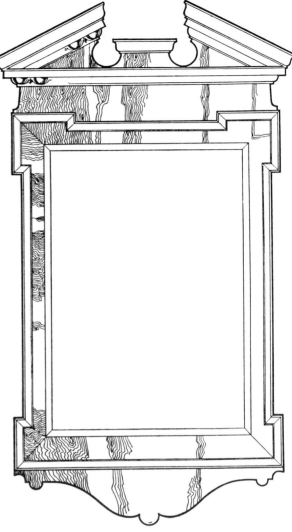

Fig. 20.3

cornice moulding. Any shrinkage will then slightly open this joint behind the moulding without affecting the rest of the work. After veneering a cut is made right through the veneer level with the joint. Note that pieces are planted on at the sides later to enable the broken shape to be worked. At the top there must be enough wood to embrace the entire shape right up to beneath the top ogee moulding which is planted on top. This is made clear from Fig. 20.2.

VENEERING

Having assembled the frame, plant on the side pieces and veneer the face. All joints in veneer should be taped to prevent them from opening as the veneer dries out. The whole shape is then marked out and the shape cut, preferably on a bandsaw. If this is not possible the shapes will have to be cut with the coping saw, and the straight parts with a fine-toothed backsaw, care being taken not to chip the veneer.

If only hand methods are used it is probably simpler to cut the shape before veneering as there is then no danger of the veneer being chipped. In this case the overhang will have to be levelled afterwards with chisel and plane.

Following this the edges are veneered, the grain running crosswise. To enable the acute bends to be veneered, damp the veneer and bend it round a dowel rod, holding it with a rubber band while it dries. It will then retain its shape and can be pressed into the shape easily. A rub with the cross-peen of a hammer will ensure close contact.

At this stage the whole job should be cleaned up ready for the application of the mouldings. Before they are glued down, however, the veneered surface should be polished. It is of course necessary to scrape away the polish locally before the glue is applied.

MOULDINGS

Accurate marking out is essential for the moulding positions as any slope or other inaccuracy is glaringly noticeable. It helps to fix the cornice first, driving in a couple of fine pins at the upper side to give definite position. The lower moulding with the break is then added, a block of wood with parallel sides being held against the cornice moulding to ensure accuracy. Alternatively pins can be tapped in above as described for the cornice mould.

In the case of the shaped moulding, this is most easily made on the spindle moulder or power router, but even so a certain amount of carving is needed at the break.

It will be realised that the cornice moulding is returned at the ends. The same thing applies to the corresponding moulding of the sloping pediment at the inner ends. At the outer ends, of course, it is cut at an angle to butt against the horizontal cornice. The simplest way to deal with the top ogee member, however, is to work each side in a single piece and plant on top, returning the ends in the solid.

At this stage the various ornaments — shell, ear pieces, and lower leaf work are prepared. To enable them to be handled they should be glued temporarily

90

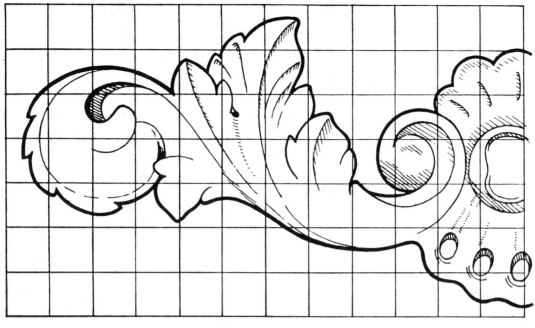

Fig. 20.4

to a block of wood with newspaper interposed to ensure easy removal.

Since the mouldings have to be gilt it is necessary to gesso them first. This is a somewhat messy process, and it is essential to protect the polished surface of the frame. This is best done with strips of masking tape stuck down all round up to the edge of the mouldings, and peeled away after the entire gilding has been completed.

In this frame the mouldings are oil-gilt and the shell, ear pieces, and bottom carving water-gilt and varnished. Finally, the ornaments are glued and pinned on, the polish being scraped away locally to enable the glue to grip. The addition of the narrow bolection moulding provides a rebate into which the mirror can fit. The mirror is held by wedges of wood glued to the edges of the frame. In this way the silvering is not touched. It should not be fixed until after gilding. For the backing a piece of plywood with the edges rounded over is used.

CARVING THE ORNAMENTS
It is advisable to fret out the wood for the applied ornaments and glue them on a temporary backboard with newspaper interposed. This strengthens the otherwise rather fragile parts during the carving, and also enables cramps to be used to hold the wood firmly.

The newspaper prevents permanent attachment to the backboard, and assists easy release of the ornament with a table knife. Fig. 20.4 shows the main shape set out in squares.

Begin with the bosting-in with which the main modelling of the wood is carried out. Thus the low parts of the leaves are cut away in free continuous sweeps, the wood between the scrolls cut back and brought to the general contour. All this is done before any attempt is made to put in any detail. This bosting process inevitably removes many of the pencil lines, and it is necessary to draw them in afresh. Endeavour to make the modelling lines of the leaves run in sweet, unbroken curves. Finally cut in the main outline, undercutting on the thicker parts. The advantage of mounting on a board is particularly felt here because the tool can be taken right down without danger of

splintering out at the bottom edge. The most useful tools for this work are the fluters and Nos. 3, 4, and 5 of varying size for both bosting-in and finishing.

The shell is not so delicate, but needs mounting to provide a means of gripping. Here again complete the main modelling first, sinking the wood from the highest point at the edges to the portion between the scrolls in a continuous sweep. Carve the entire hollow before cutting in the scallops. At the back the wood is rounded over towards the edge so that the shell looks relatively thin. The ear pieces are fretted to the outline and the hollow strapwork and scroll cut in.

EGG AND TONGUE DETAIL
When plotting the egg and tongue carving it is clearly necessary to space the repeat detail so that it balances out at the ends. To do this it is convenient to step out with dividers by trial and error. Once fixed, a templet can be cut of the main details and this used to mark out. A piece of thick brown paper of good quality, painted both sides with cellulose or French polish, is good material to use; the polish soaks right through and makes the whole quite strong. Only the chief motifs are included and the whole should be moulded up to the shape, then opened flat to enable the opening to be cut with gouges.

Stages in cutting are shown in Fig. 20.5. First a downward stab is made at the side of the egg (1) and a sloping cut made to meet it (2). It is unlikely that the full depth will be reached in one cut, and it is better to repeat the process. In all probability the gouge will have to be given a rocking or twisting movement because the shape is being cut on a rounded surface. This forms the deep hollows and frees the egg of wood

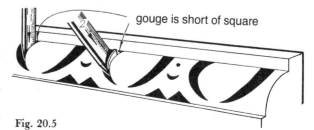

gouge is short of square

Fig. 20.5

91

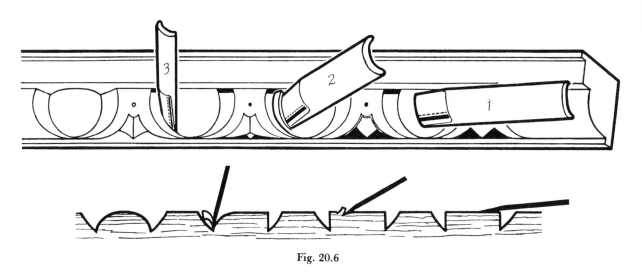

Fig. 20.6

at each side. When stabbing in do not hold the gouge immediately close against the deep adjoining square member as this may prevent a clean finish from being obtained. The final cuts are made more or less horizontally towards the square rather than downwards, and this is done after the eggs have been cut in.

To form the egg shape hold the gouge low down at the middle of the egg (1), Fig. 20.6, and, as it is pushed forward, gradually raise the handle (2) and (3) until it ends up in a vertical position as shown. It calls for practice, and it is advisable to try out the method on a spare moulding.

The tongue is cut first with downward stabs along the whole length of the curve and then deepened locally from beneath the tongue. The wood is sloped away with a single cut at each side, and the lower waste pared away beneath the tongue.

GILDING

When it's possible the ornaments are gilded separately, but when this is not possible stick strips of masking tape over the polished surface to avoid damage. A gesso foundation is needed, made from acrylic gesso, or from parchment cuttings covered with cold water and left overnight. In the morning the water is thrown away and the cuttings put into a double kettle and covered with about three times the volume of water. Allow to simmer but not boil for about 3-4 hours. Strain through nylon into a jar and allow to cool, when it should be similar in consistency to a fruit jelly.

Warm up again and add gilder's whiting, stirring constantly. The first coat should be thin, and the successive coats, which are made up fresh, of about the consistency of oil paint. Add one or two drops of linseed oil, and apply with a brush. About 6-8 coats are needed, each drying before the next is applied, but completing the whole of the coats in one day. In the

case of the oil-gilt parts only about three coats are needed.

The surface is now rubbed smooth with fine glasspaper and painted over with Armenian bole, a red gilder's earth. Prepare some warm parchment size and add the prepared bole to the consistency of thin cream. Apply 3–4 coats with a soft brush, allowing each to dry out. Take off any spots of bole, which may be left in the relief, with very fine abrasive paper and polish with coarse linen or a nail brush. In oil gilding yellow clay is used. Apply and finish off as for water gilding but with fewer coats.

OIL GILDING

Gold size is used for this. If 18-hour size is used, it is put on very thinly (no puddles or blobs) on one day and the gold leaf applied the next. However, a four-hour size can be used if the application is to be made the same day. It should have become tacky, not wet, when the gold is applied. Transfer gold is used, this being backed with tissue paper. It is pressed on to the carving, but try to take off all the gold in one application as far as possible. There will be parts that are missed, and this involves going over the missed parts a second time.

WATER GILDING

Loose leaf gold is used for this, the leaf being picked up with a gilder's tip. An area of the size of gold being picked up is wetted with weak parchment size applied with a No. 4 camel-hair mop, and the gold applied. The areas covered are bound to overlap and there will be loose flakes of gold over the whole job, but ignore these for the present. When the whole surface has been covered the gold can be burnished with an agate burnisher. Go over lightly first with little more pressure than the weight of the burnisher itself, then gradually increase the pressure as the gold takes on a brilliant burnished appearance.

LYRE-END OCCASIONAL TABLE

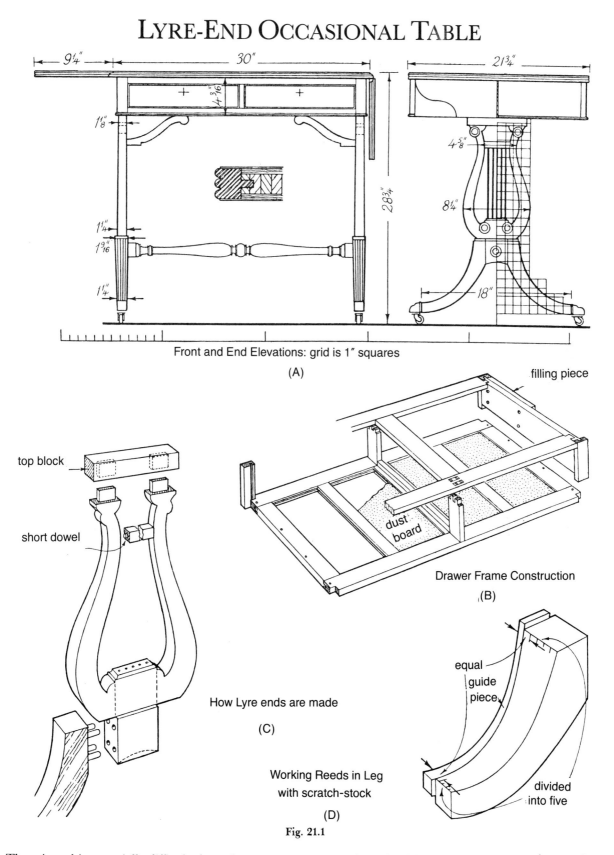

Front and End Elevations: grid is 1″ squares

(A)

top block

short dowel

How Lyre ends are made

(C)

Drawer Frame Construction

(B)

dust board

filling piece

equal

guide piece

divided into five

Working Reeds in Leg
with scratch-stock

(D)

Fig. 21.1

There is nothing specially difficult about the construction of this attractive table, but it does call for neat and careful workmanship. Anything in the nature of a crude finish is immediately obvious. A certain amount of simplification is possible, such as the omission of the curl veneer and banding on the top, but the general proportions should be retained. A top of 30 × 21¾ in closed, opening to about 48 in long is suitable for most purposes.

The top drawer frame is made up complete in itself. The shaped lyre uprights and curved legs are made separately and fixed beneath it. A turned stretcher rail joins the legs, and at the top are two small shaped bracket pieces which help prevent side racking. Mahogany is used throughout.

DRAWER FRAME

Construction of this is shown in Fig. 21.1B. A bottom frame is put together with mortise and tenon joints with grooved-in dustboards, which can be either plywood or hardboard. Having assembled it, plane the edges dead to size, and cut notches at the corners to receive the short uprights. These uprights are 1¼ in wide, but the notches are only ⅝ in wide. Thus the uprights project, enabling the sides of the frame to be flush at the inside, and at the same time enabling the hinged brackets to fit at the outside. As the brackets reach only halfway across the width a filling piece is glued and screwed on as in Fig. 21.1B. This also provides a convenient edge to which the bracket hinges can be screwed.

The ends of the drawer frame are glued and screwed on top of the ends of the bottom frame, and are tongued into the short uprights. Short drawer divisions are tenoned between the bottom frame and the top rails, which are dovetailed at the ends. It's convenient to glue the short uprights to the ends, and add them as a whole to the bottom frame when the glue has set. Finally, the two top rails with centre cross-rail tongued between are glued on. A drawer guide is glued and pinned on to the centre rail. Filling pieces are added, and the astragal moulding glued around the bottom of the whole assembly. Note that it is returned along the filling pieces and on the short uprights where the brackets occur.

There are drawers at one side only, and at the back dummy drawer fronts are fitted. The simplest way of dealing with these is to make up the two fronts as though they were to be actual drawers, and fix them between the rails with screws after polishing has been completed.

LYRE ENDS

Fig. 21.1C shows how these are made. Either of two methods can be followed. In one, the main shape is in a single piece including the square bottom block, and the upper portion is thinned down. At the top the ends are tenoned into a top block, and a horizontal rail is fitted with short dowels a short way down (the shape at this point is vertical). The dowels can be sprung in, but to avoid an accident a cramp is put over the lower part of the shaping. Without this there is danger of the wood splitting away at the bottom where the grain is short.

The general procedure is to step down the thickness first. Square the rectangular board and mark the position of the bottom block parallel with the bottom edge. From this point to the top mark the edges of the wood with a gauge, and thin down to the line. The smoothing plane can be used for the greater part, taken inwards all round. At the shoulder by the bottom block, however, the shoulder or rebate plane will have to be substituted. It will be noted from Fig. 21.1A that the arms of the lyre actually taper slightly towards the top, but this is best done after the shape has been sawn; a few shavings each side gives the effect.

While the block is still rectangular the top shoulders and tenons can be marked. A bandsaw is the best means of cutting the shape, but failing this you can use a bowsaw or jigsaw. At this stage leave the bottom outer ends of the lyre arms uncut, and a cramp can then be fixed across. This enables the short dowel holes for the top rail to be bored; get help to spring the arms sideways enough to enable the bit to be centred. Without the bottom cramp this is dangerous. The same idea is used to spring the arms apart to enable the short dowels to be slipped in. It is, of course, necessary to drill the brass rod holes first, and slip in the rods before gluing.

The other way out of the problem; the arms are made separate from the bottom block and joined at the dotted lines in Fig. 21.1C. This is simpler in that no springing is necessary, and the arms need be only 1¼ in thick maximum. Dowels are used at joints of the bottom block, the outer shaping remaining uncut to allow cramps to be applied. This method is recommended for the less experienced, as it's simpler and less liable to accident. At the top the tenons are entered into the top block (Fig. 21.1C), and the latter fixed with screws from the bottom of the drawer frame.

LEGS

These are fixed with dowels as in Fig. 21.1C. The simplest way of marking the centres is to make a template in thin metal or card; place this in position and prick through. Specially shaped blocks will have to be prepared for use beneath the cramp shoes. The reeding around the outer edges is done with a scratch stock (or spindle moulder), and it entails preparing shaped and tapered guide pieces over which the scratch stock can work as in Fig. 21.1D. A pointed cutter with hollowed sides is used to cut in the quirks, and the final rounded shape of the reeds done with glasspaper wrapped around shaped blocks.

Taper the legs towards the feet, and divide top and bottom into five. The shaped guide pieces are then tapered in thickness so that the point of the scratch-stock cutter touches the corresponding marks at top and bottom. The same guide can be used from each side of the four legs, and is then tapered afresh to enable the remaining cuts to be made.

DRAWERS

These are cock-beaded around the edges, and the fronts are veneered with curls. Normal dovetailed construction is followed. The dummy drawer fronts at the back have already been mentioned. The fronts should be veneered with curls.

TOPS

These are in blockboard with an applied edging all round (inset, Fig. 21.1A). Both sides are veneered to ensure they remain flat. The rule joint is used at the leaves, and the outer edges are reeded. Remember that the edging of the leaves must be wide enough to enable the curved corners to be cut. If possible, use curl veneer on the top, jointed across the middle, and crossband the edge.

The final job is to fit the shaped brackets between the lyre ends and the drawer frame. They are tenoned into the cross rails of the ends and fixed with screws at the rail of the drawer frame. The turned bottom rail, of course, is put in in the final assembly. It is simpler to complete all polishing when the parts are separate.

CUTTING LIST

Part	L	W	T	L	W	T
	INCHES			*MM*		
4 Rails (drawer frame)	29	2¼	⁵⁄₈	736	57	16
4 Rails (drawer frame)	20½	2¼	⁵⁄₈	521	57	16
2 Rails (drawer frame)	20½	1¾	⁵⁄₈	521	44	16
2 Ends (drawer frame)	21½	3⁷⁄₈	⁵⁄₈	521	98	16
2 Uprights (drawer frame)	4¼	2¼	⁵⁄₈	108	57	16
4 Uprights (drawer frame)	4½	1½	⁵⁄₈	114	38	16
2 Filling pieces (drawer frame)	10½	4½	⁵⁄₈	267	115	16
2 Bracket pieces (drawer frame)	10½	4½	⁵⁄₈	267	115	16
4 Dustboards (drawer frame) (hardboard or ply)	18	5¾	³⁄₁₆	458	146	5
4 Drawer fronts	13¾	3¼	⁵⁄₈	349	83	16
2 Drawer backs	13¾	2¾	³⁄₈	349	70	10
4 Drawer sides	20	3¼	³⁄₈	508	83	10

CUTTING LIST (continued)

Part	L	W	T	L	W	T
	INCHES			*MM*		
2 Drawer bottoms (hardboard or ply)	13	20	³⁄₁₆	330	508	5
2 Pieces (lyre ends)*	17½	8½	1⁹⁄₁₆	445	216	40
2 Top blocks (lyre ends)*	8	1¼	1	203	32	25
2 Rails (lyre ends)*	3½	1¼	¾	89	32	19
4 Legs (lyre ends*)	12½	4	1⁹⁄₁₆	318	102	40
1 Turned rail (lyre ends)*	30	–	1⁹⁄₁₆sq	762	–	40
2 Brackets (lyre ends)*	9¼	2	1⁹⁄₁₆	235	51	40
1 Top	31½	22	⁵⁄₈	800	559	16
2 Leaves	9¾	22	⁵⁄₈	248	559	16

(Edgings extra; adapt sizes to suit)

Working allowances have been made to lengths and widths; thicknesses are net. **Note that the above list is for solid lyre ends — if they are being built up with joints substitute the following for the items marked ***

Part	L	W	T	L	W	T
4 Arms	14½	3	1¼	368	76	32
2 Bottom blocks	6	3	1⁹⁄₁₆	153	76	40

WINDSOR CHAIR

Fig. 22.1 The completed chair – a modern version of a traditional design.

This Windsor chair is designed to overcome some of the disadvantages of the traditional construction, whose strength depends almost entirely on the seat. Unfortunately the holes for the legs and back are a source of weakness, particularly at the back where the holes are necessarily close together. Obviously the seat must not split, and elm is usually chosen for this reason. Although it is an attractive timber it has a reputation for warping and twisting. Plywood is used for the seat of this chair as it will not split and it's unlikely to warp, so a considerably thinner seat can be used, which greatly reduces the weight. Such a seat would have been difficult to shape with traditional cutting tools, but rasps with detachable blades make the hollowing a straightforward job. The contours of the ply revealed by the hollowing make the seat look attractive and interesting.

Drill the holes for the legs before shaping the seat in

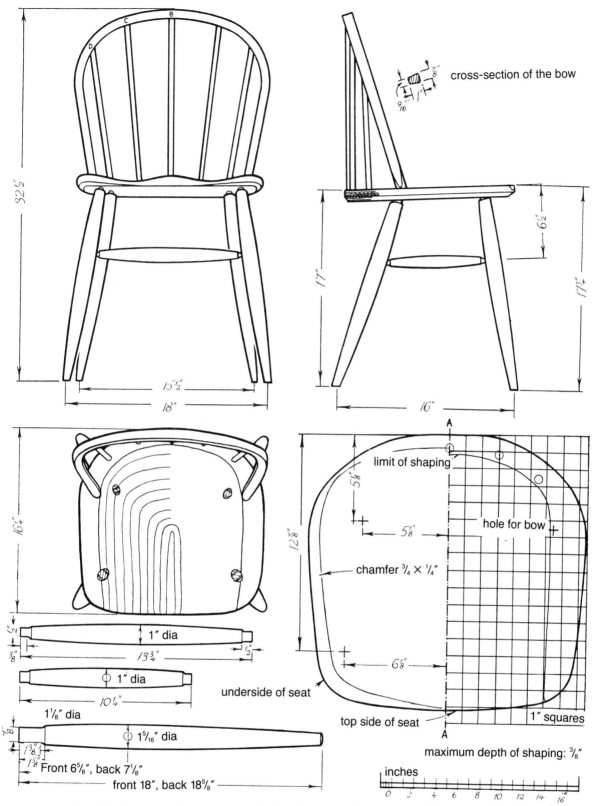

Fig. 22.2 Front and side elevations and plan; dimensions for the seat and legs are also given.

any way. Careful study of the plan view in Fig. 22.2 will show that the bottom ends of the legs have their centres level with the front or back of the seat, although the back legs are slightly inside the seat and the front legs slightly outside it. Mark the position of the holes according to the dimensions given in Fig. 22.2. Note that the holes for the back are marked on the opposite surface to the legs. Cramp the seat in the vice with the centre line A–A vertical, with a short length of two-by-one cramped behind the hole marks to prevent splitting when the bit emerges from the seat. Fix a $\frac{7}{8}$ in bit in a carpenter's brace and mark the

brace with chalk or adhesive tape a distance from the end of the bit equal to the length of the leg. If this mark is correctly positioned in relation to the sides of the seat blank, it follows that the angle will be correct. The chalk mark should therefore be on a horizontal level with the edge of the plywood sheet and offset sideways. The method of obtaining the sideways offset is shown in Fig. 22.3. Sight the chalk mark with the mark on the batten and get an assistant to sight the horizontal level. Drill the holes for the back by a similar method but from the other side.

97

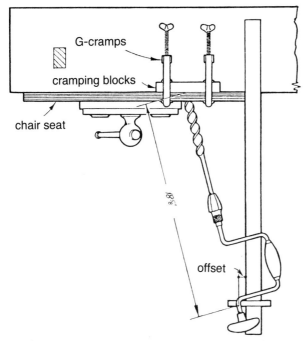

Fig. 22.3 Method of drilling holes at the correct angle.

TABLE OF OFFSETS
(Measured from $16\frac{3}{4} \times 16\frac{3}{4}$ in plywood.)
  Front legs .... $\frac{5}{8}$ in
  Back legs .... $\frac{5}{8}$ in
  Back .... Zero at 9 in from ends.

Mark the outline of the seat using the 1 in squares in Fig. 22.2 as a guide and cut to shape with a fine-toothed bow saw, bandsaw or suitable power saw. Plug the holes with temporary softwood plugs and hollow the seat with a 'Surform' drawplane. Finish either with glasspaper on a suitably shaped cork block, a belt sander, or an electric drill fitted with a circular sanding disc followed by hand finishing. Chamfer the under-side; note the shape of the chamfering at the front.

Turn the legs from $\frac{1}{2}$ in square ash or beech. This part of the job should be quite straightforward, but note that the shoulders must be rounded. Gauge the $\frac{7}{8}$ in diameter by trying the leg tops in a hole drilled in scrap, as carpenter's bits rarely drill to size. The back legs are $\frac{5}{8}$ in longer than the front, and when it's assembled the seat should have a $\frac{3}{4}$ in slope from front to back. Drill the $\frac{1}{2}$ in holes for the spindles by assembling the legs and aligning the bit according to the marks on the legs.

Make the bow from 1 in square straight-grained ash or beech. The straight grain is important. Make the mould as shown in Fig. 22.4 and fix it, and the block, to a suitable bench. Also make up the bending strap shown in Figs 22.5 and 22.6.

The steaming apparatus shown in Fig. 22.5 is based on a 6 in diameter by 4 ft drain pipe, (not plastic) readily obtainable from builders' merchants.

Steam the timber for about 30 minutes and quickly place it between the end stops of the bending bar. With as little delay as possible fit the assembly squarely into the moulding jig and pull into shape. Lock the bend with the locking bar shown in Fig. 22.6 or a suitable sash cramp or even tie the ends with rope. Leave the bend in position in the jig for 24 hours to allow it to set. Shape to the cross section shown in Fig. 22.2 and round the ends to a good fit in the seat holes.

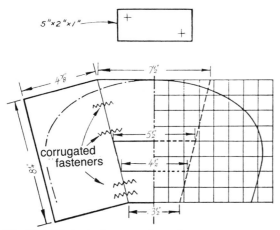

Fig. 22.4 Method of constructing a former.

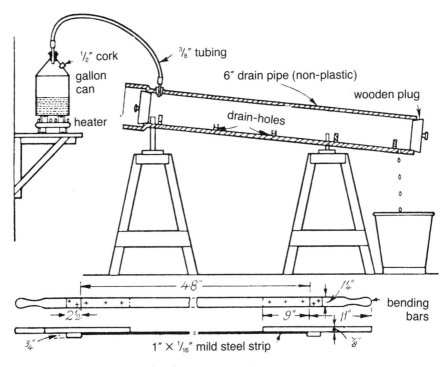

Fig. 22.5 Steaming box with bending apparatus.

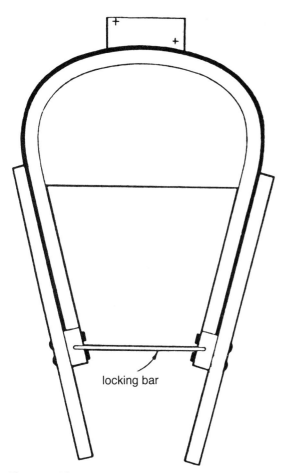

locking bar

Fig. 22.6 After steaming, the bow is locked in position around the former.

Mark the distances BC to 4 in and CD to 3¾ in (Fig. 22.2, front elevation) on the inside of the bend with dividers and mark the position of the supporting dowels on the seat. Assemble the back in position, and with a ratchet brace align the brace and bit with the dowel marks and drill shallow holes for the dowels. As the holes are shallow a slight mis-alignment is not very

important. A power drill can be used instead; you lose accuracy of alignment, but gain in convenience. Choose birch or beech dowel.

The final polishing will be more convenient if the legs and underside of the seat are polished before gluing. After gluing and wedging the legs in place, clean off the tops of the legs and polish the top surface of the seat. Polish the dowels and bow before assembly. Glue the back and dowels in position and later trim off the waste on the underside. Give the job a final polish and trim the legs for level if necessary.

As this type of chair is used either as a kitchen chair or dining chair and as such is subject to domestic accidents, a waterproof 'plastic' finish will be found very suitable. In this case the character of the wood will be best preserved by *not* filling the grain. The burnishing stage must therefore be omitted as the paste will fill the open pores, but otherwise, the maker's instructions should be followed.

CUTTING LIST

		INCHES			*MM*		
		L	W	T	L	W	T
1	Seat (birch plywood)	16¾	17¼	1	425	438	25
2	Back legs, ash or beech	19¼	trnd	1½	489	trnd	38
2	Front legs, ash or beech	18½	trnd	1½	470	trnd	38
2	Side spindles, ash or beech	10¾	trnd	1¼	273	trnd	32
1	Front spindle, ash or beech	14¼	trnd	1¼	362	trnd	32
1	Back spindle, ash or beech	48	trnd	1	1219	trnd	25

Working allowances have been made to lengths and widths; thicknesses are net.

GRANDFATHER CLOCK IN TRADITIONAL STYLE

Fig. 23.1 The design of this clockcase is straightforward and it could be made in either oak or mahogany. It is intended to house a 12 in dial which would give a 10 in sight-size. Overall height is 6 ft.

The grandfather or longcase clock has been a familiar feature in the home for about three centuries, and is still popular. Either oak or mahogany could be used, or a softwood or mixed woods painted black and picked out in gold or pastel shades.

Fig.23.2 shows how the main body is made up of a waist with base and plinth planted on at front and sides. Make this waist first.

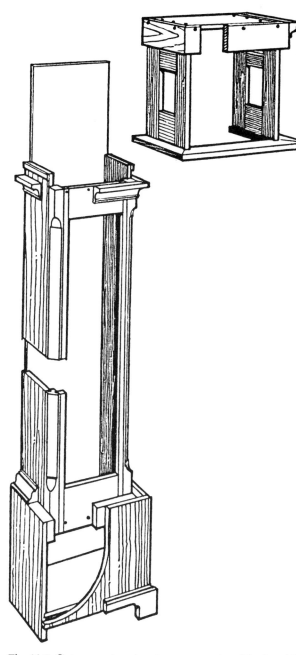

square and equidistant. Level the joints and clean them up ready for the addition of the packing pieces which are applied around the bottom to take the base. These should have the grain running vertically so that any shrinkage in the wood of the base is not resisted. Glue and screw the front piece first with the ends projecting slightly. Level these ends and then add the side pieces. The wide chamfers can also be worked; they should be left until after the body has been assembled because otherwise it would be awkward to apply the cramps.

BASE

The parts for this are now prepared. Work grooves to take the bottom, and rebates for the back, and glue these in position. The side pieces are fixed first in this case, glued and cramped down. The bottom is inserted in the same operation. Level the front edges and add the front panel. Finally the plinth and base mouldings are added.

Details of the top mouldings are given in Fig. 23.3. The section immediately beneath the hood is divided, one part being fixed to the body and the other to the hood. The latter is rebated so that no join is visible. To prevent the hood from falling forward as it is withdrawn, strips of wood are fixed to the tops of the ends so that the hood moulding fits between this and the large moulding fixed to the body (Fig. 23.2).

Before leaving the body, note that the seat board to which the movement is bolted rests on the top edges of the ends. It is lightly rebated at the ends to give it exact position, and must be substantial as it takes the weight of movement and weights. Holes are cut in it to receive pendulum and weight guts or chains. The door of the body is a solid piece of dry wood with moulding fitting in rebates around the edges. Acorn hinges are used to hang it, let wholly into the framework, the knuckles passing through the moulding and projecting well at the front.

HOOD

Construction of this is given in Fig. 23.2. The two side frames, mortised and tenoned together, are joined by the top which is screwed on. At the bottom the mitred moulding joins them. This bottom moulding should be put together independently first, the mitre being tongued, and the whole assembly screwed to the hood from beneath. Remember to allow for the door when fixing the moulding in position. Mouldings are applied around the side openings to form rebates for the glass (Fig. 23.3). At the top packing pieces are needed to form the projecting frieze. These are glued and screwed, and at the front a foundation piece the same thickness as the doors is needed first as shown in the enlarged section in Fig. 23.3. Fit the door (it has a moulded and rebated inner edge) and add the columns to the corners. These are turned and have a rebate cut out from them to fit over the door edges. To give a neat finish when the door is opened a thin mount or frame is fitted to the hood immediately behind the door. It has rounded edges as shown in Fig. 23.3.

Finally fit the back. This is screwed into the rebate in the body and projects upwards into the hood. The clock case should be screwed to the wall otherwise there is danger of its falling over. In any case the movement would probably not work properly if the clock wasn't fixed, as vibration would most likely shift it.

Fig. 23.2 Cut-away view showing construction. The hood is completely separate and is made to slide forward from the body.

WAIST

As shown in Fig. 23.3 there are two ends and a front frame tongued into corner posts, which are needed so you can work the wide chamfer. The whole thing must be tall enough to project downwards into the base, so the ends should finish 44 × 6 in, including the tongue. The front frame stands down slightly at the top (Fig. 23.2) and is 43¼ × 9 in with tongues. The tongues are ¼ in in every case. Make up the frame with mortise and tenon joints. Stiles are 1 in wide (with tongues) and rails are 4½ in (top) and 6 in bottom. Plane both ends of this frame dead straight, also the front edges of the ends so they make clean joints with the corner posts. They are then gauged for the tongues and the tongues worked. The back edges of the ends also have to be rebated to hold the back.

Cut the posts to the same length as the frame and groove them. The whole waist assembly can then be glued together, care being taken to keep the ends

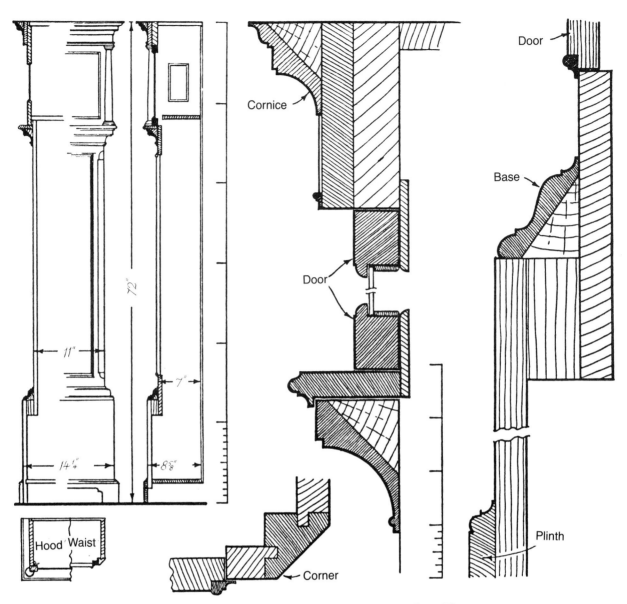

Fig. 23.3 Front elevation, side section, plan, and enlarged sections of mouldings etc.

CUTTING LIST

	INCHES			MM		
BODY	*L*	*W*	*T*	*L*	*W*	*T*
2 Ends	44¼	6¼	⅝	1124	159	16
2 Stiles	44¼	1¼	⅝	1124	32	16
1 Rail	9	5	⅝	229	127	16
1 Rail	9	6¼	⅝	229	159	16
2 Posts	44¼	sq	1¼	1124	sq	32
1 Back	70	14	⅜	1778	356	10
1 Door	33½	7¼	⅝	851	184	16
BASE						
1 Front	14	14½	⅝	356	369	16
2 Sides	16	8½	⅝	407	216	16
1 Bottom	14	8	⅝	356	203	16
1 Plinth	16	3¾	½	407	95	12
2 Plinth	10	3¾	½	254	95	12
HOOD						
4 Stiles	16½	2¼	⅝	419	58	16

CUTTING LIST (continued)

	INCHES			MM		
Part	*L*	*W*	*T*	*L*	*W*	*T*
2 Rails	6	7	⅝	153	178	16
2 Rails	6	4¼	⅝	153	108	16
1 Top	13½	7¼	½	343	184	12
1 Packing piece	13½	3¾	⅞	343	95	22
1 Packing piece	15	3¾	⅝	381	95	16
2 Packing pieces	9	3¾	⅝	229	95	16
2 Stiles	13	1⅜	⅞	330	35	22
2 Rails	12	1⅜	⅞	305	35	22
2 Mounts	13½	1⅞	3/16	343	48	5
2 Mounts	13½	1⅜	3/16	343	35	5

Mouldings and sundry small parts extra. Working allowances have been made to lengths and widths; thicknesses are net.

OAK REFECTORY TABLE

Fig. 24.1 If you can obtain the rather heavy timbers, there is a sturdy charm in these old baluster-leg tables. If you are careful you can always joint thin pieces to make up the thicker parts. Oak is to be preferred throughout, although it could be confined to the top with the other parts in beech or a similar hardwood.

The size of the top of this solid traditional table can be adjusted to suit the room it will occupy. It can be made any length from about 5 ft to 10 ft and the width from 30–36 in, the span of the feet remaining unaltered. There are several ways of finishing, perhaps the best being a medium warm oak stain, filled and sealed, and polished to a dulled antique finish. Alternatively the surfaces could be wire brushed or waxed.

BALUSTER LEGS

These are $4\frac{1}{2}$ in square finished size when planed ready for turning. If necessary, joint two pieces $4\frac{1}{2} \times 2\frac{1}{4}$ in together for each leg, dowelling them at the centre. The grain should be carefully matched, the medullary rays of both pieces running in the same direction. Avoid timber from too near the heart of the tree, as heart wood has a tendency to rise and open the joint. A careful drawing of the leg on paper or a piece of odd plywood should be made from the end elevation (Fig. 24.2) for turning showing squares and turning. An inch scale has been laid down to one side of the turning for this purpose and the minimum diameters given.

After they are turned, any shakes in the legs should be feathered, thin wedges driven in and finished off flush. A bridle joint for the top bearer (D) and tenon to enter the feet and stretcher (B) should be marked and cut as shown in Fig. 24.3. The bridle joint is not cen-

tral in the leg (see plan detail, Fig. 24.3), but kept to the outside to give more wood for the tenon of the long rail (E).

FEET AND STRETCHER

These are half-lapped together and afterwards mortised for the leg tenons; see the plan of stretcher, Fig. 24.2. The feet might come out of $4\frac{1}{2} \times 2\frac{1}{2}$ in, wood like the stretcher, with shoes joined on beneath at the shaped ends – or in any way convenient to the timber available as long as the joints are horizontal and not vertical. The shaped feet are shown plotted out in 1 in squares. This could be done with coping saw and chisel if a bandsaw is not available. The stretcher is moulded along the top edges, fading out just short of the legs (Fig. 24.3).

TOP BEARERS

When the top bearers (D) are cut to size, mark and cut the bridle joints. The bearer is central to the leg but the shoulders are deeper on the inner side of the joint to allow for as long a tenon as possible to the long rail (E). The shaping is plotted in 1 in squares as for the feet, and it could also be cut in the same way. It would be better to drive a couple of pegs through the leg into the joint after assembly.

103

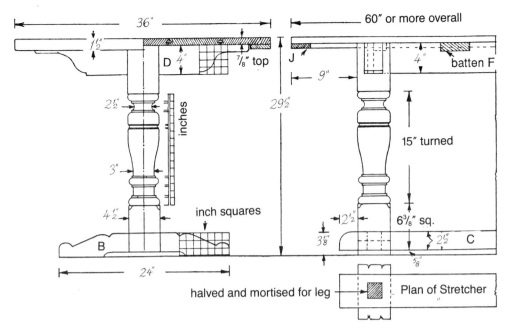

Fig. 24.2 End elevation, and part side elevation, showing dimensions. The end overhang should be increased by 1 in for every 12 in the top exceeds a length of 5 ft.

LONG RAIL

The joints of this rail into the legs should be a firm fit and the corners well blocked after assembly; see sectional plan, Fig. 24.3. This rail is inserted before the legs enter the feet and stretcher, and the shoulder lengths of both should be exactly the same.

TOP

Narrow boards are preferable, which should be well matched for grain, and joints tongued or dowelled.

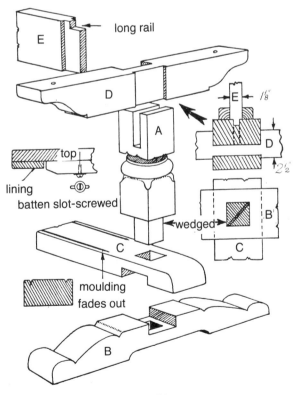

Fig. 24.3 Details of joints on table supports.

The top will look better in odd numbers of boards; use five or seven pieces (end view, Fig. 24.2). Keep the wood as stout as possible from 1 in nominal thickness, just skimming the underside. The top edges are lined to show additional thickness, and the grain of the end linings should run with the top. These are well glued and screwed on. Several battens (F) will be required across the width of the top underneath according to its length, the long rail (E) being notched away to allow the battens to pass. Alternatively the battens can be halved over the long rail, thus positioning the top. The battens are fixed and screwed centrally, but the rest of the screws should be slotted to allow shrinkage. The battens are screwed to the top with round-head screws with washers under the heads (Fig. 24.3). A gap should be left between the ends of the battens and the inner edge of the top linings. The top is secured with screws up through the bearers (D).

CUTTING LIST

			INCHES			MM		
Part			L	W	T	L	W	T
A	2	Legs	28½	trned	4½	724	trned	115
B	2	Feet	24½	4¾	3⅛	623	121	80
C	1	Stretcher	47½	4¾	2½	1207	121	64
D	2	Top bearers	24½	4¼	2½	623	108	64
E	1	Long rail	38	4¼	1⅛	965	108	29
F	3	Battens	31	4¼	1⅛	787	108	29
G	1	Top (can be jointed)	61	36½	⅞	1549	927	22
H	2	Top linings	60½	2¾	⅝	1537	70	16
J	2	Top linings	3	31¼	⅝	76	794	16

Working allowances have been made to lengths and widths; thicknesses are net.

LONG STYLE OCCASIONAL TABLE

Fig. 25.1 The completed table. The carved details can be altered to choice.

The design of this table is based on the late middle years of the 18th century, but the carved detail of the legs is a modern interpretation of the work of that period. Those who prefer could follow the earlier tradition and use acanthus leafage. The detail around the top, however, is in true period style with spiral ribbon and conventional leafage. The whole thing is oil polished and is thus not liable to be marked.

The proportions of the table are pleasing, and the size makes it useful to stand in front of a settee. Mahogany should be used throughout, and if too light it could be darkened with a proprietary stain or pota-

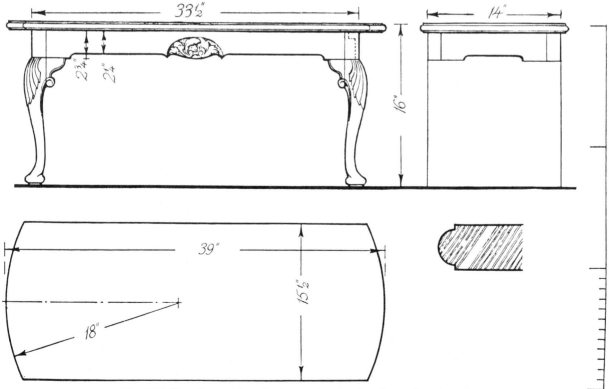

Fig. 25.2 Elevations with main sizes and scale; also plan and section of top.

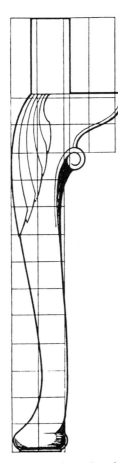

Fig. 25.3 Leg shape marked on 1 in grid.

ssium bichromate, which darkens the wood by chemical action. The legs call for square finishing not less than 2¼ in (the ears are extra and are glued on). All the rest of the wood is ¾ in thick, though ⅞ in could be used equally well.

Fig. 25.4 How to mark out the leg.

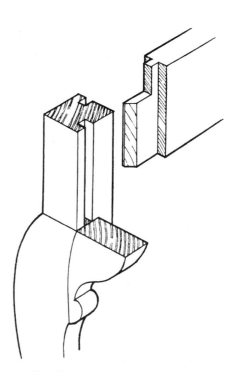

Fig. 25.5 Detail of corner joint.

LEGS

Prepare the material for each leg as a square, and turn the foot, centring the wood at both ends. Note that the turned shape is not a semi-circle, but much flatter, the point being that the curve of the leg has to flow imperceptibly into it. Make a template of the leg shape in card, and mark two adjacent faces of the square as in Fig. 25.4. Make the two cuts on one face, preferably on the bandsaw, and replace the waste pieces temporarily, holding them with gummed tape. The cuts on the adjacent face can now be made. The replacement of the lower waste piece forms a square surface on which the wood can bed, and that at the top brings back the outline which has to be sawn. It is now a case of bringing the legs to a fair shape, using spokeshave, rasp, file, and finally scraper.

When the top squares have been trued up, the mortises can be marked out and chopped. They should meet in the thickness of the wood and should have slots at the top to take the haunches of the tenons. It is advisable to put a cramp over the end of the square when chopping these mortises, to avoid splitting the wood.

At this stage the ear pieces should be glued on to enable the carving to be completed. The simplest way is to rub-glue them, and put in a dowel (mahogany) after the glue has set. Carving calls for considerable patience, as the whole of the wood around the carved knee and the side scrolls and beads has to be sunk back. The best way is to hold the wood down so that it projects at the edge of the bench.

Outline the design with a small veiner or parting tool, and cut away the groundwork evenly using a flat gouge. Afterwards a chisel is substituted to make the surface as flat as possible, and finally a narrow scraper is used to take out tool marks.

RAILS

The rails are prepared straight and square, and the tenon shoulders squared across each pair. After the tenons have been sawn they are fitted individually. All four rails are shaped at the lower edge, and the long

Fig. 25.8 Close-up drawing of edge carving.

Fig. 25.6 Detail of carving on centre of long rails.

ones have a decorative panel carved at the centre, though this detail could be omitted if you prefer. The carving is shown part-finished in Fig. 25.6. A veiner is used for the main outline of the detail and the ground-work recessed, leaving sufficient relief for the slight modelling of the leafwork.

When assembling the framework, put the opposite ends together independently, and add the long rails

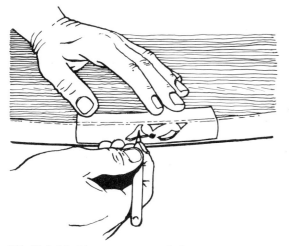

Fig. 25.7 Marking out repeats of edge carving.

afterwards. When the glue has set it is advisable to bore holes through the ear pieces into the rails and glue in mahogany dowels. Glue blocks are also rubbed in at the internal angles. Finally any irregularity at the joints is levelled, and the top edges made true.

TOP

This is prepared as a rectangle and the end curves marked out from the centres shown in Fig. 25.2. To avoid damaging the top, drive a nail into a waste piece of wood and cramp this down over the top so that the nail is over the centre. A strip of wood pivoted on the nail can be used as a beam compass to mark the shape. After sawing and cleaning up the edge is worked to the astragal section shown in Fig. 25.2.

CUTTING LIST

		INCHES			MM	
	L	W	T	L	W	T
4 Legs	17	2½	2¼	432	64	58
8 Ear pieces	3	2¼	¾	76	58	19
2 Rails	33	3	¾	838	76	19
2 Rails	13½	3	¾	343	76	19
1 Top	39½	15¾	¾	1003	400	19

Working allowances have been made to lengths and widths; thicknesses are net.

SETTLE-TABLE

The design is reproduced by kind permission of Mrs Lyle, Barrington Court, near Ilminster, Somerset.

The combined settle-table is unusual as an early example of dual-purpose furniture. In one guise it acts as a side-table for serving food, and by re-arranging and re-fixing the top it becomes a settle.

You can tell it is intended as a side-table because of the following two features; first, the back edge of the top lines up with the back edge of the crosspiece (Fig.26.2), whereas there is an overhang at the front edge; and second, there is a slot cut through each crosspiece and a peg can be pushed through to engage in a hole in the arm at each end. This allows you to slide the top towards you when sitting at the table and gives you more leg-room – quite a normal characteristic of this kind of table.

The individuality of the design, however, lies in the fact that you can withdraw the pegs, take the top off and re-position it as a settle-back by inserting each peg through its slot into a second hole bored through the back end of each arm, as shown in the end elevation, Fig.26.2. The result is a settle with a wooden seat and back which only needs some cushions to make it comfortable.

Probably first made in the early or mid-17th century settles of this style are often called 'monks' benches', but there's no evidence that they were particularly favoured by monks.

CONSTRUCTION
The top couldn't be simpler. It consists of three pieces of oak, laid alongside each other and nailed to the two crosspieces. The inevitable would happen, of course, in olden times; and the pieces have shrunk across their widths with resulting gaps and splits.

If you are concerned with authenticity you can do

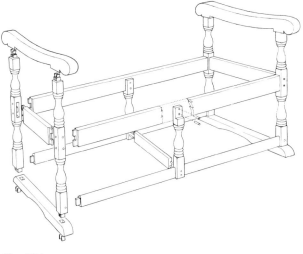

Fig. 26.1

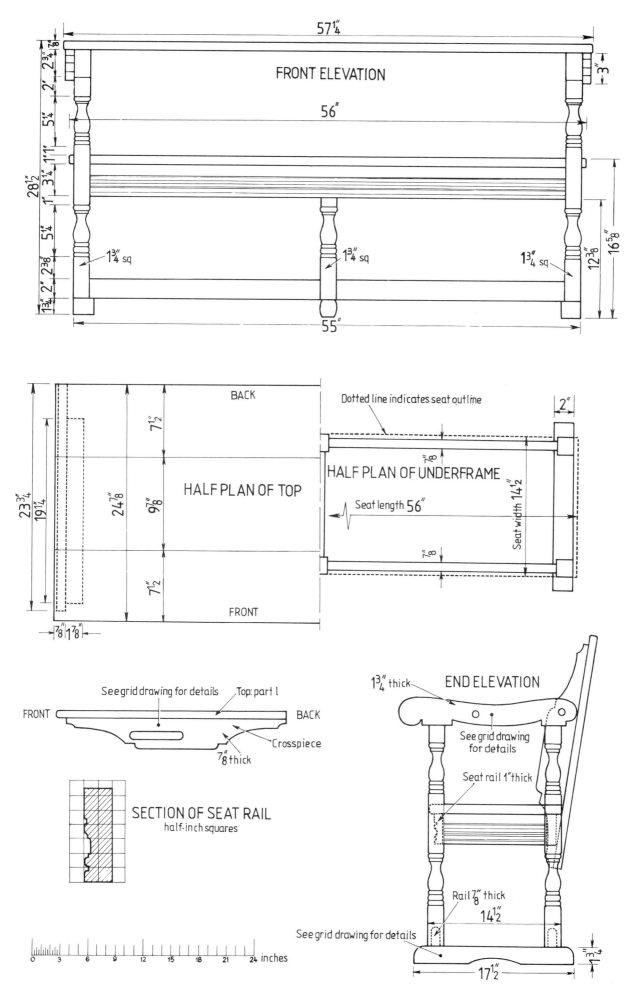

FRONT ELEVATION

$57\frac{1}{4}''$

$3''$

$56''$

$28\frac{1}{2}''$

$1\frac{3}{4}''$ sq

$1\frac{3}{4}''$ sq

$1\frac{3}{4}''$ sq

$16\frac{5}{8}''$

$12\frac{3}{8}''$

$55''$

BACK

$7\frac{1}{2}''$

HALF PLAN OF TOP

$24\frac{7}{8}''$

$9\frac{7}{8}''$

$23\frac{3}{4}''$

$19\frac{1}{4}''$

$7\frac{1}{2}''$

FRONT

$\frac{7}{8}''$ $1\frac{7}{8}''$

Dotted line indicates seat outline

$2''$

$\frac{7}{8}''$

HALF PLAN OF UNDERFRAME

Seat length $56''$

Seat width $14\frac{1}{2}''$

$\frac{7}{8}''$

See grid drawing for details   Top: part I

FRONT

BACK

Crosspiece

$\frac{7}{8}''$ thick

SECTION OF SEAT RAIL
half-inch squares

$1\frac{3}{4}''$ thick

END ELEVATION

See grid drawing for details

Seat rail $1''$ thick

Rail $\frac{7}{8}''$ thick

$14\frac{1}{2}''$

See grid drawing for details

$1\frac{3}{4}''$

$17\frac{1}{2}''$

0 3 6 9 12 15 18 21 24 inches

Fig. 26.2

109

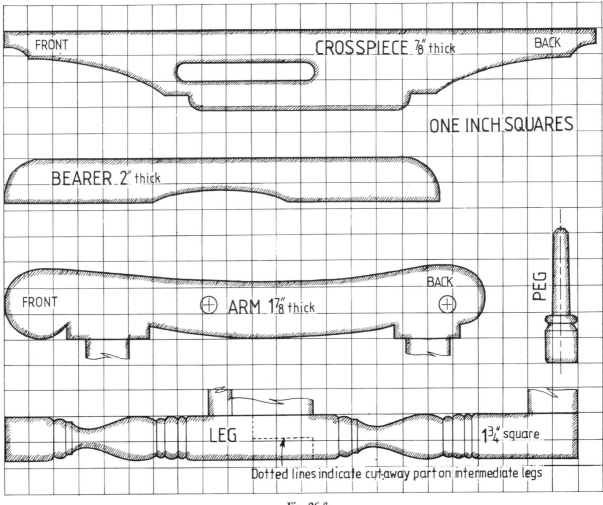

FRONT CROSSPIECE ⅞" thick BACK

ONE INCH SQUARES

BEARER 2" thick

FRONT ⊕ ARM 1⅞" thick BACK ⊕ PEG

LEG 1¾" square

Dotted lines indicate cut-away part on intermediate legs

Fig. 26.3

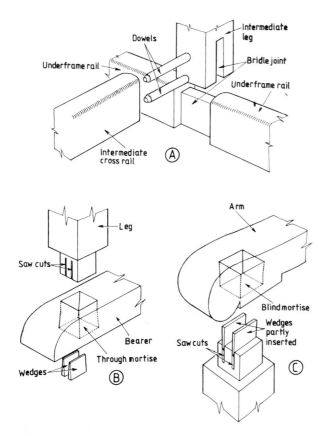

Dowels
Underframe rail
Intermediate leg
Bridle joint
Underframe rail
Intermediate cross rail
Ⓐ

Leg
Saw cuts
Bearer
Through mortise
Wedges
Ⓑ

Arm
Blind mortise
Saw cuts
Wedges partly inserted
Ⓒ

Fig. 26.4

the same, but shrinkage plates (Fig. 26.5A) would be better. Fig. 26.5B shows how the plate is first screwed to the crosspiece, sunk slightly below the surface (say ¹⁄₃₂ in or so) which means that the crosspiece and the top will be in close contact. Use a round-head screw to fix the plate to the underside of the top; the slot will allow movement without the top splitting.

Fig. 26.1 shows the various joints used. You will see the framing uses mortise-and-tenon joints, all pegged; the joints on the seat rails are double tenons.

The wedged tenons on the tops and bottoms of the legs need cutting carefully. The tenons at the top ends are blind and call for a slightly different treatment from the bottom ones which are through tenons; Fig. 26.4 shows both kinds, B at the bottom and C at the top of the leg. Points to note are: the saw-cuts to accept the wedges should only extend two-thirds of the tenon length; the mortise should be slightly splayed as shown to allow for the expansion of the tenon when the wedges are driven home, but the splay only extends for two-thirds of the mortise depth, the same as the length of the saw cuts; and judge the size of the wedges nicely. They mustn't be too thin to expand the tenon properly, nor should they be too thick so they force the tenon apart prematurely and jam it before it's fully home.

The tops of the intermediate legs are cut away to accept the seat rails, and the joints are pegged right through (Fig. 26.1). At the bottom they are bridle-jointed over the underframe rails as shown at Fig. 26.4A, and the joints are pegged right through with dowels, which also fix the intermediate cross-rail.

Like the top, the seat consists of two pieces nailed to the end seat-rails and notched round the legs. This is obviously another case for using shrinkage plates along the end seat-rails; fixing to the front and back seat-rail can be by pocket-screwing (Fig. 26.5C), if you don't mind a gap opening up in the middle of the seat. If you prefer comfort to authenticity, pocket-screw at the front and use shrinkage plates everywhere else.

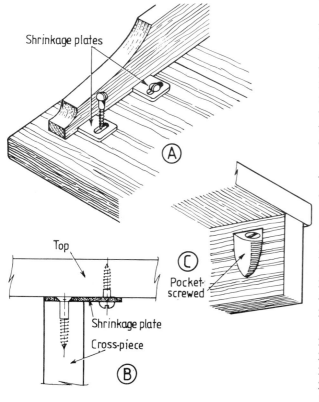

Fig. 26.5

All the seat rails have moulded faces, the profile of which is shown in Fig. 26.2. This would probably have been worked with a combination of moulding planes and scratch-stocks, but life is easier with a spindle moulder or a router to speed things up.

The only other components are the two pegs (detail, Fig. 26.3) which call for straightforward woodturning.

Furniture like this almost always began its life 'in the white' — free from any kind of polish. Hundreds of years' worth of wax polish would have been applied, of course, and you can do the same thing; use any good quality proprietary wax polish.

You can see from the main drawing that the piece would have had heavy wear, particularly on the front under-frame rails where the wood would be worn away to about half the original size. If you want to give your reproduction the same appearance you can use a rasp to simulate the wear, restricting it to the front under-frame rail and the edges of the legs, where feet would normally scuff the wood. The edges of the arms were also notched and bruised, and so were all the edges of the top.

CUTTING LIST

		INCHES			MM		
		L	W	T	L	W	T
1	Top	57¾	25⅛	⅞	1467	638	23
2	Cross-pieces	24¼	3⅜	⅞	616	86	23
1	Seat	56½	14¾	1	1435	375	25
2	Arms	19¾	3	1⅞	502	76	48
4	Legs	23½	1¾	1¾	597	51	45'
2	Intermediate legs	13½	2	1¾	343	51	45
2	Long seat rails	53¾	3½	1	1365	89	25
2	End seat rails	13⅝	3½	1	347	89	25
2	Underframe rails	53¾	2¼	⅞	1365	63	23
2	Bearers	17¾	2	2	451	51	51
1	Intermediate cross-rail	11½	2¼	⅞	292	63	23

Working allowances have been made to lengths and widths; thicknesses are net.

CHIPPENDALE LIBRARY TABLE

The original on which this table is based stands in the library at the great house of Stourhead, Wiltshire. It could be used for writing, display or occasional purposes. It has a mahogany top and legs; usually, the top is quite plain and bears no inlays or marquetry, its only decoration consisting of a triple-beaded edge (see detail, Fig. 27.4). The frame and drawer-rails are in oak, the latter having mahogany lippings on the edges. Chippendale seems to have designed the drawer too wide ($40\frac{3}{8}$ in) – even when empty, quite an effort is needed to span it and withdraw it. Further, the drawer-bottom is all in one piece without a central muntin. It would be more practical to fit twin drawers side-by-side.

The table is intended to be free-standing because

the back is a dummy replica of the front, exactly the same except that there is no lock and no escutcheon.

The drawer-frame construction is conventional, except that the kickers (which are softwood) are screwed and glued to the ends. To fix the top, slot-screw up through kickers to allow for shrinkage in the width (C, Fig. 27.2), and pocket-screw along the top rails.

Details of the brassware are shown in Fig. 27.2 at B, D and E; it's not likely that you will be able to get identical fittings, but at least you will have an idea of the kind of things to look for.

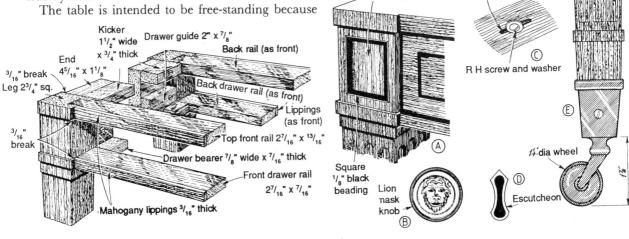

Fig. 27.1

Fig. 27.2

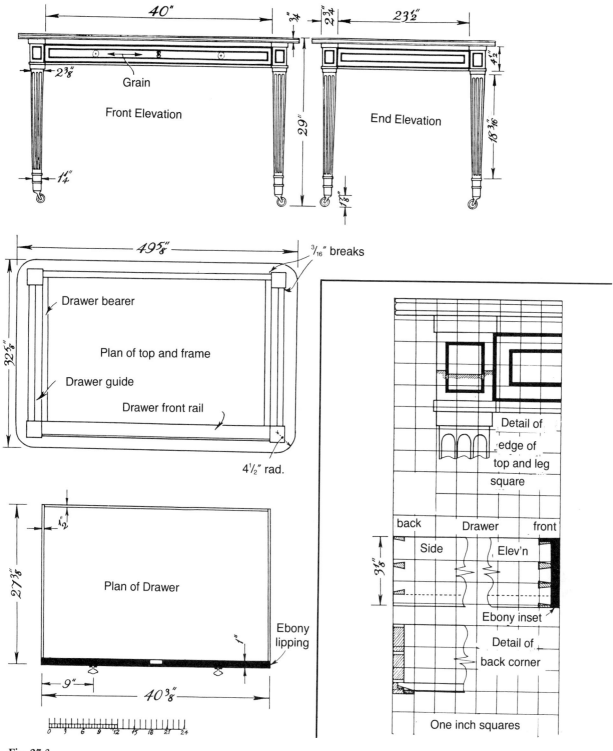

Fig. 27.3

CUTTING LIST

	INCHES			MM		
	L	W	T	L	W	T
1 Top	$50\frac{1}{8}$	$32\frac{7}{8}$	$\frac{3}{4}$	1273	835	19
4 Legs	$28\frac{3}{4}$	3	$2\frac{3}{4}$	730	76	70
1 Top front rail	$41\frac{1}{2}$	$2\frac{11}{16}$	$\frac{13}{16}$	1054	68	21
1 Back front rail	$41\frac{1}{2}$	$2\frac{11}{16}$	$\frac{13}{16}$	1054	68	21
1 Back drawer rail	$41\frac{1}{2}$	$2\frac{11}{16}$	$\frac{11}{16}$	1054	68	18
2 Ends	$24\frac{1}{2}$	$4\frac{9}{16}$	$1\frac{1}{8}$	623	116	29
2 Drawer bearers	$24\frac{1}{2}$	$1\frac{1}{8}$	$\frac{7}{16}$	623	29	11
2 Drawer kickers	$24\frac{1}{2}$	$1\frac{3}{4}$	$\frac{3}{4}$	623	45	19
2 Drawer guides	24	$2\frac{1}{4}$	$\frac{7}{8}$	609	58	22

CUTTING LIST (continued)

Part	INCHES			MM		
	L	W	T	L	W	T
1 Drawer front	$40\frac{7}{8}$	$3\frac{3}{8}$	1	1038	86	25
2 Drawer sides	$27\frac{1}{2}$	$3\frac{3}{8}$	$\frac{1}{2}$	698	86	12
1 Drawer back	$39\frac{7}{8}$	$3\frac{3}{8}$	$\frac{1}{2}$	1013	86	12
1 Drawer bottom	40	$27\frac{1}{2}$	$\frac{1}{2}$	1016	698	12
1 For lipping	276	1	$\frac{3}{16}$	7008	25	5

Working allowances have been made to lengths and widths; thicknesses are net.

REGENCY LIBRARY TABLE

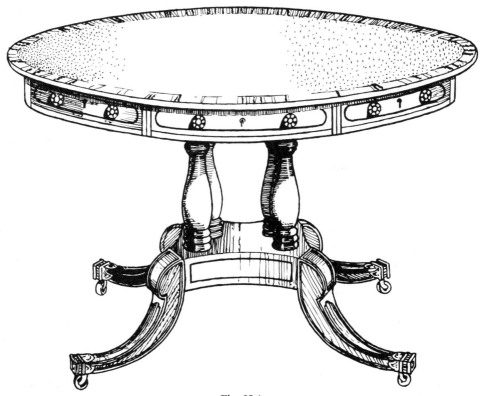

Fig. 28.1

The heyday of circular-topped tables was the Regency period and the early years of Queen Victoria's reign – about 1810–40. One of the best known types is the rent table, which usually had 4 drawers – one for each quarter of the year – and often included a small till for money in the centre of the top.

This piece could also be called a drum or capstan table because of its appearance. It was probably used in the library, the baize-lined top allowing books to be moved about without fear of scratching or marking any polish. The design has been simplified a little; the original had carved tapering and spiralling reeds on the pillars, and boldly carved acanthus leaves on the knees of the claw legs.

LEGS AND PILLARS

Solid mahogany was used for the legs and pillars; also for the top and bottom blocks – in the latter case the block is deepcut from $3\frac{1}{2}$ in thick solid plank so that the grain runs vertically (Fig. 28.2C and D). Probably this was done so that the sockets which accept the dovetails on each of the legs would be as strong as possible. Details of the dovetails are shown in Fig. 28.3 at B and H.

The sides of the legs are routed out to a depth of about $\frac{3}{16}$ in. You should be able to do this with a machine router, and chop the corners out by hand. However, the routed area on the knee is a different proposition because it is curved; it will almost certainly have to be done by hand, or with a curved base

and guides for the router. Another piece of hand work is the raised beading on the front of the legs, which is carved in the solid. There is a sketch of the original castors at C, Fig. 28.3, it's highly unlikely that you will be able to find any of this design, but there are several different patterns of this kind of socket castor on the market. Don't forget you may have to alter the size of the toe (Fig. 28.4C) to fit the castor you have chosen.

Turning up the four pillars should be straightforward enough, and there is a pattern for you to follow – Fig. 28.4A. The pins at top and bottom are for fixing into the top and bottom blocks. The top block is a plain piece of solid mahogany, 2 in thick, with two opposite edges bevelled off on the underside (Fig. 28.2B).

CIRCULAR CASE

Now we come to the circular case which comprises the upper and lower tops and the drawers. On the original table both tops are in pine, the upper one 45 in diameter and the lower one 43 in. Both are $\frac{3}{4}$ in thick, the upper top has a $\frac{7}{8}$ in crossbanding round the edge.

As you can see from Fig. 28.2 there are four drawers, and Fig. 28.3 F and G give further details. Two parallel divisions rails run right across, and there are four smaller division rails at right angles to them. This arrangement gives four drawers, and four quadrant-shaped spaces, which are left empty. Their fronts are finished in just the same way as the drawer-fronts, even to the extent of dummy handles and escutcheons.

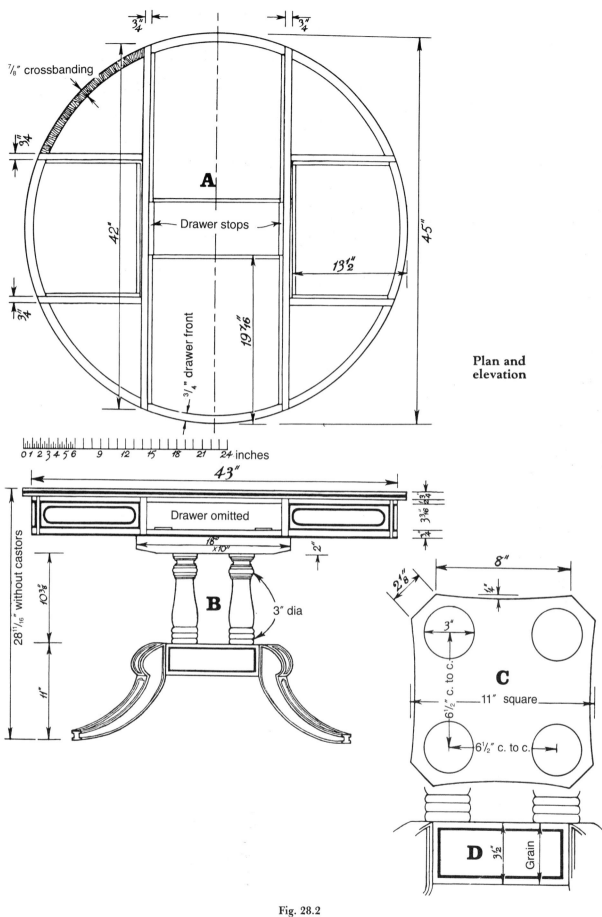

Fig. 28.2

These division rails, Fig. 28.3E, are pine except at the ends, where a piece of vertically grained oak is jointed on. The show-wood face is veneered in mahogany.

This is not a construction that greatly appeals, and the job offers a great opportunity to try MDF. It would be ideal for making up the entire case, tops and all, as shown at Fig. 28.3A. You will notice that buttoning the top down is recommended as well as gluing the stub tenons; the divisions could be tenoned right through the lower top, and the tenons wedged from beneath.

115

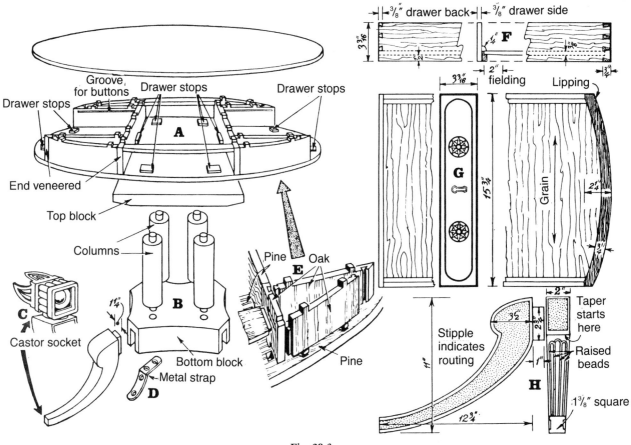

Fig. 28.3

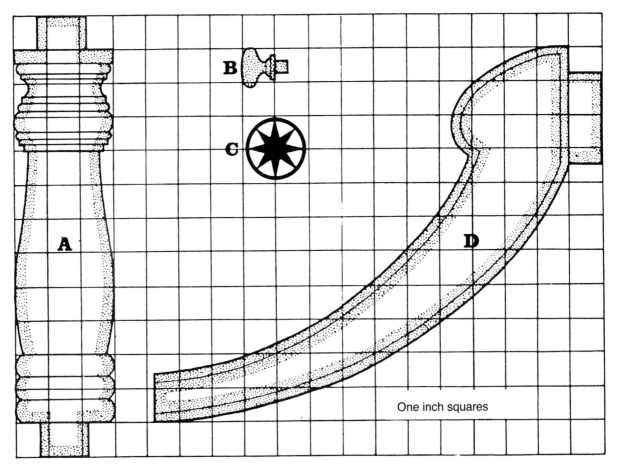

Fig. 28.4

116

The edges of both tops and the ends of the rails will need to be veneered, of course. The rails should be fixed and buttoned to the upper top before gluing on the lower top, or it will be hard to get at the buttons.

DRAWERS
Details of the drawers are shown in Figs. 28.3F and G. They follow traditional construction, with lap-dovetails at the front corners; as the drawer-fronts are curved, a flat has to be planed off each inside front corner to enable the dovetail joints to be made. On the original the grain in the oak drawer-fronts runs vertically and they are veneered with horizontally grained mahogany. The method of making them depends on what timber you have available – obviously, they will almost certainly have to be deep-cut from solid timber in order to achieve the curve. If you are using mahogany you may be able to have the grain running horizontally and dispense with the veneer. The drawer-bottoms are grooved into the back of the drawer-fronts and supported by slips along the sides; they run out at the back and the grain runs from side to side (Fig. 28.3G). Note that a black lipping is laid on the upper edges of the drawer-fronts.

BANDINGS
Finally comes ornamentation, which mainly consists of inlaid black bandings. Beginning with the top, there is the cross-banding around the edge – already mentioned; in addition, a $\frac{3}{8} \times \frac{1}{16}$ in black banding is inlaid into the edge itself. Oak, suitably ebonised, will make good bandings and lippings.

The rest of the bandings are all the same – black, and $\frac{3}{16} \times \frac{1}{16}$ in, they are arranged as shown in Fig. 28.2B and D. A profile of the knob handle is illustrated in Fig.28.4B, plus details of the inlaid patera which surrounds the knob. Again this is simplified considerably, as the original was a complicated sunburst design; a dark wood such as ebony (or ebonised oak) for the centre, rosewood for the rays and the outer circle, and a light-coloured wood such as holly or sycamore for the infill would be a good combination.

The details of decoration have been left rather vague, precisely because it will give you the chance to adapt such things to suit your own tastes, tools and expertise.

CUTTING LIST

	INCHES			MM		
	L	W	T	L	W	T
1 Upper top (grain long way)	46	$45\frac{1}{2}$	$\frac{3}{4}$	1168	1155	19
1 Lower top (grain long way)	46	$43\frac{1}{2}$	$\frac{3}{4}$	1118	1105	19
4 Pillars	14	$3\frac{1}{2}$	3	356	89	77
4 Claw legs	$18\frac{1}{4}$	$5\frac{1}{2}$	2	464	140	51
1 Top block	19	$10\frac{1}{2}$	2	483	267	51
1 Bottom block	12	$11\frac{1}{2}$	$3\frac{1}{2}$	305	292	89
2 Top carcase rails, long	43	$5\frac{1}{8}$	$\frac{3}{4}$	1092	130	19
4 Top carcase rails, short	14	$5\frac{1}{8}$	$\frac{3}{4}$	356	130	19
2 Drawer stops	$7\frac{1}{8}$	1	$\frac{5}{8}$	182	25	16
4 Drawer fronts	$16\frac{3}{4}$	$3\frac{5}{8}$	$\frac{3}{4}$	425	92	19
4 Drawer sides, long	$20\frac{3}{8}$	$3\frac{5}{8}$	$\frac{3}{8}$	518	93	9
4 Drawer sides, short	$14\frac{1}{2}$	$5\frac{5}{8}$	$\frac{3}{8}$	368	93	9
4 Drawer backs	$16\frac{3}{4}$	$2\frac{3}{4}$	$\frac{3}{8}$	425	70	9
2 Drawer bottoms, large	$19\frac{1}{2}$	$15\frac{3}{4}$	$\frac{3}{8}$	495	400	9
2 Drawer bottoms, small	$13\frac{3}{8}$	$15\frac{3}{4}$	$\frac{3}{8}$	340	400	9
Drawer slip from one piece	112	1	$\frac{1}{4}$	2844	25	6
Drawer quadrant moulding from one piece	112	$\frac{3}{4}$	$\frac{1}{4}$	2844	19	6
Drawer stops from oddments						

Working allowances have been made to lengths and widths; thicknesses are net.

GEORGIAN-STYLE POLE SCREEN

The original of this fire-screen was probably made about 1760, judging from the trumpet-shaped turned column and the pad feet.

Fire-screens were a peculiarly English invention as they were intended to shield the body from the fierce heat of an open fire – on the Continent, room heating was by closed stoves, so the problem did not arise. This screen can be moved up or down, and during the summer it could be used to mask the empty fireplace.

The piece is made in mahogany throughout. The principal dimensions are given in the rear elevation, Fig. 29.2. Beginning with the turned column, the first point to note is that it is split in two as marked in the

illustration; it would be extremely difficult to turn the whole thing, and in fact it is unnecessary. The main column (A. Fig. 29.2) is turned first, and a 1 in diameter by 1¼ in-long pin is turned on the bottom end. The shaft which supports the screen tapers very slightly from ⅞ in at the lower end to a bare ⅞ in at the top, which enables the catches on the back of the screen to slide up and down freely. Again, a pin needs to be turned on the lower end of the shaft; this can be ⅝ in in diameter by 1 in long, and is glued into a corresponding hole in the top of the column. If you have a suitably sized screw-box and tap, it is good practice to thread the parts so that they can be screwed together.

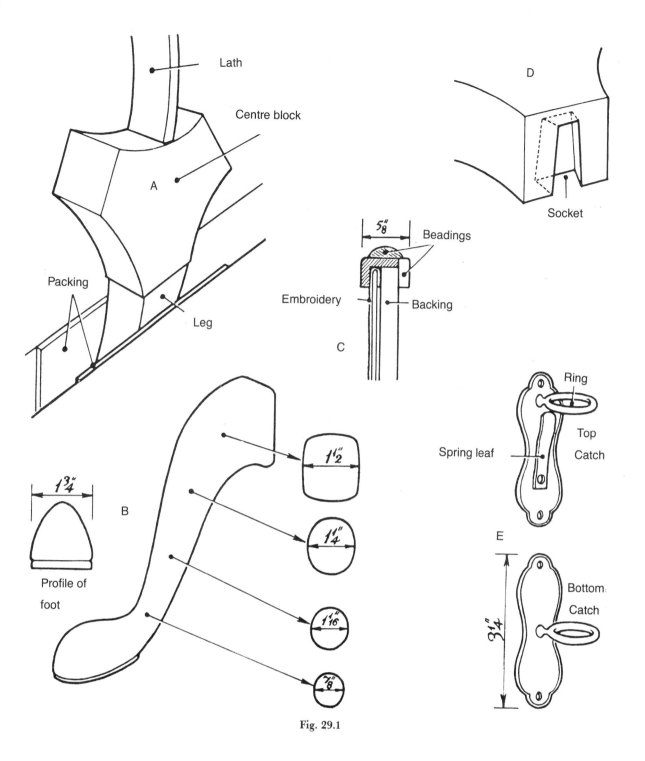

Fig. 29.1

Before the column and shaft are finally assembled and glued up, however, you need to make up the tripod stool, as this will be difficult enough without having the column in the way.

The central block is cut from a piece 5 in square and 2⅛ in thick. The plan is shown at C, Fig. 29.2. The best way to cut the shape is on a bandsaw, and the same goes for the shapes of the legs. Allow yourself a good margin when sawing out the legs, say ¼ in all round, as they will need a lot of bench work with spokeshave and rasp – and don't forget to allow the extra for the dovetail on each one; E. Fig. 29.2, gives the shape. It would be best to mark out a template first and use it as a pattern; you will no doubt be able to nest the shapes into each other to save timber, but you should make sure that the grain on each one runs in the direction shown by the arrow. A sketch of the leg is shown at B, Fig. 29.1, to help you to shape it.

The trickiest part of the work is to cut a dovetail on the end of each leg to fit into a slot in the central block. A plan of the joint is shown at C, Fig. 29.2, a side elevation at E and a front at F; there is a perspective view in Fig.29.1 (D). This makes a very strong joint – yet it is still the weakest point of the whole piece, which is why it is frequently reinforced with a metal plate such as that shown at B, Fig. 29.2. This is most easily made by cutting out a cardboard pattern and fitting it over the leg and centre-block assembly, marking where the screw holes need to be drilled and then sticking it to a piece of thin steel plate which can be cut and shaped with a hacksaw and files.

Another problem is cramping the leg and centre-block assembly while the glue sets. You will find one solution in Fig. 29.1 (A), where the leg is held in the bench vice suitably protected from bruising and a lath is wedged between the centre block and the ceiling – the lath must be cut a little over-length, of course, so that is is slightly curved and exerts pressure.

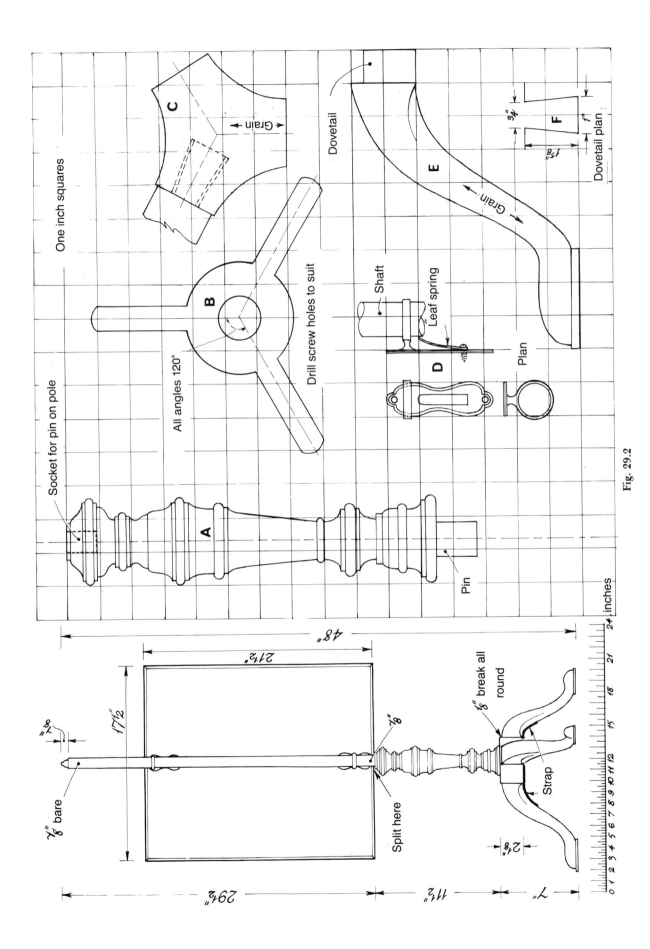

One inch squares

Socket for pin on pole

All angles 120°

Drill screw holes to suit

Grain

C

B

A

Pin

Dovetail

Grain

E

F

Dovetail plan

3/4"

1"

1⅝"

Shaft

Leaf spring

D

Plan

48"

21½"

17½"

29½"

1/8" bare

Split here

7/8"

1/8" break all round

Strap

2⅛"

11½"

7"

0 1 2 3 4 5 6 7 8 9 10 11 12 15 18 21 24 inches

Fig. 29.2

120

The screen itself is a perfectly straightforward frame which contains the embroidery; normally it is not glazed, because of the risk that the glass might crack with the heat. The embroidery itself is mounted on a piece of hardboard or thick mounting board, overlapping at the edges by at least an inch; the excess can then be fixed down with an adhesive tape such as carpet tape – or, better still, laced across diagonally with strong thread. The frame itself needs to be at least $\frac{5}{8}$ in thick, as shown in Fig. 29.1 (C) – which also indicates a suggested arrangement; the mouldings and beadings are all mitred at the corners, and the beadings are pinned and glued to the frame moulding. In addition, the back beading can be pinned to the backing; the latter should be at least $\frac{1}{4}$ in thick, as it has to form a good anchorage for the screws which hold the catches.

Fig. 29.2 (D) shows measured front and side elevations and a plan of the top catch. You will see from Fig. 29.1 (E) that, while the top catch has its ring attached near the top and a leaf spring screwed on, the bottom catch has no leaf spring, and the ring is set centrally – it acts merely as a guide. The rings are $1\frac{1}{8}$ in in outside diameter and $\frac{1}{4}$ in thick. In use the leaf spring scrapes against the wooden shaft, its springiness holding the screen wherever it is moved. The fitting is not ideal, as the shaft is gradually worn away by the leaf spring; moreover, supply is a problem, so you would have to make it up yourself. If you are not too worried about things being historically authentic, an alternative is to sink a length of steel wire (or a narrow steel strip) into the shaft, and then screw the magnetic sections of two magnetic catches to the screen; this too will enable you to slide the screen up and down and leave it at any height you wish.

CUTTING LIST

	INCHES			MM		
	L	W	T	L	W	T
1 Centre block	$4\frac{3}{4}$	$5\frac{1}{8}$	$2\frac{1}{8}$	121	130	54
1 Pillar (including pin)	$13\frac{1}{4}$	$2\frac{7}{8}$	$2\frac{5}{8}$	337	74	67
1 Shaft (including pin)	31	$1\frac{1}{8}$	$\frac{7}{8}$	787	27	23
3 Legs, each from a piece	$11\frac{3}{4}$	$3\frac{5}{8}$	2	298	93	51
Frame moulding, from total length	80	to choice		2032	to choice	

Working allowances have been made to lengths and widths; thicknesses are net.

CORNER DISPLAY CABINET

This design, which is late 18th century in appearance, would look best in a mahogany-type timber. There are several West African woods which are loosely called 'mahoganies', and one of these would be suitable. Some examples are abura, afrormosia, agba, gedu nohor, guarea, makore, sapele, and utile. Assuming that you will use manufactured board with veneered faces for the cupboard door and the ends, you will need to match the mahogany pieces to the veneer on the board, and this obviously determines the timber.

CONSTRUCTION

This is not an easy piece to make up, and you'll find that accurate preparation is the principal key to success, particularly on the long edges.

Starting with the plinth, there are mitred joints between the plinth front rail and the plinth corners. These are $67\frac{1}{2}$ degrees, not 45 degrees, and the joints are loose-tongued; that is, a slot is made longitudinally along each meeting edge and a tongue glued in (Fig. 30.2).

In the same drawing you can see the groove-and-rabbet joint between the plinth corner and end; also the way in which the plinth end is rebated into the rear post – this latter joint can be reinforced by screws.

Turning to Fig. 30.4 you will see that the carcase panels of the cupboard fit inside the plinth frame and rest on bearers which are glued and screwed inside the frame $\frac{3}{4}$in down from the upper edge. For further strength you can insert screws as shown to hold the

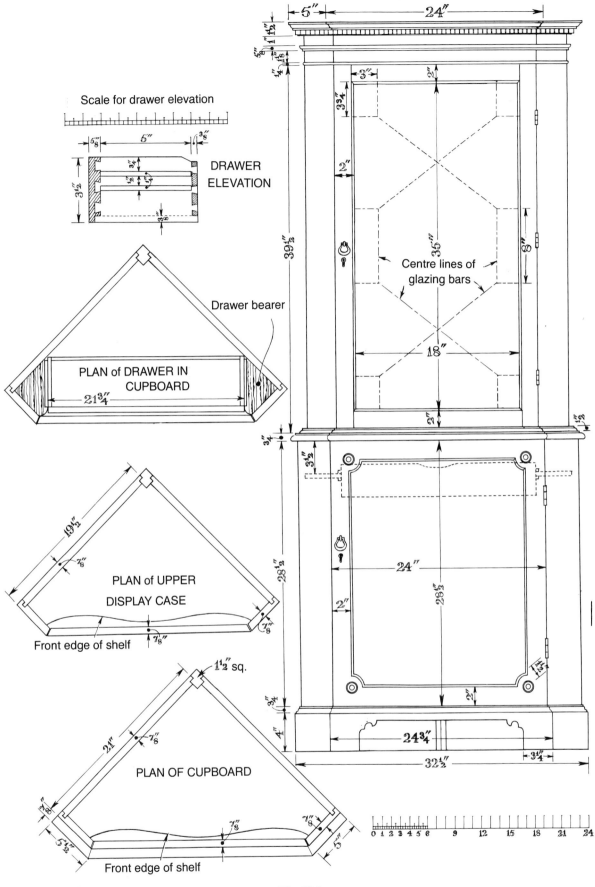

Scale for drawer elevation

DRAWER ELEVATION

PLAN of DRAWER IN CUPBOARD

Drawer bearer

PLAN of UPPER DISPLAY CASE

Front edge of shelf

PLAN OF CUPBOARD

Front edge of shelf

Centre lines of glazing bars

Fig. 30.1

bottom edges of the carcase panels against the inside of the plinth frame.

There is a slightly different arrangement along the inside upper edge of the plinth front rail, where a ³⁄₄ in bearer is screwed and glued to it, flush with the upper edge. This means that when the cupboard bottom is laid on top of it, the ogee moulding masks the edge. Returning to Fig. 30.4, the cupboard bottom is housed into trenches cut ³⁄₄ in away from the lower edges of the panels; the trenches themselves need to be ³⁄₄ × ¹⁄₄ in wide and deep. The cupboard bottom can, of course, be notched around the rear post.

123

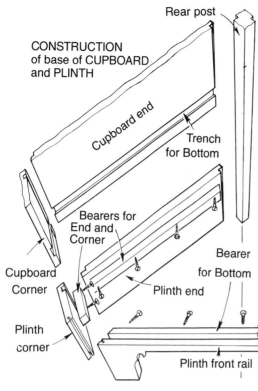

CONSTRUCTION
of base of CUPBOARD
and PLINTH

Rear post

Cupboard end

Trench
for Bottom

Bearers for
End and
Corner

Cupboard
Corner

Plinth end

Plinth
corner

Bearer
for Bottom

Plinth front rail

Fig. 30.2

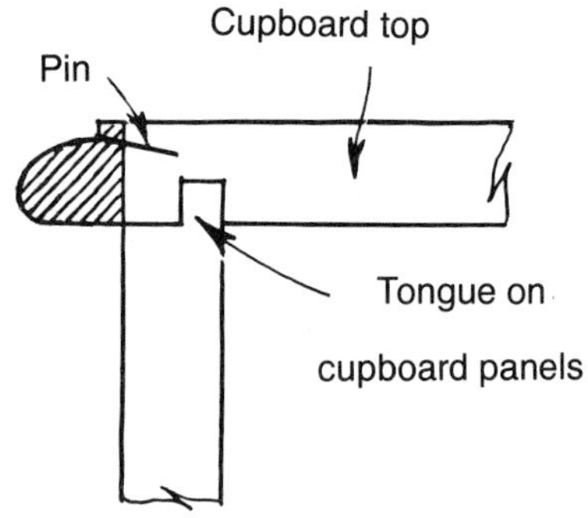

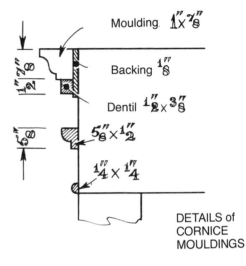

Pin

Cupboard top

Tongue on
cupboard panels

Fig. 30.5

Moulding $1'' \times 7''_8$

Backing $1''_8$

Dentil $1''_2 \times 3''_8$

$5''_8 \times 1''_2$

$1''_4 \times 1''_4$

$1''_2$

$6''_8$

DETAILS of
CORNICE
MOULDINGS

Fig. 30.6

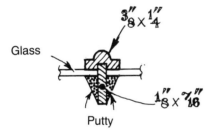

$3''_8 \times 1''_4$

Glass

$1''_8 \times 7''_{16}$

Putty

BARRED DOOR MOULDING

Fig. 30.3

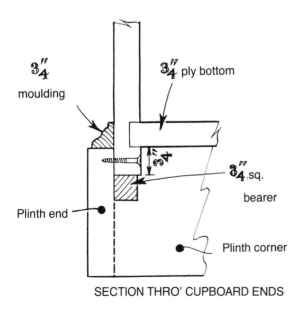

$3''_4$ moulding

$3''_4$ ply bottom

$3''_4$

$3''_4$ sq. bearer

Plinth end

Plinth corner

SECTION THRO' CUPBOARD ENDS

Fig. 30.4

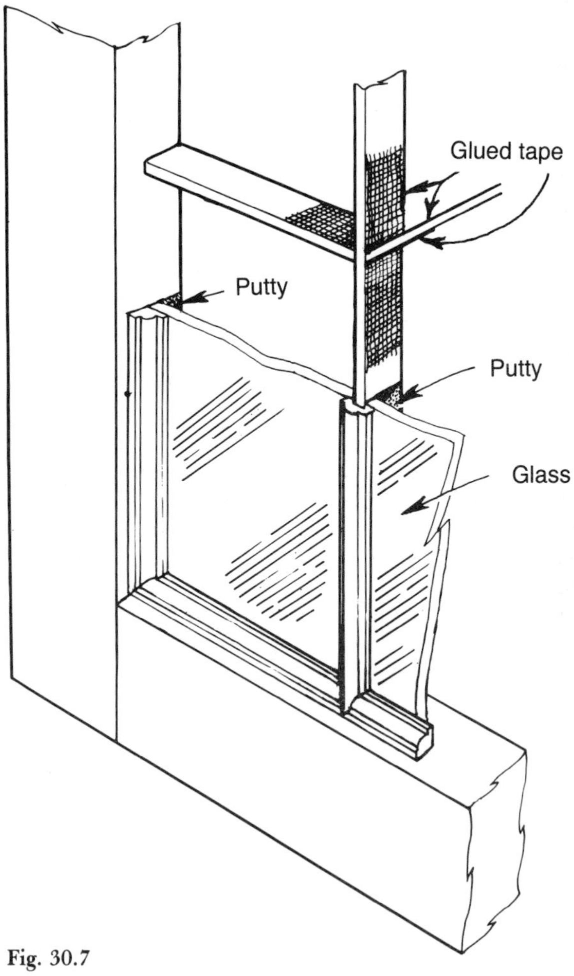

Glued tape

Putty

Putty

Glass

Fig. 30.7

124

The cupboard top is a ³⁄₄ in manufactured board, veneered with a lipping pinned and glued on as shown in Fig. 30.5; this section also shows how tongues are formed on the upper ends of the cabinet corners and ends which fit into grooves on the underside of the top.

A solid piece of ³⁄₄ in board is also used for the door, and if necessary, you may have to veneer the edges. Also, you may be doubtful about screws driven direct into the board to secure the hinges; if so, you could sink small pieces of hardwood dowel flush with the inside of the door and screw into them.

You will need to rout out a channel to accept the ³⁄₁₆ in beading on the door; the small circular ornaments are, of course, turned paterae. The drawer is optional but if you do decide to include it, details are given in Fig. 30.1. As it is a comparatively small one and only intended to carry light loads, it runs on triangular-shaped bearers screwed and glued into the corners, and these help to strengthen the carcase.

The bottom edges of the corner and end panels of the display case are cut away by a ¹⁄₂ × ¹⁄₂ in rebate which houses the ¹⁄₂ in ply bottom, and this joint can be reinforced by gluing and screwing — the screw heads will be hidden by the surbase moulding which is pinned and glued on afterwards. A cornice rail is mitred and loose-tongued at the top between the corner panels, and ¹⁄₂ in plywood top lies in a ¹⁄₂ × ¹⁄₂ in rebate formed around the top edges of the case panels and the cornice rail. It can be screwed and glued in place in the same way as the case bottom, and the screw heads will again be hidden by the applied cornice moulding.

How many shelves you fit depends, naturally on your own requirements; they are shown with serpentine front edges only as a suggestion and you could adopt any design you please.

The case door is made up in the conventional manner using mortise and tenon joints, and bearing in mind that it is barred and glazed, it must be absolutely true and the diagonal dimensions exactly equal. As you can imagine making up the bars and fixing in the glass panes is the trickiest job of all and it is essential that you start with a perfect door frame as a basis.

Start by cutting and fitting a piece of hardboard to fit exactly into the door aperture, minus the quadrant beading which is later fitted around the edges. Mark the centre lines of all the bars on to the hardboard and cut all the bars to length and mitre their ends as appropriate. Note, however, that the thin slats which are ¹⁄₈ × ⁷⁄₁₆ in are mortised into the back of the door by ¹⁄₂ in or so, and allowance must be made for this. Figs. 30.3 and 30.7 show details of the assembly and you will see in Fig. 30.7 that the joint intersections can be reinforced by strips of fabric which have been soaked in glue — an old bandage is a very suitable material for this.

Finally, the glass is put into place with putty; it can be an ordinary linseed oil putty to which a little gold size has been added for extra strength and hardness. Alternatively there are proprietary mastic putties available.

CUTTING LIST

	INCHES			MM		
	L	W	T	L	W	T
1 Cupboard door	29½	24¼	⅞	749	611	22
1 Plinth front rail	25¾	4¼	⅞	654	108	22
2 Corner plinth rails	6½	4¼	⅞	165	108	22
2 End plinth rails	22	4¼	⅞	559	108	22
1 Rear post	79	1¾	1¼	2006	45	32
2 Cupboard corner panels	31¼	5¼	⅞	794	133	22
2 Cupboard end panels	31¼	20⅜	⅞	794	518	22
1 Cupboard bottom	30¾	17½	¾	782	445	19
1 Cupboard top	32⅜	18⅝	¾	823	473	19
1 Case bottom	28½	15⅞	½	724	403	12
2 Case corner panels	45	4¾	⅞	1143	11	22
2 Case ends	45	18⅞	⅞	1143	479	22
1 Case top	28½	15⅞	½	724	405	12
1 Front cornice rail	23½	4¾	⅞	597	121	22
2 Case door stiles	40	2	⅞	1016	51	22
2 Case door rails	21	2	⅞	533	51	22
Cupboard shelf (each)	30	16¼	⅜	762	413	9
Case shelf (each)	27½	14¾	⅜	698	375	9
2 Drawer bearers	7	3¾	½	178	95	12
1 Drawer front	22¾	3¾	⅝	578	95	16
1 Drawer back	22¾	6¾	⅜	578	172	9
2 Drawer sides	6¾	3¾	⅜	172	95	9
1 Drawer bottom	22	6	⅜	558	152	9
4 Drawer runners	6	½	¼	152	12	6
Plinth moulding from one piece	36¾	1	¾	934	25	19
Lipping for cupb'd top from	36¾	1	¾	934	25	19
Surbase moulding from	35	¾	½	889	19	12
Cornice mldg, top, from	77	1¾	1½	1955	45	38
Cornice mldg, dentil, from	71	¾	⅜	1803	19	9
Cornice mldg, backing, from	70	1¾	⅛	1778	45	3
Cornice mldg, frieze, from	71	⅞	½	1803	22	12
Cornice mldg, bottom from	70	½	¼	1778	12	6
Case door beading, from	108	½	¼	2742	12	6
Glazing bar (ovolo), from	121	⅝	¼	3072	16	9
Flat beading, from	127	¹¹⁄₁₆	¼	3224	18	3

Working allowances have been made to lengths and widths; thicknesses are net.

'GIMSON' LADDER-BACK CHAIR

This handsome chair was made in the Pinbury workshop by Gimson/Barnsley about 1895 and then used by Sidney Barnsley in his own workshop.

The chair is made in ash throughout, and although the construction is pretty obvious from the drawings there are several points to note.

The front legs and underframe spars are straightforward turnery, but the back feet will almost certainly be too long to turn between centres. This means shaping them by hand, which involves planing them as far as possible to a hexagonal section, finishing off with a drawknife or spokeshave. Each backfoot will then need mortising to take the tenons on the ends of the ladder rails, and the mortises should be about $\frac{1}{2}$ in deep as

shown in the front elevation, Fig. 31.1. The end elevation of the same drawing shows that each ladder is set at a slight angle to the vertical, the angle being the same for each ladder.

As is usual with this type of chair, the underframe spars are mortised into the legs (Fig. 31.1, front elevation) and the front legs have pins turned on their upper ends which penetrate the arms and show on the upper surface.

Fig. 31.2 shows the plan and section of an arm, which needs to be hand-benched to shape; it has a square $\frac{7}{8}$ in tenon on the back end which is mortised into the backfoot and pegged, with the head of the peg being allowed to show. Also in Fig. 31.2 is an elevation

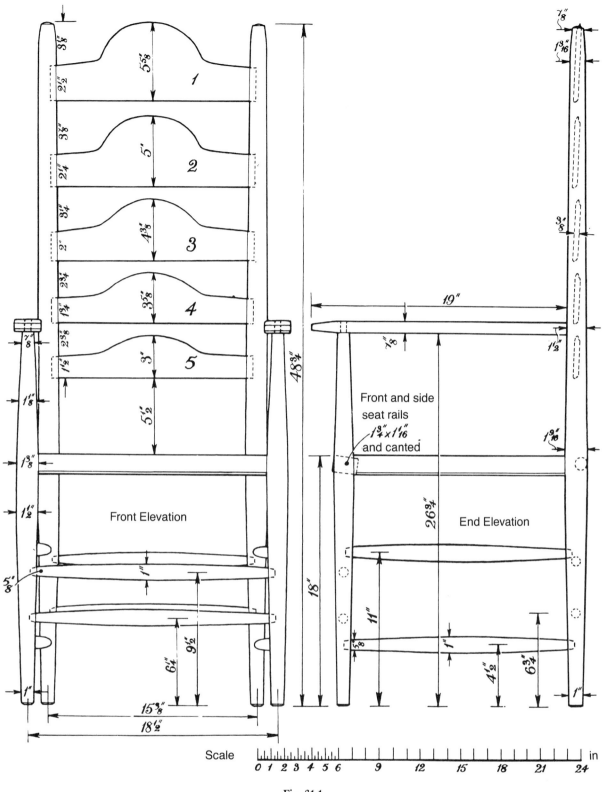

Fig. 31.1

of the top ladder rail, together with its section; note that the bottom edge is rounded off while the top edge is profiled as shown. They are also slightly curved, and you may have to steam-bend them to shape, which should not be too difficult as ash bends readily.

The trickiest part of the chair is the seat construction. First, the back seat rail is actually a turned cylinder, ¾ in diameter, which is tenoned into the backfeet at each end – this tenon need only be a pin of, say, ½ in diameter and ½ in long. The side and front rails are bareface-tenoned into the backfeet and the front legs; the most important feature is that they are

all canted at a slight angle from the horizontal as shown in the end elevation, Fig. 31.1. Note, too, that their outside edges are slightly curved (see seat plan, Fig. 31.2).

Rush seating is a craft in itself, and rather than rely on necessarily skimpy instructions here, it's a far better idea to read it up from one of the many books available on the subject, or take a short course.

A chair like this, which has a definite 'farmhouse' air about it, would probably best be finished with a simple wax polish. To do so, start by giving it a good coat of shellac (clear french polish) which will seal the

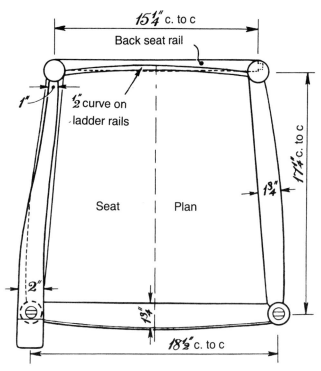

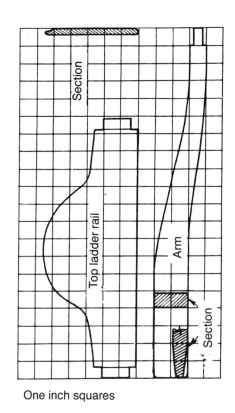

One inch squares

Fig. 31.2

end-grain and help prevent grime from entering the grain, and then apply any good proprietary wax polish, which must be non-silicone. Thereafter it's a matter of frequent applications plus plenty of elbow grease.

CUTTING LIST

Part	INCHES			MM		
	L	W	T	L	W	T
2 Backfeet	49¼	1¹³⁄₁₆	dia	1251	46	dia
2 Front legs	28⅛	1⅝	dia	714	41	dia
2 Arms	20⅛	2¼	⅞	511	57	23
1 Ladder rail, No 1	15¾	5⅞	⅜	400	149	10
1 Ladder rail, No 2	15⅝	5¼	⅜	397	134	10
1 Ladder rail, No 3	15½	4⅝	⅜	394	118	10
1 Ladder rail, No 4	15⅜	3⅞	⅜	391	98	10

CUTTING LIST (continued)

Part	INCHES			MM		
	L	W	T	L	W	T
1 Ladder rail, No 5	15⅜	3¼	⅜	391	82	10
1 Front under-frame spar	18½	1¼	dia	470	32	dia
1 Front under-frame spar	18¾	1¼	dia	476	32	dia
1 Rear under-frame spar	15½	1¼	dia	394	32	dia
1 Rear under-frame spar	15¾	1¼	dia	400	32	dia
2 Side under-frame spar	17⅜	1¼	dia	441	32	dia
2 Side under-frame spar	17½	1¼	dia	445	32	dia
1 Back seat rail	15¼	1	dia	387	25	dia
2 Side seat rail	17½	2	1¹⁄₁₆	445	51	27
1 Front seat rail	18¼	2	1¹⁄₁₆	464	51	27

Working allowances have been made to lengths and widths; thicknesses are net.

CARLTON HOUSE WRITING TABLE

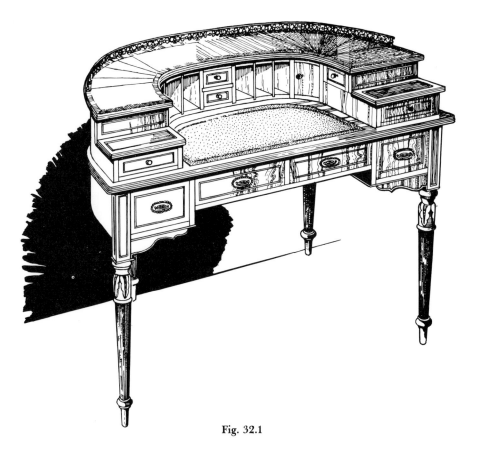

Fig. 32.1

The Carlton House lady's writing table was so called by the firm of Gillow and Co, who made one in 1796, presumably for the Prince Regent who was engaged in refurbishing the Carlton House. There is a similar design in Sheraton's *Drawing Book,* where it is described as a 'Lady's Drawing and Writing Table', and variations continued to be made well into the Victorian period, often with a shelf underframing.

This is, of course, a composite design and there is no reason why you should not alter it to suit your own choice. As an example, the legs illustrated with their carved bulbs may well present difficulties, and two alternatives are shown in Fig. 32.5A and B. The first one has a reeded bulb and shaft, and although this calls for considerable handwork, at least it is straightforward use of gouges. The second example is the elegant square tapered leg with a spade toe; note that the taper is heavier on the inside edge than on the outside, to avoid a pin-toed appearance.

Another feature which can be altered is the gallery, and you might care to substitute the scalloped wooden one shown at Fig. 32.5C for the metal design shown in Fig. 32.1.

Satinwood was usually the wood chosen, but as this is very expensive and difficult to obtain in any but small sizes, the logical alternatives are mahogany or walnut. Construction is shown in Fig. 32.4, and the greatest problem will be to form the curved panels; in the old days these might have been built up 'brick' fashion (as shown in Fig. 32.5D) and veneered, but you will find it easier to laminate them in a former. You could use three laminations of $\frac{1}{4}$ in ply with the grain running vertically which could be bent cold to the necessary curve. This method has the advantage that you can allow one or other of the plies to protrude and form a tongue which can be glued into a groove to make a strong joint. The tops, if solid, could be made up from multi-ply with an edging pinned and glued on.

At the intersections the rails in the main frame are housed into each other (Fig. 32.3 half plan) and the housings can run right through, as they will not be seen once the top has been fixed on, which can be done either by buttoning or pocket screwing. The drawer rails should be mortised and tenoned into the legs, and the stiles and muntins (parts 38 and 39) can be glued and screwed in place.

From the half plan of the stationery unit in Fig. 32.2, you can see that the curved section extends between the two divisions (part 31), and the two side drawer sections are separate but connected by the bottom and the tops. Note that the small drawers are set at right angles so that they open inwards towards the centre of the table top. All the divisions are housed into the top

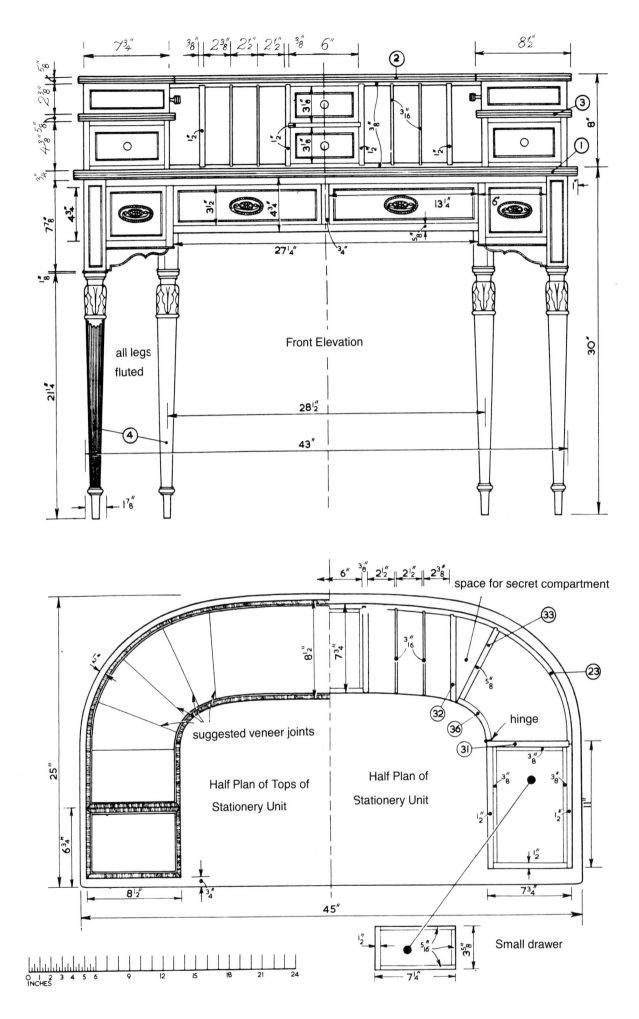

Fig. 32.2

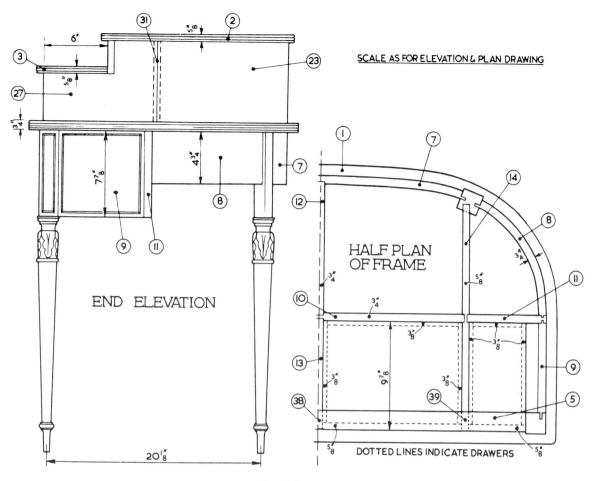

SCALE AS FOR ELEVATION & PLAN DRAWING

END ELEVATION

HALF PLAN OF FRAME

DOTTED LINES INDICATE DRAWERS

Fig. 32.3

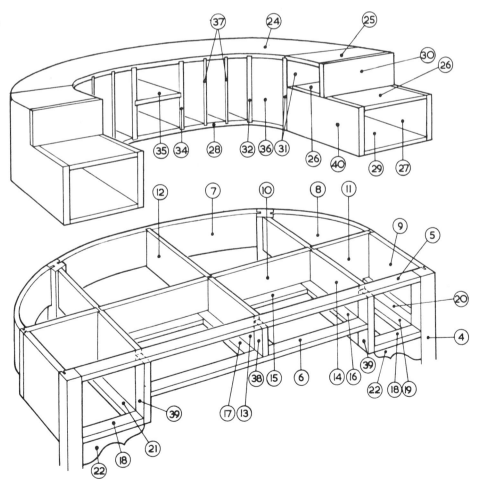

Fig. 32.4

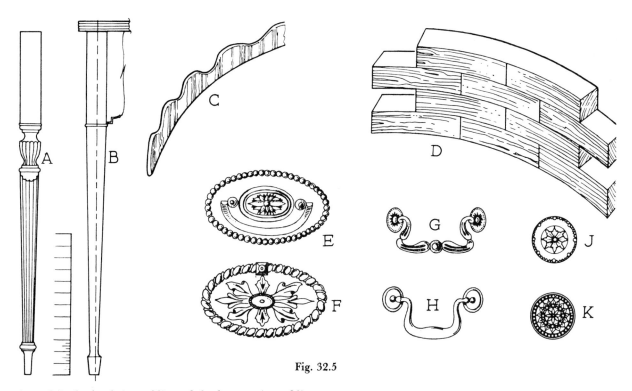

Fig. 32.5

(part 24), the back (part 23), and the bottom (part 28). You could adapt the division in the inside of the curve (part 33) to incorporate a hidden door giving access to the 'secret compartment'; this was often accomplished by fitting a panel tightly into an aperture cut into the division. The only way to remove it was to prise it open with a pointed instrument inserted in a small hole provided.

The table centre is laid with leather (or simulated leather) held down with a suitable adhesive; a tooled border looks attractive and gives a finished appearance. Crossbanding was widely used at this period, and the boxwood stringing on the drawer fronts is also very much in character. A selection of handles (E, F, G, and H) and knobs (J and K) is shown in Fig. 32.5. The range is so wide that we can only give an indication of the style.

CUTTING LIST

Part				INCHES			MM		
				L	W	T	L	W	T
1	1	Table top		46	$25\frac{1}{2}$	$\frac{3}{4}$	1168	648	19
2	1	Stationery unit top		45	$24\frac{1}{2}$	$\frac{5}{8}$	1143	616	16
3	2	Stationery unit sub-tops		$9\frac{1}{2}$	$7\frac{1}{4}$	$\frac{5}{8}$	242	185	16
4	4	Legs		$30\frac{1}{4}$	$2\frac{1}{8}$	$1\frac{7}{8}$	769	54	48
5	1	Upper front rail		$40\frac{1}{2}$	$2\frac{1}{4}$	$\frac{5}{8}$	1028	58	16
6	1	Lower drawer rail		$28\frac{1}{2}$	$2\frac{1}{4}$	$\frac{5}{8}$	724	58	16
7	1	Back rail segment		$28\frac{1}{2}$	$5\frac{1}{4}$	3	724	133	76
8	2	Back rail segments		$13\frac{1}{2}$	$5\frac{1}{4}$	$3\frac{3}{4}$	343	133	95
9	2	Ends		9	$8\frac{1}{4}$	$\frac{3}{4}$	229	210	19
10	2	Centre rails		$28\frac{1}{2}$	$5\frac{1}{4}$	$\frac{3}{4}$	724	133	19
11	2	End centre rails		$8\frac{1}{2}$	$8\frac{1}{4}$	$\frac{3}{4}$	216	210	19

CUTTING LIST (continued)

Part				INCHES			MM		
				L	W	T	L	W	T
12	1	Central division, back		13	$5\frac{1}{4}$	$\frac{3}{4}$	330	133	19
13	1	Central division, front		$9\frac{1}{2}$	$5\frac{1}{4}$	$\frac{3}{4}$	242	133	19
14	2	End divisions		$19\frac{1}{2}$	$8\frac{1}{4}$	$\frac{5}{8}$	495	210	16
15	2	Back drawer rails		11	$2\frac{1}{4}$	$\frac{5}{8}$	279	58	16
16	2	Drawer bearers		$9\frac{1}{4}$	$2\frac{1}{4}$	$\frac{5}{8}$	235	58	16
17	2	Drawer bearers		$9\frac{1}{4}$	$2\frac{1}{4}$	$\frac{5}{8}$	235	58	16
18	2	Front drawer rails, small		$6\frac{3}{4}$	$2\frac{1}{4}$	$\frac{5}{8}$	172	58	16
19	2	Drawer bearers		$9\frac{1}{4}$	$2\frac{1}{4}$	$\frac{5}{8}$	235	58	16
20	4	Drawer guides		$9\frac{1}{4}$	$1\frac{1}{2}$	$\frac{5}{8}$	235	38	16
21	2	Drawer bearers		$9\frac{1}{4}$	$2\frac{1}{4}$	$\frac{5}{8}$	235	58	16
22	2	Brackets		$6\frac{1}{2}$	$2\frac{1}{4}$	$\frac{5}{8}$	165	58	16
23	1	Stationery unit back		54	$5\frac{1}{4}$	$\frac{1}{2}$	1371	133	13
24	1	Stationery unit top		46	26	$\frac{5}{8}$	1168	660	16
25	2	Stationery small drawer tops		$8\frac{3}{4}$	6	$\frac{5}{8}$	242	185	16
26	2	Stationery large drawer tops		$11\frac{3}{4}$	9	$\frac{5}{8}$	305	229	16
27	2	Stationery ends		$11\frac{1}{2}$	8	$\frac{1}{2}$	292	203	13
28	1	Stationery bottom		$44\frac{1}{4}$	8	$\frac{5}{8}$	1124	203	16
29	2	End bottoms		$11\frac{3}{4}$	$7\frac{1}{2}$	$\frac{5}{8}$	298	191	16
30	2	Small cupboard fronts		$8\frac{3}{4}$	$3\frac{1}{2}$	$\frac{5}{8}$	222	89	16
31	2	Divisions		$8\frac{1}{2}$	$8\frac{1}{4}$	$\frac{5}{8}$	216	210	16
32	2	Divisions		$8\frac{1}{4}$	$8\frac{1}{4}$	$\frac{5}{8}$	210	210	16

CUTTING LIST (continued)

Part	*INCHES* *L*	*W*	*T*	*MM* *L*	*W*	*T*
33 2 Internal divisions	$8^1/_4$	$7^1/_2$	$^5/_8$	210	191	16
34 2 Drwr cupbd divisions	$8^1/_4$	$8^1/_4$	$^1/_2$	210	210	13
35 1 Cupboard division	$7^1/_2$	$8^1/_4$	$^1/_2$	191	210	13
36 2 Doors	$8^1/_4$	$4^1/_2$	$^5/_8$	210	115	16
37 4 Pigeonhole divisions	$8^1/_4$	$8^1/_4$	$^3/_{16}$	210	210	5
38 1 Muntin	$4^3/_4$	$2^1/_4$	$^3/_4$	121	57	19
39 2 Muntin	$6^1/_2$	$2^1/_4$	$^3/_4$	165	57	19
40 2 Small cupboard panels	$11^3/_4$	5	$^1/_2$	292	127	13
Drawer material						
2 Deep drawer fronts	$5^7/_8$	5	$^5/_8$	149	127	16
4 Deep drawer sides	10	5	$^3/_8$	254	127	10
2 Deep drawer backs	$5^7/_8$	5	$^3/_8$	149	127	10
2 Deep drawer bottoms	10	$5^5/_8$	$^3/_{16}$	254	143	5
2 Long drawer fronts	$13^3/_4$	$3^3/_4$	$^5/_8$	349	95	16
4 Long drawer sides	10	$3^3/_4$	$^3/_8$	254	95	10

CUTTING LIST (continued)

Part	*INCHES* *L*	*W*	*T*	*MM* *L*	*W*	*T*
2 Long drawer backs	$13^3/_4$	$3^3/_4$	$^3/_8$	349	95	10
2 Long drawer bottoms	$13^3/_4$	$9^3/_4$	$^3/_{16}$	349	248	5
2 Staty drwr fronts, large	$7^1/_4$	$3^3/_8$	$^1/_2$	184	86	13
4 Staty drwr sides large	$10^3/_4$	$3^3/_8$	$^3/_8$	273	86	10
2 Staty drwr backs, large	$7^1/_4$	$3^3/_8$	$^3/_8$	184	86	10
2 Staty drwr bottoms, large	$10^3/_4$	$7^1/_4$	$^3/_{16}$	273	184	5
2 Staty drwr front, small	$4^1/_8$	$2^5/_8$	$^1/_2$	105	67	13
4 Staty drwr sides, small	$7^1/_2$	$2^5/_8$	$^5/_{16}$	191	67	8
2 Staty drwr backs, small	$4^1/_8$	$2^5/_8$	$^5/_{16}$	105	67	8
2 Staty drwr bottoms, small	$7^3/_4$	$3^7/_8$	$^5/_{16}$	197	99	8

Working allowances have been made to lengths and widths; thicknesses are net.

ITALIAN-STYLE CARD TABLE OF THE 18TH CENTURY

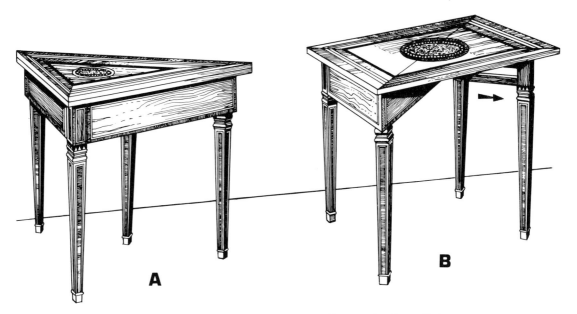

Fig. 33.1 (A) shows the table closed; (B) open with extension leg pulled out.

The fact that this very unusual piece of furniture closes into a triangular shape makes it ideal as a piece of corner furniture.

The decoration here is greatly simplified, the original having the two ovals in the top filled with marquetry designs depicting scenes from classical mythology; both the rails and legs also carried marquetry swages and pendants.

TABLE FRAMING
This is shown in Figs. 33.2, 3, 4 and 5. Bearing in mind that the rails and legs are mainly covered in veneer, the choice of timber is made easier as so little of it is showwood. One of the West African woods such as abura, agba, or sapele would be a good choice, remembering that as well as being used for the legs and frame it will also be employed for the top where the edges will be seen and where it will act as a groundwork for the veneer.

Fig. 33.3 gives the best overall view of the frame construction and you will see that the extension leg operates on the simplest of principles, as it simply pulls out of its housing in the frame. A more detailed view of this housing is shown in Fig. 33.4, and it comprises the four rails (F) and (G), which are glued and screwed together in pairs, as illustrated. Rails (F) are glued and housed into the frame rails (D), and rails (G) are glued and screwed into the same frame rails. The other end of each rail (F) is mortised and tenoned into the end of each of the back frame rails (E). A point to note is that the rails (G) do not extend to the same length as the rails (F), being shorter so that the leg (E) can butt against them when the extension is closed – Fig. 33.2 (half plan of frame) and Fig. 33.3 display this feature best.

The frame rails (D) are mortised and tenoned into corner leg (C) at one end while their other ends are mitred and glued to the ends of back rail (E), thus forming the other two corners of the triangular frame. These corners are further strengthened by two factors, the first being that the upper ends of the legs (C) are cut away to fit snugly into the angle of the corner where they are well glued into place. The second factor is the block (K) which is halved and glued into the rails (D) and (E), and also screwed to the top of leg (C); the whole arrangement is illustrated in Fig. 33.5.

MAKING THE LEGS
These are, at first sight, straightforward tapered legs with square tops, but if you look at the rear elevation in Fig. 33.2, you will see that the two ball-faced members at the tops, and the smaller mouldings around the toes, are all applied, as they project beyond the dimensions of the leg squares.

Forming the legs should be easy enough as they can either be bandsawn to shape or planed. If you do decide to plane them you will need to make a box into which each leg will fit, and then put a wedge-shaped packing under the toe end so that it will stand proud of the box sides by the amount of taper required. You can then plane the side of the leg down flush with the side of the box, thus imparting the correct amount of taper. You will find the box invaluable, too, when you come to rout out the ground-work for the crossbanded veneer.

THE LEG EXTENSION
This has four component parts, namely leg (B), two rails (H) which are mortise-and-tenoned into the leg and, finally, the strip (J) which is mortise-and-tenoned

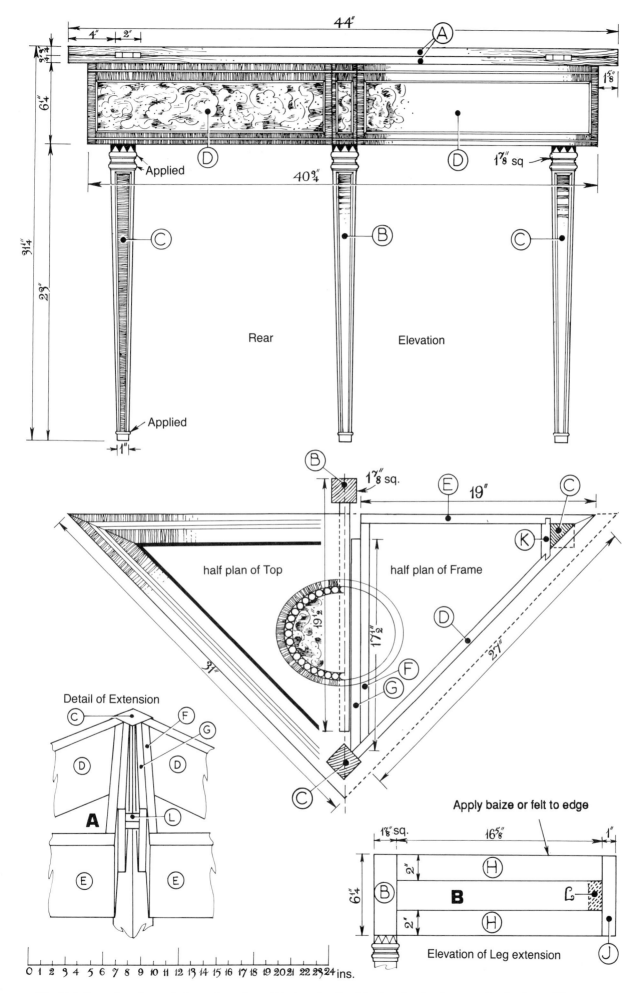

Fig. 33.2 Rear elevation and plans of top. Inset (A) gives details of the housing for the extension leg frame. The measurements for the extension leg are shown at (B).

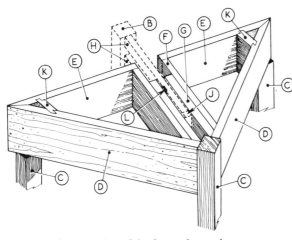

Fig. 33.3 Construction of the frame; lettered parts are referred to in the cutting list.

to the rails (H). This strip acts as a stop to prevent the whole extension being withdrawn completely, as it engages with a block (L) which is dowelled between the two rails (G). Details are shown in Figs. 33.2 and 3. Apply a strip of baize or felt to the top edge of the upper rail (H) so that it cannot mark the table top when it is open.

THE TOP

On the original design the edges of the top were crossbanded except for the hinged ones, where it would be impracticable to do so.

One half of the top (the half which opens) may be veneered on both sides, while the other half (which is fixed to the frame) is veneered on one side only. The conclusion is that this fixed half should have a counter-veneer laid on the opposite side to the show veneer. This counter-veneer could be something like gaboon or obeche veneer and should be laid at right angles to the grain of the solid top. Naturally, if you are not going to veneer the tops this counter-veneering can be disposed with.

Fig. 33.5 Framing-in of front legs.

Next you have to accommodate any movement of the half of the top which has to be fixed, and this can be accomplished by either using buttons or shrinkage plates (Fig. 33.6). Of the two, I prefer shrinkage plates as they are so easy to fix; remember to use a round-

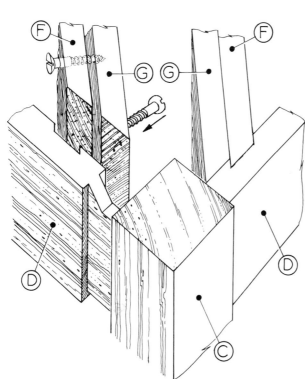

Fig. 33.4 Framing-in of back leg.

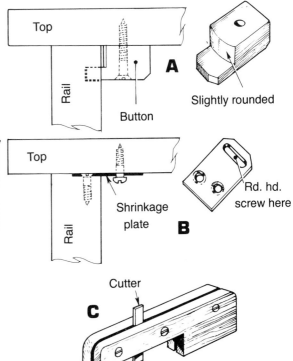

Fig. 33.6 Details of a table top fixing button are shown at (A), while the fixing of a shrinkage plate is illustrated at (B). A scratch stock is shown at (C).

head screw in the slot and do not tighten it down hard but just enough to hold the top firm and yet allow for any lateral movement.

DECORATION

This consists mainly of crossbandings, stringings, and rectangular and oval panels; the tops can either be veneered or not, as you wish. Although you can use a router to cut the grooves for the stringings, a home-made scratch-stock will do the job just as efficiently. Fig. 33.6 shows how to make one using a piece of old saw-blade filed to shape as a cutter. But you will certainly need a router to sink the oval panels on the table tops, and a rabbet plane could clear away ready for the edge bandings.

The box in which you planed the legs can also be used to hold them while you cut away the ground for the crossbanding; again, you can use either a router or a scratch-stock for this job, although you may need to chop out corners with a chisel.

Choice of veneers is yours. Holly is a good choice for the white stringing, but there are alternatives; plus small pieces of burr veneer for the panels. Burr walnut, bird's-eye maple or amboyna would be suitable. The small triangles at the tops of the legs are black and white and can be laid directly on to the leg itself as a goundwork.

A tip to remember when laying the stringings: the grooves for these should be cut just deep enough so that when the stringing is laid it stands proud by a tiny amount — the thickness of a piece of paper is about right. Then when you press them in with the head of a hammer, they will go down under pressure flush with the surrounding surface.

FINISH

Obviously you will need as clear a finish as possible to show up the beauty of the veneers, and one of the best is to first of all brush on a coat of clear french polish, followed (when dry) by two or three coats of a clear plastic lacquer. Allow each coat to set for 24 hours and then rub it down lightly with very fine (flour) glass-paper before applying the next. With the last coat, allow it to set thoroughly and then rub it down very lightly with fine steel wool dipped in wax.

CUTTING LIST

Part				INCHES			MM	
			L	W	T	L	W	T
A	2	Tops from one piece	31½	31¼	¾	800	794	19
B	1	Leg	30¼	2⅛	1⅞	768	54	48
C	3	Legs	30¼	2⅛	1⅞	768	54	48
D	2	Side rails	28	6½	¾	711	165	19
E	2	Back rails	19½	6½	¾	495	165	19
F	2	Outer housing rails	18	6½	¾	457	165	19
G	2	Inner housing rails	18	6½	¾	457	165	19
H	2	Leg exten-sion rails	17⅝	2¼	⅞	448	58	22
J	1	Extension end block	6¾	1¼	⅞	172	32	22
K	2	Struts	4	6½	⅞	102	165	22
L	1	Stop block	2½	1¼	⅞	64	32	22

Working allowances have been made to lengths and widths; thicknesses are net.

GEORGIAN-STYLE BOOKCASE

Fig. 34.1

This bookcase-cupboard is a composite design, which could possibly be called Basic Chippendale. It does adapt itself quite well to the use of manufactured boards (suitably veneered, of course) for the carcases and the cupboard doors.

GENERAL DESCRIPTION

The piece is made up in mahogany, and although the drawings show carcases which employ solid timber,

quite often they were framed-up panels with oak or softwood rails and panels, particularly for the shelves.

There are four main components; the plinth, the cupboard, the bookcase, and the cornice. In practice, they were not fixed together but rested on top of each other; a moulding was planted around the base of each carcase to position it and locating battens were also used. This stacking of the components had two advantages – there is the obvious one that dismantling

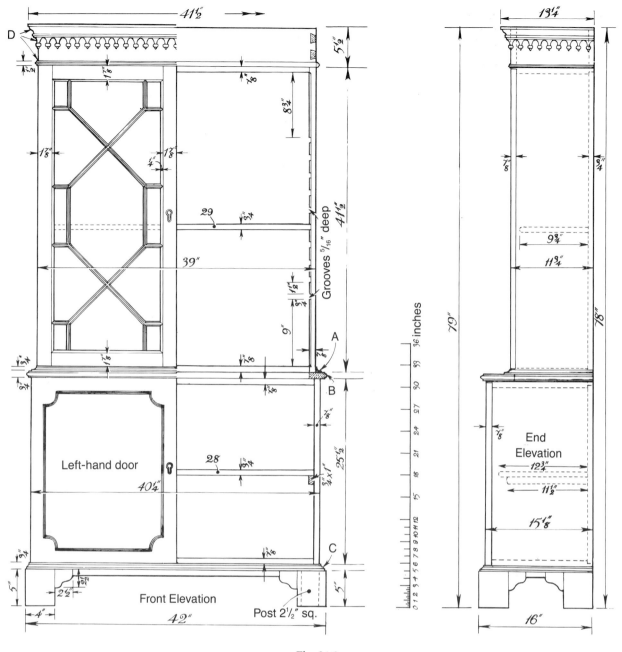

Fig. 34.2

the components for removal is easy, but there is also the important benefit that any splitting or shrinkage is confined and cannot spread to the others.

Normally the cornice would have carried an additional dentil moulding but this is omitted as the overall height of the design has been restricted to 79 in to easily fit into the average room height of 90 in.

THE PLINTH

Details are shown in Figs. 34.3 and 4. The four corner posts are joined by rails (2) and (3); the dovetail joint is shown in Fig. 34.4 (A) and (B). Plinth feet (4) are mitred at the corners and glued to the posts, and brackets (6) are glued and dowelled on (Fig. 34.4C). Quite often a 'staff' bead was worked on one of the meeting edges of each pair of plinth feet, to mask any opening of the joint.

Glue in strip 7 between the brackets at the front, and also a similar one (7A) at the back. Brackets are omitted at the back; note that the plinth feet are usually slightly tapered. Although this is not shown,

it's worthwhile screwing in corner braces to strengthen the whole framing.

Next, there is the three-sided frame consisting of parts 8 and 9, which is screwed and glued down on to the plinth frame. The corners are mitred and tongued (Fig. 34.4D), and are positioned to be set back at the front and the sides by the thickness of the moulding (C).

THE CUPBOARD CARCASE

As this is made of solid timber, the corner joints are all lap-dovetailed (Fig. 34.4E) so that no traces of the joints appear on the ends. The locating battens (10) are screwed and glued to the underside of the carcase and they fit between the inside edges of rails (9) and butt against the back edge of rail (8).

Work a rebate all around the back edges of the carcase which will accept the back framing; it needs to be ³⁄₄ in deep by ³⁄₈ in wide so that the back frame can be screwed in.

The sub-assembly consisting of parts 14 and 15 can be screwed and glued to the top (13) of the carcase; the

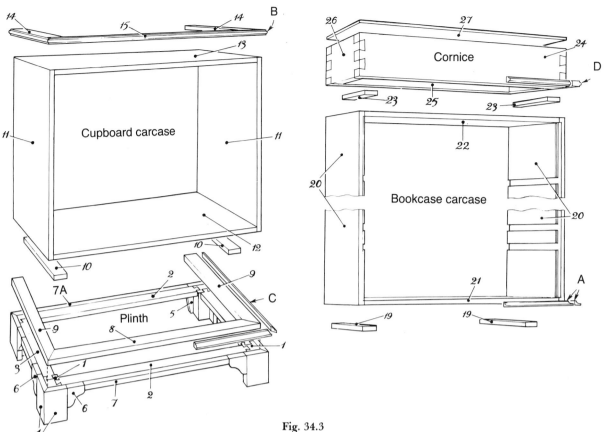

Fig. 34.3

front piece (15) runs the full width, and the rails are tenoned into the back of it. Use a moulding plane, spindle moulder or router to work the outer edges to profile, Fig. 34.4F.

THE BOOKCASE CARCASE
Again this is made of solid timber, and the corners are lap-dovetailed together. The main complication is the trenching of the ends (20) for the shelves; they are $\frac{5}{16}$ in deep, and other details are given in Fig. 34.2. A point to note is that the front edge is moulded as shown in Fig. 34.4F; at the back the trenching will run out into the rebate which has been made for the back framing.

Locating battens (19) can be screwed and glued to the underside in the same manner as for the cupboard carcase, and similar battens (23) are fixed to the top to locate the cornice.

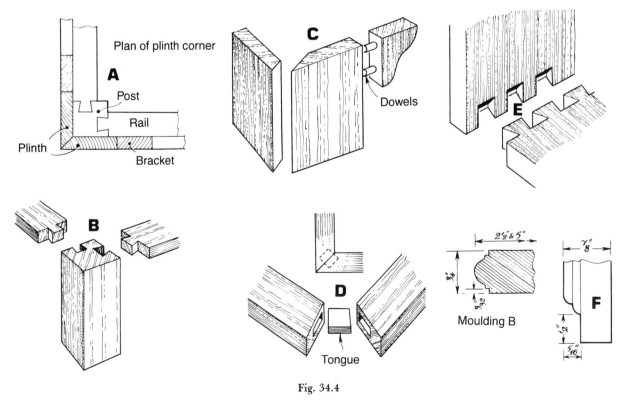

Fig. 34.4

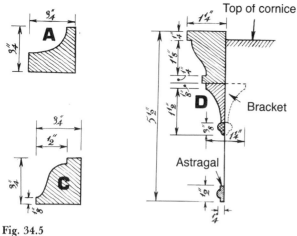

Fig. 34.5

THE CORNICE

This can be made up in solid oak, or fully seasoned softwood, with through dovetails at each corner. Naturally, whatever timber you use must be thoroughly dried as the ends and the front are veneered over the dovetails and any movement would be damaging.

The top (27) needs to be exactly the same size as the outer dimensions of the cornice, as it is screwed and glued down on to it; the edges are concealed by mouldings which are applied later.

MOULDINGS

Having constructed the carcase, we can turn to the mouldings, which are shown in Fig. 34.5, in profile.

Both mouldings (A) and (C) are pinned and glued only on the horizontal faces, the vertical faces which butt against the carcase edges being left dry. By this means they hold the carcases in position, but any movement of shrinkage or swelling of the carcases will not be transmitted to them. All corners are, of course mitred.

Turning now to the cornice mouldings, which are all fixed after veneering, first of all the small half-inch astragal beading is pinned and glued on, with the corners mitred.

The next moulding to be fixed should be the topmost one which stands up $\frac{1}{8}$ in proud of the cornice so that it hides the edges of the top. Once more the corners are mitred.

The arcaded moulding (C) is made up of two components – the main bracket part, and the small knob-like finial at the bottom of each bracket. Make the main bracket moulding by profiling a length to shape, and then cutting out the shapes with a fretsaw or jigsaw; the cuts are not made right through but only up to the flat so that, when finished, the length of moulding resembles arcading.

Split turnings can be used for the finials, and these are made up by gluing two small blocks of wood together with a piece of paper between them, and turning this assembly to shape, when the two pieces can easily be parted.

You may be confronted at this juncture with the same problem as the old craftsmen had to overcome – namely how to polish the arcaded moulding without getting gummy deposits in the nooks and crannies. To solve this, they polished both the moulding and the veneered cornice separately, and then laid the moulding dry into the position and scribed round it with a sharp point. When the moulding was removed the scribed outline remained and the polish was scraped away. Next, they warmed up a metal plate (so that the glue would not chill, but this need not be the case with a modern adhesive) and spread a thin coating of glue on it. Then they drew the back of the moulding across the plate (which they called a sticking board) so that it picked up a thin film of glue; when stuck down there was no excess glue to clean away.

THE CUPBOARD DOORS

Details are given in Fig. 34.6. They consist of a straightforward framing with orthodox blind mortise and tenon joints (Fig. 34.6B), with a $\frac{1}{4} \times \frac{1}{4}$ in groove cut centrally all around the inside of the framing (Fig. 34.6A); the grooves can also be used to accept the tenons at each corner, but will have to be made deeper locally. The panel, of course, is flush with the frame at the front, and the grooves for its tongues must be deep enough to allow a movement space. Although not illustrated, corner braces can be glued in at the back of the panel if required.

Each door carries two $2 \times \frac{1}{2}$ in brass hinges, and a lock is fitted to the right-hand door only. The latch engages into a groove cut in the meeting edge of the left-hand door, although both doors have escutcheons around the keyholes, the one on the left being a

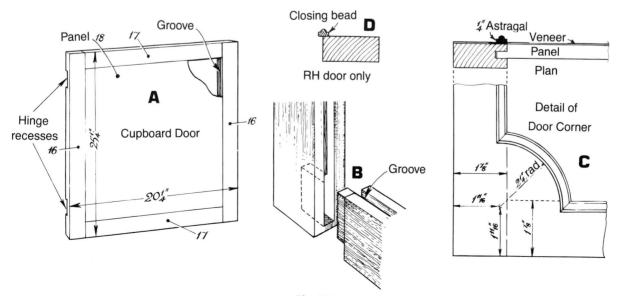

Fig. 34.6

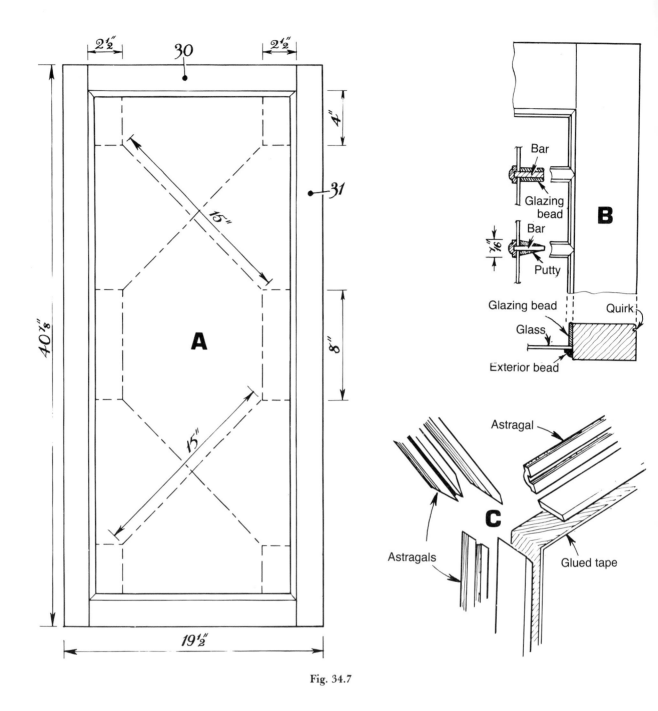

Fig. 34.7

dummy. Additionally, the left-hand door carries two bolts, one at the top and one at the bottom.

The doors are veneered all over, but of course you will probably prefer to lay the central piece first, following on with laying the borders and the corners, particularly if you want to use cross banding for the borders. Almost certainly the astragal beading will need to be bent in hot water, and details of the corner measurements are given in Fig. 34.6C.

Lastly, glue a length of the astragal beading to the edge of the right-hand door (Fig. 34.6D) to act as a closing bead.

THE BOOKCASE DOORS

We can soon deal with the door frames, as they are made just like the cupboard doors; the lock, escutcheons, and bolts are the same, the only exception being that each door carries three hinges, not two. A nice decorative touch is to work a small quirk on the hinging edges, as in Fig. 34.7B.

Fig. 34.7A gives measurements of the centre lines for the glazing bars, but these are a *guide only* and you

should adapt them to your own door when you have framed it up. In any case cut out hardboard templates around which you can assemble the beadings.

Figs. 34.7B and 34.7C illustrate the method used. In Fig. 34.7B you will see that a small exterior bead is pinned and glued to the inside of the frame, all round. Although the bead is set slightly below the frame surface in this design, quite often an alternative bead was used which protruded slightly.

Having done this, turn the door frame over face downwards, and assemble the bars, gluing them around the hardboard templates. It is a good idea to reinforce them (as many craftsmen did) with strips of linen soaked in glue or adhesive: you will, of course, need to mitre the joints as in Fig. 34.7C. You can then use either of two ways to hold the glass in, both of which are shown in Fig. 34.7B. One is to employ flat beads which are glued to the sides of the bars; the other is to use linseed oil or putty with a little gold size mixed in. The puttying method has little resiliency and if the frame shrinks or swells, the result is a cracked pane.

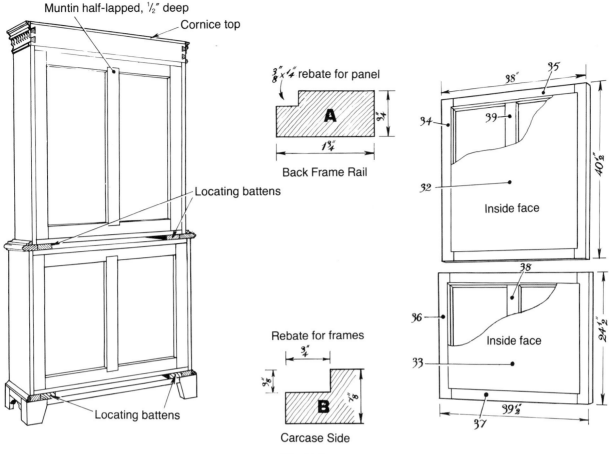

Muntin half-lapped, ½″ deep
Cornice top
$\frac{3}{8}″ \times \frac{1}{4}″$ rebate for panel

A

Back Frame Rail

Locating battens

Rebate for frames

B

Carcase Side

Locating battens

Inside face

Inside face

Fig. 34.8

The last step is turn the door frame over again, face upwards, and put in the glass, finishing by gluing on the astragal beadings.

THE BACK FRAMES AND SHELVES
These are illustrated in Fig. 34.8, but it should be pointed out that this construction is not historically correct. The fact is that the backs of many of these old pieces were crude – sometimes they were composed of softwood boards nailed on and covered (inside) with silk or some other fabric to hide the roughness; sometimes they were built up from boards which were rebated and lapped; sometimes they comprised a framing with fielded panels; and sometimes the styles were mixed on the same piece.

Note that the panels are rebated into the framing so that the inside surface is flush all over (Fig. 34.8A) so avoiding the need to notch out the shelves to fit around the framing; the muntins are half-lapped into the rails and glued. The panels are pinned and glued in place.

Now, to the shelves. These were solid (as shown in Fig. 34.2) or softwood or oak, lipped at the front edge with mahogany; the book-shelves rest in the trenchings, while the cupboard shelf (or shelves) rests on bearers.

FINISH
To be historically true, this should be a linseed oil finish of several applications well rubbed in, and followed by polishing with beeswax. After 50 years or so of repeated waxing and rubbing, you will achieve a patina like that on an authentic piece! However, you can build up a good finish by using a good quality wax (no silicones) furniture polish over three or four coats of linseed oil; each coat must be well rubbed in and left to dry for a week or so before applying the next.

You will find that this treatment considerably darkens the colour, and perhaps you should forget history and use two or three coats of clear plastic lacquer, each allowed to cure and being lightly glass-papered before applying the next. But instead of glasspapering the last coat, cut the surface back to a satin finish by rubbing very lightly with steel wool dipped in wax.

CUTTING LIST

Part			INCHES			MM		
			L	W	T	L	W	T
1	4	Posts	5½	2¾	2½	140	70	64
2	2	Plinth rls, frnt and back	37¼	2	¾	934	51	19
3	2	Plinth rls, end	11¼	2	¾	286	51	19
4	6	Plinth feet, frnt and ends	5½	4¼	⅞	140	108	23
5	2	Plinth feet, back	5½	4¼	⅞	140	108	23
6	6	Brackets	3	2¾	⅞	76	70	23
7	1	Front strip	29½	1	⅞	749	25	23
8	1	Front rail	40¾	2	¾	1035	51	19
9	2	End rails	15⅜	2	¾	391	51	19
10	2	Locating battens	13⅞	2	¾	353	51	19
11	2	Cupboard ends	26	14½	⅞	661	368	23
12	1	Cupboard bottom	40¾	15⅜	⅞	1035	391	23
13	1	Cupboard top	40¾	15⅜	⅞	1035	391	23
14	2	End rails	11½	2¾	¾	293	70	19

143

Part			INCHES L	W	T	MM L	W	T
15	1	Front rail	42½	5¼	¾	1079	133	19
16	4	Cupboard door stiles	25¾	2⅛	⅞	654	54	23
17	4	Cupboard door rails	18½	2⅛	⅞	470	54	23
18	2	Cupboard door panels	22½	17¼	½	572	438	13
19	2	Locating battens	11½	2	¾	293	51	19
20	2	Bookcase ends	42	11⅛	⅞	1066	283	23
21	1	Bookcase bottom	39½	11⅛	⅞	1003	283	23
22	1	Bookcase top	39½	11⅛	⅞	1003	283	23
23	2	Locating battens	10½	2	¾	267	51	19
24	1	Cornice front	39½	5¾	⅞	1003	146	23
25	1	Cornice back	39½	5¾	⅞	1003	146	23
26	2	Cornice ends	12¼	5¾	⅞	312	146	23
27	1	Cornice top	39½	12	⅛	1003	305	3
28		Cupboard shelves, each	39¼	13	¾	997	330	19
29		Bookcase shelves, each	38⅜	10	¾	975	254	19

Part			INCHES L	W	T	MM L	W	T
30	4	Bookcase door rails	17¾	2⅛	⅞	451	54	23
31	4	Bookcase door stiles	41⅜	2⅛	⅞	1051	54	23
32	1	Bookcase back panel	38¼	35½	¼	972	902	6
33	1	Cupboard back panel	22¼	37	¼	565	939	6
34	2	Bookcase back stiles	41	2	¾	1041	51	19
35	2	Bookcase back rails	35	2	¾	889	51	19
36	2	Cupboard back stiles	25	2	¾	635	51	19
37	2	Cupboard back rails	36½	2	¾	927	51	19
38	1	Cupboard back muntin	21½	2	½	546	51	13
39	1	Bookcase back muntin	38½	2	½	978	51	13

Working allowances have been made to lengths and widths; thicknesses are net.

GRANDMOTHER CLOCKCASE

Fig. 35.1

A well-proportioned clock case can look well in either a modern or traditional setting, and this version is veneered in English walnut with motifs in holly and ebony, with mouldings from solid walnut. The drawings show an arrangement of the case with the principal dimensions added. The dial, hands, and clockwork are not included, as this work is quite separate from clock-case making.

A height rod with widths is shown, (Fig. 35.2) from which you should make a full-size copy. Each piece is numbered and the size will be found in the cutting list. Any sound, well-seasoned timber can be used for the framing. Having made a full-size drawing, check the sizes of the timber from this, as any alteration to the

size of the clock will correspondingly alter the sizes on the cutting list.

Prepare the timber to the sizes given, the mortises being ¼ in or 5/16 in and the frames made up as shown in the exploded drawing. The frame that forms the front for the doors has a bevel cut on the right-hand stile for the door, allowing the door to open on the edge of the moulding.

No. 19 is the wide stile for the waist door, and this gives even margins when the moulding is applied to the door. Check the plywood thickness and the rebates, as they must finish flush.

The plinth frames are mortised together and loose tongued, the plywood being lipped at the top edge,

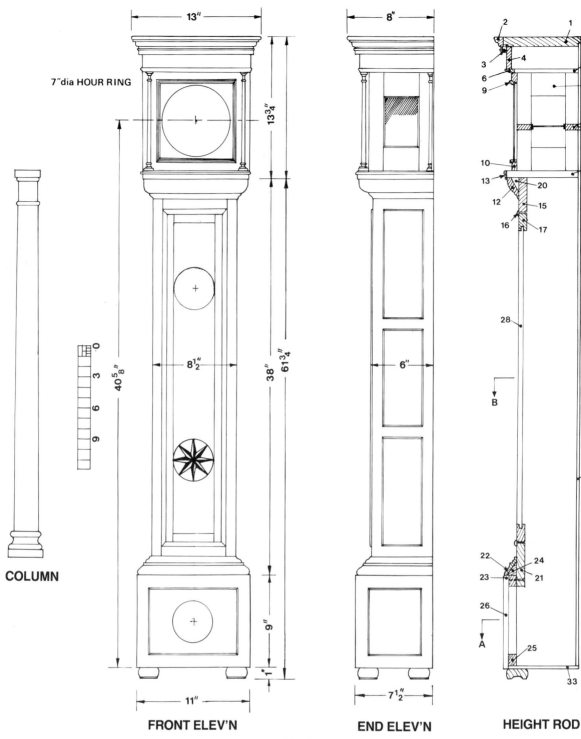

COLUMN

FRONT ELEV'N

END ELEV'N

HEIGHT ROD

7"dia HOUR RING

Fig. 35.2

then mitred round, pinned and glued. Keep the frame up from the bottom $\frac{1}{4}$ in for the plywood base. In the hood assembly, the side frames and door are mortised $\frac{1}{4}$ in or $\frac{3}{16}$ in.

Both pieces of ply (part 14), are glued together to give approximately $\frac{5}{8}$ in for the moulding. Part 13 is worked and fitted. Parts 5 and 6 are prepared and glued together for the plywood base for the hood. Part 14 is cut to allow tongues to be fitted so that the hood will slide forward to give access to the clock, as shown. The two assemblies 5 and 6, 13 and 14, are screwed to the side frames, thus making the carcase for the hood. The cornice can then be built up as shown, part 4 being mitred at the corners. The veneer that forms the drip is built up as shown. The mouldings for the clock can be made by hand moulding planes and scratch stock, but if a spindle moulder is available it will save a

good deal of work. Do be careful to remove the machine marks.

The hood door moulding, No. 9, because it is small, should be fixed to a board so that it can be worked. The mouldings for the top and bottom of the waist are fitted after the veneering, as are the mouldings for the glass in the hood side frames. The columns can be turned at any time along with the feet; the square caps at the bottom and top of the columns are brass.

Toothing the surfaces to be veneered is most important, and check surfaces for any dents or raised edges, as any mark will show through the veneer. Selection of veneer to be used is a personal choice. The illustration shows fine figured veneer for the panels in the sides, the plinth, and door, with straight grain for the cross-banding. The lines are boxwood.

Scotch glue in bead form is used for laying the

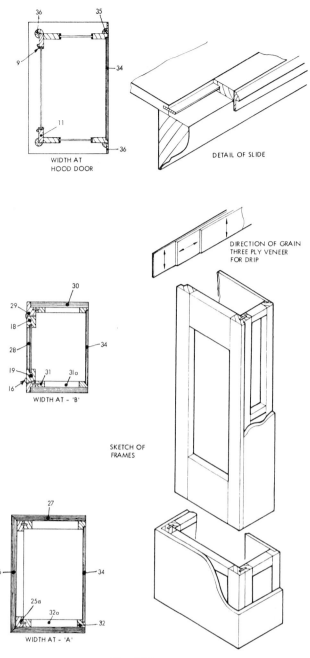

WIDTH AT
HOOD DOOR

DETAIL OF SLIDE

DIRECTION OF GRAIN
THREE PLY VENEER
FOR DRIP

SKETCH OF
FRAMES

WIDTH AT – 'B'

WIDTH AT – 'A'

Fig. 35.3

glass in the sides. The hood door can also be hung and the columns fitted to the corners. The quarter that remains fits in the back edge of the hood with a thin backboard.

Now for the waist door. The hinge pin position must be given some thought, as the door must open round the moulding. You need special hinges with wider leaves to allow the hinge to come well forward.

For the finishing, bleached shellac is used throughout. Six coats in all are applied, with flour paper and then fine wire wool to rub down between coats. When the surface is sealed, a light waxing is given for a final finish. It remains to cut and fit the glass, add the feet (ensuring that the case stands straight), and fit the $\frac{1}{4}$ in ply back, which will have to be cut in to fit the waist and screwed home. Drill a hole in the back of the case, about 33 in from the bottom, which is for screwing the case to the wall.

veneer, freshly made up for each stage as stale glue can give problems. Tape all edges with gummed tape.

For the geometric motifs a pad of veneers comprising holly, ebony, burr walnut and a backing piece are glued together. Thin the glue and leave the pad under pressure to dry. Make three copies of the design, glue one to each pad and cut it out using a piercing saw with a fine blade. Separate the cut pieces with a hot knife and re-assemble them on a sheet of paper with Scotch glue, then leave them under pressure to dry. When they are set firm, cut them into position in the door and the plinth, and mark out the circle with a sharp knife; re-heat the waste veneer with an electric iron and remove it, fit in the motif and tape it well down.

The removal of the tape and cleaning up follows. The cabinet scraper is the best tool for this, as it will not tear the veneer. Garnet paper is used in the later operations from grades 2/0 to 5/0, damping down to raise the grain between glasspapering.

Mouldings for the top and bottom of the waist can now be mitred and fitted, along with the beads for the

CUTTING LIST

Part			L	W	T	L	W	T
			INCHES			*MM*		
			L	*W*	*T*	*L*	*W*	*T*
1	1	Hood top	$11\frac{1}{4}$	$7\frac{3}{4}$	$\frac{7}{8}$	286	197	22
2	1	Top moulding cornice	36	$\frac{7}{8}$	$\frac{7}{8}$	914	22	22
3	1	Drip back	36	$\frac{11}{16}$	$\frac{3}{8}$	914	18	10
4	1	Frieze rail	30	2	$\frac{1}{2}$	762	51	12
5	1	Hood lining, gaboon ply	11	$6\frac{1}{2}$	$\frac{3}{8}$	279	165	10
6	1	Frieze moulding	30	1	$\frac{3}{8}$	762	25	10
7	4	Hood side rails	$4\frac{1}{2}$	$2\frac{1}{4}$	$\frac{1}{2}$	115	58	12
8	4	Hood side stiles	$10\frac{1}{2}$	$1\frac{1}{2}$	$\frac{1}{2}$	267	38	12
9	4	Hood door mouldings	9	$\frac{3}{8}$	$\frac{3}{8}$	229	10	10
10	2	Hood door rails	$8\frac{3}{4}$	1	$\frac{1}{2}$	223	25	12
11	2	Hood door stiles	$10\frac{1}{2}$	$1\frac{3}{16}$	$\frac{1}{2}$	267	30	12
12	1	Top waist moulding	30	$2\frac{3}{8}$	$\frac{1}{2}$	762	60	12
13	1	Tower hood moulding	30	$\frac{3}{4}$	$\frac{1}{4}$	762	19	6
14	2	Hood base pieces, ply	11	$7\frac{1}{2}$	$\frac{5}{16}$	279	191	8
15	1	Waist top frame rail	$7\frac{1}{2}$	$2\frac{15}{16}$	$\frac{7}{8}$	191	75	22
16	1	Waist door moulding	84	$\frac{1}{2}$	$\frac{3}{16}$	2132	12	5
17	2	Waist door rails	$60\frac{1}{8}$	$1\frac{7}{8}$	$\frac{7}{8}$	1527	48	22
18	1	Waist door stile	34	1	$\frac{7}{8}$	864	25	22
19	1	Waist door stile	34	$1\frac{3}{16}$	$\frac{7}{8}$	864	30	22
20	1	Softwood fillet for Part 12	30	$1\frac{5}{8}$	$\frac{7}{8}$	762	42	22
21	1	Waist frame	$7\frac{1}{2}$	4	$\frac{7}{8}$	191	102	22
22	1	Lower waist moulding	30	$2\frac{1}{4}$	$\frac{1}{2}$	762	58	12
23	1	Lipping	30	$\frac{1}{2}$	$\frac{1}{4}$	762	12	6

Part			L (INCHES)	W	T	L (MM)	W	T
24	1	Softwood fillet for Part 22	30	$1\frac{1}{4}$	$1\frac{1}{8}$	762	32	28
25	2	Plinth front rails	$8\frac{1}{2}$	1	$\frac{3}{4}$	216	25	19
25a	2	Plinth front stiles	10	1	$\frac{3}{4}$	254	25	19
26	1	Base front panel, gaboon ply	12	$8\frac{3}{4}$	$\frac{1}{2}$	305	223	12
27	2	Base end panels, gaboon ply	8	$8\frac{3}{4}$	$\frac{1}{2}$	203	223	12
28	1	Waist door panel, gaboon ply	$28\frac{3}{4}$	$4\frac{1}{2}$	$\frac{1}{2}$	730	115	12
29	2	Waist frame stiles	41	$1\frac{1}{4}$	$\frac{7}{8}$	1041	32	22
29	2	Waist frame stiles	41	$1\frac{1}{4}$	$\frac{7}{8}$	1041	32	22
30	2	Side frame pieces, ply	41	$5\frac{5}{8}$	$\frac{1}{2}$	1041	143	12

Part			L (INCHES)	W	T	L (MM)	W	T
31	4	Side stiles	41	$\frac{7}{8}$	$\frac{1}{2}$	1041	22	12
31a	6	Side frame rails	4	$\frac{7}{8}$	$\frac{1}{2}$	102	22	12
32	4	Plinth stiles	10	$\frac{3}{4}$	$\frac{3}{4}$	254	19	19
32a	4	Plinth rails	$5\frac{1}{4}$	$\frac{3}{4}$	$\frac{3}{4}$	133	19	19
33	1	Bottom	$10\frac{1}{2}$	7	$\frac{1}{4}$	267	178	6
34	1	Back	60	10	$\frac{1}{4}$	1524	254	6
35	2	Columns	12	$\frac{7}{8}$	$\frac{7}{8}$	305	22	22
36	2	Backboards	$10\frac{1}{2}$	1	$\frac{1}{8}$	267	25	3
37	1	Piece for glass beading	144	$\frac{1}{4}$	$\frac{1}{8}$	3656	6	3

Also required: 1 pair solid drawn $\frac{1}{4}$ in brass butts; 1 pair solid drawn 2 in wide-leaf brass butts; 1 cut cupboard lock, $1\frac{1}{2}$ in with keys; 1 spring catch; 1 escutcheon cover; 8 oz glass for hood door and sides.

Sizes shown are net and extra material should be allowed for waste in cutting and working. The normal allowance is $\frac{1}{2}$ in on lengths, and $\frac{1}{4}$ in on widths; thicknesses are net. All timber is walnut unless marked otherwise.

GATE-LEG TABLE

Fig. 36.1

Gate-leg tables, like Windsor chairs, are one of the few designs which have come down through the centuries virtually unchanged. In the case of the gate-leg table the secret lies in the fact that it opens up to provide seating for four people as a dining table, yet it can be folded up to stand against a wall as a very convenient side-table.

An interesting feature of this design is the plain stiles on the inner sides of the gates. These are usually turned or otherwise decorated to match the other legs, but these were not. The old craftsman might well have reasoned that as these stiles were to all intents and purposes hidden, why incur the expense of having them turned? It is quite an attractive feature, as the forest of turned legs one often sees on this kind of table can seem repetitive.

The table is made in solid oak throughout, but there is no reason why you should not make it up from ordinary softwood if solid oak is too expensive or difficult to get. If you decide on softwood, bring the wood indoors for a month or two before you begin work on it so that it stabilises itself to the normal indoor moisture content and temperature. The spare room is a good place for storage, or even under the bed!

In the actual design, the centre bed is one piece of solid oak, and each flap comprises two pieces rub-jointed together. Using softwood will probably entail joining two pieces for the bed and two pieces for each of the flaps; make sure that the end-grain of one piece is opposed to that of its fellow as shown in the diagram

at inset A, Fig. 36.3. This is done because when a length of timber 'cups' and shrinks it will take up a curve which follows that of the original tree. The best joint would probably be an ordinary tongue-and-groove, taken right through, and the fact that the joint will show on the ends is not detrimental as the old-time craftsmen were not fussy about concealing joints.

Construction is really straightforward as all framing joints are mortise and tenon, and each one is pegged. The inner plain stile (part no. 4) on each gate has to swivel, of course, and this is accomplished by using a metal pin sunk into each end – an ordinary metal bolt cut to length would suffice.

A notch has to be cut out of the bottom of each gate leg (part no. 5) to fit over the bottom rail (part no. 8), and the rail itself is also notched to match. A block (part no. 10) is glued and screwed to the inside of each top rail (part no. 6) to form a base into which the metal pin can be sunk at the top. Also, a short length of $\frac{3}{8}$ in dowel is let into the underside of each flap to prevent the flap from being opened too far.

To fix the top, two buttons along each end will allow for any shrinkage of the top across the grain; as the timber will not shrink or swell in its length, pocket-screwing can be used on the long sides.

The traditional finish is wax, applied and well rubbed in over a few centuries! However, as you will probably want to use the table for dining it would be advisable to use a modern polyurethane lacquer which will resist most of the hazards of everyday use. Dilute

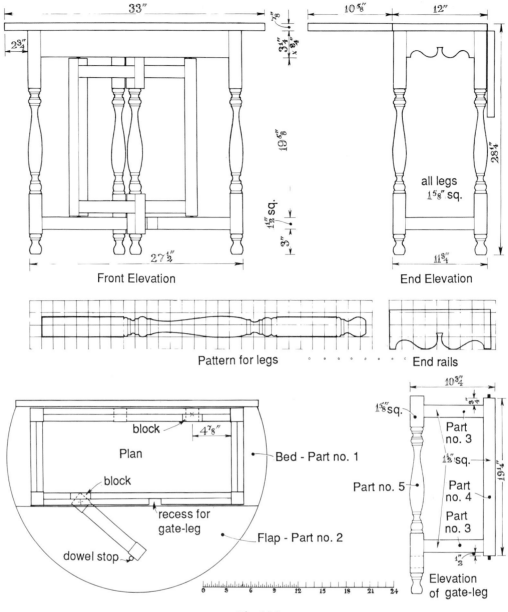

Front Elevation

End Elevation

Pattern for legs

End rails

block

4⅞"

Plan

Bed - Part no. 1

block

recess for
gate-leg

Flap - Part no. 2

dowel stop

1⅝"sq.

Part
no. 3

1¼"sq.

Part no. 5

Part
no. 4

Part
no. 3

Elevation
of gate-leg

Fig. 36.2

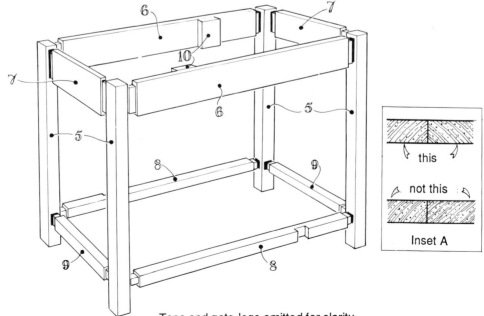

this

not this

Inset A

Tops and gate-legs omitted for clarity

Fig. 36.3

the first coat by about half with white spirit, as this will get the lacquer well into the grain and form a good base for the ensuing two or three coats of undiluted lacquer. Each coat should be well rubbed down (when the lacquer has set) before applying the next. Finish by rubbing on a good quality wax polish, making sure it is a non-silicon type.

CUTTING LIST

			INCHES			MM		
Part			L	W	T	L	W	T
1	1	Centre bed	33½	12¼	⅞	851	311	22
2	2	Flaps	33½	10⅞	⅞	851	277	22
3	4	Gate top and bottom rails	9¾	1¾	1½	248	45	38
4	2	Gate stiles	19¾	1¾	1½	502	45	38

CUTTING LIST (continued)

			INCHES			MM		
Part			L	W	T	L	W	T
5	2	Gate legs	24⅝	1⅞	1⅝	625	48	42
6	2	Frame rails, long	26	3½	¾	660	89	19
7	2	Frame rails, short	10¾	3½	¾	273	89	19
8	2	Underframe rails, long	26	1¾	1½	660	45	38
9	2	Underframe rails, short	10¾	1¾	1½	273	45	38
10	2	Blocks	3¾	2¾	1½	95	70	38

Working allowances have been made to lengths and widths; thicknesses are net.

Acknowledgements

The Publisher would like to thank the following for the inclusion of their designs in this book.

1   Oak Coffee Table   *C. Hayward*
2   Regency-Style Dressing Table   *V. Taylor*
3   Shield Mirror   *Author unknown*
4   Sheraton-Style Sideboard with Serpentine Front
      P. Chillingworth
5   Medieval Aumbry   *P. Barton*
6   Southern Huntboard   *Dr Justis*
7   Gate-Leg Table with Bow Front   *W. L. Rowson*
8   Farmhouse Kitchen Chair   *W. L. Rowson*
9   Side Table in Walnut   *W. L. Rowson*
10   Linen Chest   *N. Haigh*
11   Child's Turned Armchair   *W. L. Rowson*
12   Period Tripod or 'Snap' Table   *C. Hayward*
13   Oak Cradle   *D. Bryant*
14   Cutlery Cabinets in Mahogany and Oak
      W. L. Rowson
15   Mahogany Corner Cupboard   *W. L. Rowson*
16   Child's High Chair   *W. L. Rowson*
17   Period 'Hutch' Cupboard   *J. L. Ford*
18   Nest of Tables   *W. L. Rowson*
19   Ladderback Chair   *W. L. Rowson*
20   Architectural-Style Mirror Frame   *C. Hayward*
21   Lyre-End Occasional Table   *C. Hayward*
22   Windsor Chair   *L. W. Gorman*
23   Grandfather Clock in Traditional Style   *C. Hayward*
24   Oak Refectory Table   *Author unknown*
25   Long Style Occasional Table   *C. Hayward*
26   Settle-Table   *V. Taylor*
27   Chippendale Library Table   *V. Taylor*
28   Regency Library Table   *V. Taylor*
29   Georgian-Style Pole Screen   *V. Taylor*
30   Corner Display Cabinet   *V. Taylor*
31   'Gimson' Ladder-Back Chair   *V. Taylor*
32   Carlton House Writing Table   *V. Taylor*
33   Italian-Style Card Table of the 18th Century
      V. Taylor
34   Georgian-Style Bookcase   *V. Taylor*
35   Grandmother Clockcase   *A. R. Bishop*
36   Gate-Leg Table   *V. Taylor*